Writing for Animation, Comics, and Games

Writing for Animation, Comics, and Games

Christy Marx

Focal Press
Taylor & Francis Group

NEW YORK AND LONDON

First published 2007

This edition published 2013
by Focal Press
70 Blanchard Road, Suite 402, Burlington, MA 01803

Simultaneously published in the UK
by Focal Press
2 Park Square, Milton Park, Abingdon, Oxon OX14 4RN

Focal Press is an imprint of the Taylor & Francis Group, an informa business

Notices

Practitioners and researchers must always rely on their own experience and knowledge in evaluating and using any information, methods, compounds, or experiments described herein. In using such information or methods they should be mindful of their own safety and the safety of others, including parties for whom they have a professional responsibility.

To the fullest extent of the law, neither the Publisher nor the authors, contributors, or editors, assume any liability for any injury and/or damage to persons or property as a matter of products liability, negligence or otherwise, or from any use or operation of any methods, products, instructions, or ideas contained in the material herein.

Library of Congress Cataloging-in-Publication Data
Marx, Christy.
  Writing for animation, comics & games / by Christy Marx.
    p. cm.
  Includes bibliographical references and index.
  ISBN-13: 978-0-240-80582-5 (pbk. : alk. paper)
  ISBN-10: 0-240-80582-8 (pbk. : alk. paper) 1. Animated films—Authorship. 2. Comic books, strips, etc.—Authorship. 3. Video games—Authorship. I. Title.
  PN1996.M446 2007
  808.2'3—dc22   2006021435

British Library Cataloguing-in-Publication Data
A catalogue record for this book is available from the British Library.

ISBN 13: 978-0-240-80582-5 (pbk)

Transferred to Digital Printing in 2014

Dedication

To Randy, LOML

Acknowledgements

I owe a great many thanks to a great many people who helped and supported me during the writing of this book.

My deepest thanks to my editor, Amy Jollymore, who has the patience of a saint and then some, ably assisted by Doug Shults. Thanks to Paul Temme and Brandy Lilly for the final shepherding to completion.

Thanks to my excellent beta readers: Anne Toole, Randy Littlejohn, Ellen Guon Beeman, and Heather Ash. Any leftover mistakes are entirely my fault.

Thanks for invaluable input from Ellen Guon Beeman, Kurt Busiek, Peter David, Maureen McHugh, Terry Rossio, Sarah W. Stocker, Len Wein, Marv Wolfman and many more than I can name.

Special thanks to Wendy Pini, Stan Sakai and Kurt Busiek for permission to reprint art from their books.

Thanks and appreciation to the helpful people at Blizzard Ent., Linden Labs, Marvel Ent., and Ubisoft who granted me permission to use material. Thanks to the virtual Anhayla Lycia for the use of her Second Life image.

Much thanks to the terrific team of staff members at the WGA, and my fellow professionals in the Animation Writers Caucus and the New Media Caucus.

Contents

Preface

Writing is easy. All you do is sit down at a typewriter and open a vein.

—Walter Wellesley "Red" Smith

If you've opened this book, you either are a writer, consider yourself to be a writer, or are determined to become one. Not any old kind of writer, but a professional writer. And not any old kind of professional writer, but one who writes for animation or comics or videogames or maybe all three.

It can be done. It can be done if you're driven enough, passionate enough, persistent enough, and too plain stubborn to be easily turned aside.

One hopes you're not here for the status, at least not in the "real" world. Even someone as wildly successful as Stephen King is treated with scorn by some in the literary establishment because he writes "pop" fiction. You can guess the esteem with which an animation writer or comics writer or game writer is held outside their fields.

In fact, a lot of people seem oblivious to the fact that the products of these media are written at all, leading to this particular exchange that I've had more times than I can count:
"What do you do?"
"I write animation."
"Oh, you're an artist"
"No, I write animation."
"Do you draw the pictures, too?"
"No, I write the script. You know: the action, the dialogue."
Blank look.

One also assumes you're not here looking to get rich. Although it's certainly possible to earn a living, the odds of becoming wealthy from working in these fields are against you. Writing is hard work. Getting a job writing is even harder.

If you're the type of person who reads this and says, "I don't care. I love animation! I love comics! I love games! I have things to say. I have stories to tell. I have words to shape. I must write."—then I greet you with open arms. Welcome to the madhouse. Let's start the tour.

Introduction

I write when I'm inspired, and I see to it that I'm inspired at nine o'clock every morning.

—Peter De Vries

This book is designed to be useful to three main categories of readers:

1. The student or amateur who wants to break into one or more of these fields.

2. The writing professional working in another field who wants to move into one of these fields (for example, the TV writer who wants to write games, or the book writer who wants to write animation).

3. The nonwriter professional who works in a related area of these fields and wants to move into writing (for example, an animator who wants to turn scriptwriter, or a game tester who wants to write game stories).

Think of this as your nuts-and-bolts manual for what a writer needs to know to create scripts for animation, comics, or games so that they're in the right format and follow the right rules. This book is totally writer-centric, not an all-inclusive guide to related areas such as art or programming.

It is about the craft of writing, the practical rules, guidelines, tips, and tricks that will prepare you to approach these fields on a professional level of competency.

What this book will not do is teach you how to write. I'm assuming that you know your basic three-act structure; that you know how to create a character with motivations, needs, and desires; that you know how to type, spell, and use correct grammar. If you don't know these things, close this book and turn your attention to learning the fundamentals of writing. Find your voice. Practice your art. When you've done that, you're ready for the craft guidance you'll find here.

Overview

The most valuable of all talents is that of never using two words when one will do.

—Thomas Jefferson

In the course of a twenty-plus-year career in writing, I have discovered that the most valuable action I could take as a writer was to diversify. This is especially true when writing in more-volatile fields such as animation, comics, and games, where the companies, the business, the corporate hierarchies, and the entire field can change radically in a short time. Animation in particular tends to be cyclical both in content (comedy vs. action-adventure) and in opportunity (booms and busts). It's tremendously useful, if not downright lifesaving, to have several arrows in your writer's quiver.

This book concentrates on the three fields of animation, comics, and games for these reasons, discussed in more detail below:

- Similarity of craft

- Convergence of media

- Crossover of writers

Similarity of Craft

Animation, comics, and games fall into the category I think of as "shorthand" writing. This is in contrast to prose writing, where a writer can write plot, description, and dialogue to any length, and can cover all of the senses—sight, sound, touch, taste, smell—using both external storytelling (description, dialogue) and internal storytelling (thought processes, emotional description).

This specialized form of "shorthand" writing requires the discipline to write within a structured format; to pare description down to an absolute minimum; to boil dialogue down to a pithy essence; and to tell concise, tightly plotted stories.

Animation, comics, and games are visual media, in which the writer must have a strong ability to visualize the story, to see it in the mind's eye, and to translate that vision to paper. Because these are visual media, bear in mind an important, long-standing rule: show, don't tell.

Granted, these guidelines could apply to live-action film and TV scriptwriting as well. One of the significant differences between live action and animation/comics/games is who reads and interprets the final shape of the material. In live action, you are writing primarily for the producers and directors, who will then shape and interpret that material. This is especially the job of the director, who is the main filter for determining how the script will be converted to a film or TV show. In animation/comics/games, you are writing more directly for the artists. They are the ones who will interpret and create what you've written. True, there are still producers and sometimes directors involved, but it is the storyboard artist and animators who interpret your animation script; the comic book artist who interprets your comic book script; and the designers, animators, and programmers who interpret your games script. It's more about communicating to your cocreators than about trying to sell your words to a film or TV executive.

Two of the formats—animation and games—require exterior writing techniques. Everything must be conveyed primarily via two senses: sight and sound.

Comics are an exterior/interior storytelling form that allows more latitude in conveying information about the other senses and the character's thoughts, but it must all be done within the communication realm of one sense—sight.

Another aspect these three formats share is that they're dominated by the same genres. Broadly speaking, those are fantasy, science fiction, and action-adventure (I include superheroes in one or more of these categories). They require writers who understand these genres and are adept at writing within their boundaries. If you want to write for animation, comics, and games, you probably already have an interest in these genres. You'll want to stay current on them because you'll be expected to understand references to other books, movies, TV shows, or games in those genres. It's not unusual for the people who hire you to depend on those references and comparisons to convey what they want you to infuse in the current project.

This is not to exclude other genres such as sports games, causal games, sims, and so forth. By their nature, sports games or sims don't translate well into animation or comics. These genres are important parts of the videogame medium, but it's fantasy, science fiction and action-adventure that provide the most connections among the three media covered in this book.

Convergence of Media

The process of corporate acquisitions and mergers continues to accelerate, steamrolling across the media landscape. Far from creating a level playing field, this process is reducing the diversity of creative markets and putting control of our media into far too few and too powerful hands. Animation studios, comic book companies, and game studios are absorbed by media giants and become another cog in a huge media machine.

As you can tell, I view this type of consolidation as not beneficial for either the creative person or the general public. Like it or not, convergence has taken over these fields. One big corporation can publish the comic and novelization, produce the movie or TV series, and create the game—all based upon one property that they own and control. Consider two characters: Batman and Spider-Man. Both were published as comic book characters long before being adapted for television, movies, and animated series. Batman's publisher, DC Comics, is part of the massive Warner Bros. empire. Thus, we see many variations of Batman appearing on TV, in movies, in games, in books, in toys, and every other kind of licensing you can imagine. Spider-Man's publisher, Marvel Comics, hasn't become a part of an entertainment giant (yet), but they have formed an entertainment division and have forged alliances with studios, media producers, and licensors to reach the same end.

Conversely, games such as *Lara Croft: Tomb Raider, Mortal Kombat, Resident Evil,* and *Final Fantasy* are turned into movies. TV series such as *Alias, CSI,* and *Law and Order* are being done as games, with *CSI* also being done as a comic. Add this factoid: in 2003, Warner

Bros. entered into an agreement with cable-TV channel G4, which covers the videogame business. G4 agreed to be Warner's advance "scout," to locate games that could be turned into movies.

In this world of convergence, the smaller, independent companies struggle to survive. The smart ones recognize how important it is to control a property, rather than only doing work for hire that is owned by someone else. As often as not, the smaller studios are themselves acquired by new media conglomerates who seek to pull together various assets (animation studios, publishing arms, game developers, a means of distribution) to make sure their products reach the widest audience.

Selling a property can come down to finding the initial platform on which to launch it and expand from there. For example, Platinum Studios was formed specifically to use the format of comics as the initial platform to put an idea in front of the public, then use the comic book/graphic novel to sell the idea to movies and TV. The big money is in film and TV, but the published comic gives the publisher a property that they control and can sell to get at that big money. One such project was *Men in Black,* so you can see that this is a successful strategy.

Convergence isn't limited to visual media. Over the years, I have developed or written animation based on dolls, action figures, remote-controlled cars, interactive toys, comic books, arcade games, pulp fiction, a TV series spin-off, and a classic science fiction novel.

Everywhere you look, you see convergence. Games are made into movies, TV series, and comics. Comics are made into movies, TV series, and games. Movies and TV series are made into animation series, comics, and games. The marketing ties among these three fields—animation, comics, and games—have never been stronger or more directly related.

Consequently, the reality you face more and more as a writer is the megacorporation domination of the remaining markets in which you can work. This domination has narrowed down the number of markets, raised the stakes so that the big corporations are more fearful of taking risks, and increased the tendency of the corporations to create product based on their own properties rather than seeking original work. Knowing the formats in this book increases your odds of getting ahead in one or more of the converged media.

Crossover of Writers

Comic books have been a major source of material for animated TV series for decades. Gradually, comic book writers living in New York City migrated to Los Angeles to take advantage of their backgrounds in the comic book field to start working in animation. Famous comics writers such as Roy Thomas, Steve Gerber, Len Wein, and Marv Wolfman were among this early wave of writers who had the foresight to cross over to a new but related medium. It was a comic book story credit that gave me my break to write animation, and it was my background as a scriptwriter that opened the door to writing games.

Live-action scriptwriters have crossed over to write animation, big names in TV such as Joss Whedon and J. Michael Straczynski have written comics, and writers have moved from comics into TV series and games. Not only are the fields themselves converging, but the writers being tapped for those fields are more frequently writers who see the potential in writing for these other fields, or do it simply because they have a love for it.

To me, it's no coincidence that the greatest crossover of writers occurs among animation, comics, and games. This crossover occurs for the very reasons I delineated earlier—similarity of craft and knowledge of the genres.

This leads to one final reason I chose to cover these three fields in one book—because I can. Many writers have worked in two of the three fields, but it's still unusual for someone to have a large degree of experience in all three. I've had some rare and wonderful opportunities, not to mention dollops of luck, which enabled me to create and write animation, to create and write comics, and to design and write games. This background has given me the experience and perspective to bring it all together in one place—a one-woman convergence, if you will.

To that, I'll add this caveat: every writer has a different range of experience from which to draw, and no one book can give you everything. I would advise you to read more than one book about writing for these fields. In the last chapter of each section, you'll find recommendations for other books.

Now for Some Advice . . .

In each section, I will have advice and tips that are specific to animation, comics, or games. What I want to give you here is general advice that applies to all of them. The topics are as follows:

- Attitude
- Deadlines
- Collaboration
- Get a Life
- Gender and Age
- Personal Rewards and Responsibility

Attitude

For the student, beginner, or nonprofessional, it's important that you cultivate the attitude of a professional even before you get your first job. A professional understands that writing for animation, comics, and games is a job. You are expected to perform to certain standards, to know your craft, to know about the business, to listen well, to come up with creative solutions to notes and suggestions, and to do it with a businesslike attitude.

Although you do want to have faith in your creative vision, you also need to have the wisdom to pick which battles are truly vital enough to take a stand that could cause conflict. The most common mistakes a nonpro makes are to react defensively to requests for changes as though personally wounded; to refuse to make changes that are required; to fight over every little thing instead of knowing which battle is worth fighting; to worry that everyone is out to rip her off or steal her brilliant idea; or to behave in a touchy, oversensitive manner.

If you have a defensive attitude, get rid of it. If you want to be an artiste, rent a garret and write poetry. If you have a thin skin, emulate the rhino. Remember that notes and feedback are not a personal attack on you. These are professional fields where your job is to give the employer what they want when they want it. It's about getting the job done, meeting deadlines, and doing a great job of writing in the process.

When you absolutely need to take a stand to protect the integrity of your work, take it. Be prepared to make a strong professional argument to prove your point. You can't simply say, "Because I think so."

You can and will have a lot of fun writing for these fields, but never forget that it is, first and foremost, a job, and that you must act like a professional.

Deadlines

There are few things more vital to succeeding in these fields than meeting deadlines. Animation schedules are tight, and have a tremendous amount of money tied up in getting each phase of the project done in a timely manner—not to mention having storyboard artists, animation studios, actors, and many other stages of the production dependent on getting the script in time. If you're sloppy about getting a comic book done on time, the sales slip and you'll be regarded as unreliable, and you can cause major headaches for your artist, colorist, letterer, and editor.

Games also have big money riding on tight deadlines, along with a host of programmers, artists, animators, composers, and others whose deadlines will be affected by a writer not meeting a deadline.

Make it a hard-and-fast rule to never miss a deadline. If you truly find yourself in an unavoidable situation, talk it out with the person who hired you. Never take the avoidance route or refuse to return phone calls. I learned that the hard way.

What it gets down to is this general rule: a decent writer who always turns in a usable script on deadline will get more work than a brilliant writer who doesn't make deadlines.

Collaboration

These three fields require a high degree of collaboration with artists, producers, story editors, directors, programmers, and any number of other people in both the executive and creative ends of the business. This is most emphatically true for animation and games.

Depending on the project, you will receive notes and feedback from any variety of people. In animation, from story editor, producers, more producers, the producer's pet sitter, maybe a toy executive—whoever is allowed to have a say. In comics, primarily the editor, but your artist must feel that he or she is an integral part of a team, not a hired hand. In games, you might get feedback from anyone on the design team—publisher, producer, designers, programmers, animators, and so on.

For all three fields of writing, you need good people skills. Among those people skills are the ability to listen, the ability to clearly communicate your own ideas, the ability to praise and find constructive ways to give feedback, flexibility in adjusting your own ideas to the needs of the project, a good sense of humor (a small amount of self-deprecating humor can go a long way), and the ability to set aside temperament and ego for the good of the project. It also helps if you genuinely enjoy interacting with other people and can show interest in their goals, desires, wants, and needs.

Thoughtfulness pays. Express your thanks, send a card, and give flowers or cute gifts when someone helps you out. Let people know that you're aware they exist, and that includes the receptionist at the front desk or the person in accounting who helped you get reimbursed for expenses on a trip.

Get a Life

Most of the above is advice pertaining to the business end of the writing game. This section is about the creative end. I've encountered a few too many writers whose only influences seem to be limited to the one medium they want to work in. You need to know your medium well, of course, but you also need to have a breadth and depth of other influences and experiences.

Experience life, read, talk to people, listen to how people talk. The worst mistake writers in these fields make is not being grounded in the real world. These areas of writing require diverse knowledge that includes understanding political systems, religious systems, mythology, economics, geography, how cultures develop, and many other aspects of world creation. You should read and study other cultures, mythologies, and histories from ancient to modern. This will also help you acquire an ear for coming up with names that are appropriate to what you're writing.

If you write about shooting guns, go to a range and fire some guns. If you write about archers, loose an arrow or two. Fly a plane. Go scuba diving. Take some martial arts. You will have a better handle on many of the things you write about if you at least attempt to *do* some of them.

Gender and Age

There is another commonality to animation, comics, and games that I want to touch upon, without laboring over it. They remain male dominated, both on the creative end and the customer end. This is more true for games and comics, less so for animation.

When you evaluate the images, characters, and stories that are put forth, it's easy to see why the male-dominated fields churn out male-dominated types of entertainment. It becomes a self-fulfilling prophecy. "We have to make X game or X comic because we have X audience." But if all they put out is X games and X comics, then they never will attract the other 50 percent of the potential audience—girls and women. As a writer, it's your job to think about who it is that you're writing for, but it's also your job to push the boundaries and look for ways to reach new audiences.

There is also the issue—in the United States—that these media are "for kids." Animation, comics, and games all suffer in this country from the attitude that they are for children. Trying to break that barrier and create an adult art form in this country has been an uphill battle, to put it mildly—yet there's no good reason for this except that we as a culture have generated this mind-set—and why? Why should we equate visual storytelling in any medium with only children's entertainment?

There has been far more progress than I honestly expected to see during my career. We have *The Simpsons, King of the Hill, Adult Swim*, adult-rated comics, and a recognition of an older audience for games. All the same, there remains a large sector of society that wants to throw comic book retailers into jail for selling adult comics to adults, to sue game companies for the content of games, and to heavily control the content of animation. This is a dangerous form of censorship in which the narrow-minded want to determine for everyone else what is "adult" and what isn't. You need to be aware of this issue. More than that, I urge you to take a stand against censorship before you find your own creations on the list of "banned" works.

Having said that, the realities of the audience—or what is perceived to be the audience— must still be addressed when you sit down to write a script. That is one more part of your job.

Personal Rewards and Responsibility

I'd like to end this section by noting that the personal rewards of pursuing creative work can be immense, but there is some level of responsibility that comes with the job. Some people write to earn the respect of their peers, some to win awards, some yearn for status, and some are simply driven to do it. Seeing your name on the TV screen, on a book, on a game box can also be its own reward.

Whatever the motivation, there is nothing quite like hearing from the people who experience your work, the people that actually make it possible for any of us to have careers as writers. I'll never forget the sheer ecstasy I felt when I was standing in a comic book store and I heard someone behind me raving to the store owner about this fantastic story he'd just read . . . and I was able to turn around and say, "Thanks! I wrote that!"

Or the profound impact of knowing that an animation series has touched and shaped lives far beyond simple entertainment, even inspired people to pursue their own creative dreams or come to terms with some difficulty in their lives. Or getting email from someone who was moved to pursue an area of study because he was so intrigued by material in my adventure game.

Examine what drives you as a writer, but never forget that your work is reaching the eyes or ears of people of every age and type who can be impacted by it in a positive or negative way. It's rewarding to hear from people for whom your work had a positive impact, but accepting that your work can have a positive impact means accepting the contrary reality that your work could have a negative impact. I don't mean the rare, unintended incident where a troubled soul uses your work as inspiration to commit a wrongful act. The Beatles certainly never had Charles Manson in mind when they wrote "Helter Skelter." This doesn't change the truth that what you write has the potential to impact another person's life.

It's far too easy to shrug off taking responsibility for your work by saying: "It's just a game. It's just a cartoon. It's just a comic book."

They can be far more than that, and they can change lives for the better without preaching or moralizing. Merely writing about the human condition, the choices we all face, and the consequences of those choices can be enough. Whether your work will do that or how it does that is up to you. Know what you want your impact to be. Don't ignore your responsibility to shape minds and move hearts.

Animation

CHAPTER 1

History/Evolution of Animation

Animation—or cartoons, if you will—has a long, rich history. In order to understand how scriptwriters entered the picture and came to be where they are today, this section will briefly look at how cartoons developed.

In 1914, the marvelous artist Winsor McCay lovingly crafted line-art animation in a masterpiece known as *"Gertie the Dinosaur."* It was the first time someone had created a true character for the screen and had the character act out a little story.

One artist doing all the work was both painstaking and time-consuming, so the next step in the evolution was the development of animation studios where teams of artists would work on projects, leading to specialization. Soon you had artists who did storyboards, character animation, backgrounds, painting cells, or other jobs. However, one area of specialization that never developed in these early studios was an actual scriptwriter. Artists, animators, and other members of the creative team worked out the gags or storylines collectively. In some studios, there was a bullpen of writers whose jobs were to generate ideas and gags, which were then worked up in storyboard form, but the writers didn't write scripts as we think of scripts today.

The Fleischer brothers' sing-along cartoons beginning in 1924 and Disney's *Steamboat Willie* in 1928 were important milestones. They advanced animation styles and the use of sound and music at a time when sound was still new and revolutionary even for live-action films. Although Disney's *Snow White* wasn't the first animated feature ever created, it set a new high in the level of art, sophistication of character development, and memorable music. On the early animation features, there are people credited with the story and adaptation, but no actual animation script was part of the process. It was a fluid process of storyboards and story concepts being worked out in some combination of images and written word.

Other than the Disney features, most animation through the 1950s consisted of short pieces made to run in front of feature films, relying mostly on visual gags and jokes. As interest in theatrical shorts waned, many movie studios shut down their animation-production arms. This led William Hanna and Joe Barbera, who had formed HB Enterprises in 1944 (later Hanna-Barbera Productions), to focus on animation for the new medium of television starting in 1957. Initially, the studio turned out five- to seven-minute cartoons, giving birth to *Yogi Bear* and

Huckleberry Hound. Then came the next evolutionary step—the half-hour animated sitcom of *The Flintstones*, debuting in 1960.

Producing animation for television, particularly in this longer format, was vastly different from making theatrical shorts. The need to turn out longer shows week after week on extremely tight budgets had a profound effect on both the quality of the animation and the need to streamline the process. Animators accustomed to working out gags for short pieces couldn't maintain the volume of work that was required for the longer shows.

During the 1960s, these business-driven necessities led for the first time to the hiring of actual scriptwriters—people who knew how to type out a script that could be handed to the storyboard artists. Other studios—such as Filmation, DePatie-Freleng, and Ruby-Spears—sprang up to create animated TV series, and the step of hiring scriptwriters to first create the script was at long last integrated into the creative process.

Thus, the role of scriptwriters in the field of animation is relatively recent, given the entire history of the art form. At times, there has been an underlying tension between those who write and those who draw—I've encountered a similar tension in game design as well. Some artists may argue that only someone who can draw should be writing animation, while some writers might feel that artists don't truly understand how to write. Each side of this argument has its pros and cons, but what it gets down to is that this is a storytelling medium. You can be a great visual storyteller who writes scripts, as well as a great storyteller who draws animation, or you can be any combination of the two.

Attempts have been made for a show to go back to creating animation the old way. I haven't seen those efforts succeed for regular, half-hour series, however. Although some talented artists create their own shows and do the writing themselves, they are the exceptions. Today, the dominant method for creating a feature or television animation project is to begin with a written script, which then goes to storyboards and art design.

Another significant evolutionary step is taking place—the development of CGI (computer-generated images, frequently shortened to just CG) animation, also called 3-D. The groundbreaker in creating top-quality CG shows was Mainframe Entertainment in Vancouver, British Columbia, Canada. In 1994, Mainframe's TV series *ReBoot* was the first all-CGI series. Initially, CG was more expensive than traditional cel, or 2-D, animation, but as the technology and techniques continued to advance, CG became more and more an integral part of TV and feature animation. Pixar's *Toy Story* in 1995 showed that a CG feature could match the success of a 2-D feature, further driven by the enormous success of *Finding Nemo*.

In fact, these features were so successful that both DreamWorks and Disney have since announced that they have virtually abandoned 2-D production in favor of 3-D, decisions that continue to be hotly debated by writers, animators, and others in the field of animation. The one thing that doesn't change, whether the project is done in 2-D or 3-D, is the need for strong stories, compelling characters, and well-written scripts. The fact that the Oscars now include a category for best animated feature supports the need for top-quality writing in an art form that continues to mature.

Genres and Categories

Animation has become wonderfully diverse and open to new forms of production (Flash animation, for example). Here is a rundown of the realms of animation production that provide opportunities for you as a writer.

Features

Features, or long-form animation, can be made for three major markets:

- Theatrical
  The powerhouse studios for animation features are Disney, Pixar, and DreamWorks, but many other studios compete in this arena, including smaller, independent companies, as well as studios in Canada, France, Australia, Japan, India, Ireland, and elsewhere.

- Direct-to-video
  Some major studios have a separate division to create direct-to-video animated features. There are smaller, independent companies that also create direct-to-video.

- Television
  There isn't a lot of feature-length animation made specifically for TV. Although this does happen from time to time, it's not a regular market. Early in 2004, Warner Bros. announced an in-house division to produce four TV movies per year, most likely to be based on the studio's existing properties.

Television

There was once a thriving market for syndicated animation. Syndication refers to selling directly to as many individual TV stations as possible the rights to broadcast a program—rather than selling the rights to a network, which then itself broadcasts the program. Syndication of animation has all but vanished from the scene. The current outlets are networks and cable, though animation is seen less and less on network channels. The big cable channels such as Fox, Disney, Nickelodeon, and the Cartoon Network have taken over as the main outlets. Showtime, the Sci-Fi Channel, and others are experimenting with adult-level animated shows.

Animation for television tends to break out by age groups more than anything else. We have finally reached the stage where we can divide animation into shows for children and shows for adults.

Children's Animation

When shows are evaluated for ratings, the age groups are broken down into:

- kids 2 to 11
- kids 6 to 11
- twins 9 to 14

In development, there are loose guidelines that differ somewhat from the above. It's more common to break the categories down into roughly:

- preschool and very young (2–8)
- young heading toward twin (8–12)

I rarely encounter someone asking me to develop or write children's animation for older than 12, an age when kids begin to shy away from this type of animation.

Animation for the youngest audience is usually geared toward soft, safe shows with educational content. Laws protect young children from content deemed potentially harmful. One such statute is the Children's Television Act of 1990, which limits the amount of advertising that a broadcaster can air during children's programming. The Federal Communications Commission (FCC) has laid down guidelines that require stations to air an average of no less than three hours a week of "educational" programming, though what gets approved as educational has been the source of much controversy.

The older group has a wider menu:

- comedy *(SpongeBob SquarePants, Looney Tunes)*

- humorous action-adventure *(Jackie Chan Adventures, Kim Possible)*

- serious action-adventure *(X-Men, Teen Titans, He-Man)*

- anime *(Pokémon, Yu-Gi-Oh!, Dragon Ball Z)*

Educational, comedy, and action-adventure are viable markets for breaking into animation writing. The anime shows are done in Japan and don't provide work for outside writers, except for one specialized job:

- ADR: This stands for additional dialogue recording. English-speaking writers are hired to write the English-language dialogue to either be dubbed over the Japanese dialogue or used as subtitles.

Animation for Adults

The types of shows being done for an adult audience range all over the spectrum. Here's a partial list:

- sitcoms and satire

- edgy anthropomorphic animals

- science fiction

- fantasy

- cyberpunk

- contemporary, mainstream life with a twist

- sexy, naughty action-adventure

- weird, off-the-wall humor

- adaptations of comic books or comic strips

One comment needs to be made regarding the sitcom-style animation shows that run in prime time, such as *The Simpsons* or *King of the Hill*. Although they're produced using animation as the medium, such shows are written in the same way as sitcoms, meaning they use a staff of in-house writers (who sit together in a room working out the shows) with experience in live-action sitcom and comedy. These shows almost never, if at all, use animation writers.

To get a better sense of the prime-time writing process, I recommend purchasing the May 2003 issue of *Written By*, the monthly magazine of the Writers Guild of America, west (WGAw). This issue features articles about animation, including one about the writing staff of *King of the Hill*. You can purchase back issues of *Written By* magazine by calling the WGA Publications Department (323-782-4522) to make sure that the particular issue that you want is available. Then send $5 to *Written By* at the WGA, 7000 Third Street, Los Angeles, California, 90048. The $5 price includes domestic postage. If you're in Canada or overseas, you should call and inquire about postage.

If your interest lies strictly in these types of shows, this book won't help you. The only advice I can give on this topic is that prime time is one of the most difficult areas of writing to break into. You'll need to study how live-action sitcoms are written and developed, and you'll need to write two or three brilliantly funny spec scripts for existing shows. A "spec" (for speculative) script is a sample script based on an existing show. You write this script on your own to show how well you can handle matching the sensibilities of the show and the dialogue of the characters. You must live in Los Angeles and get an agent who can represent you well in this specialized area of the business.

A few prime-time non-sitcom animation shows (for example, *Batman*) have shown a bias against using animation writers and a preference for using live-action writers, even though these are done along the lines of other animated shows. This says something about how even writers coming from the field of animation can view animation writers.

Anime

I want to touch a bit more upon the impact of anime on the current animation market. As I said, anime is created and produced in Japan and has become wildly popular, not to mention profitable, for the American market especially. "Anime" covers a lot of territory. *Pokémon* (a fun action show for kids) is quite a different thing from *Cowboy Bebop* (harder edged for adults) in look, tone, content, and intended audience. It's a good idea to become acquainted with a range of anime, both the type intended for children and the type intended for adults.

This explosion in popularity has had ripple effects. The desire to draw upon both the visual and storytelling techniques of anime has definitely had an effect on Western animation. I've already had one situation where it was taken for granted that I knew what the distinctive qualities and features of anime are, and that I could incorporate them into the script. Be prepared for a producer or story editor to ask for something to be done in an anime style. Don't be afraid to ask the story editor or producer what elements of anime he or she wants you to incorporate.

In some cases, the influence is mainly visual: the oversize eyes, small chins, small nose, small mouth, the hair and clothes flowing elegantly or aggressively in the wind, an action shot of the character that is static while a streaked color background flashes past to simulate motion, and various other visual themes common to most anime. There are also cultural differences that can trip up a Western viewer. For example, to the American audience, crossed eyes indicate silliness; to the Japanese audience, they indicate ferocious anger or readiness for battle.

In some cases, there are stylized anime emotional cues—a character emanating heart symbols to indicate being lovesick, wavy streaks down a character's face to indicate crying, a character's eyes turning into stars to indicate being bedazzled, and so on.

When the influence reaches the writing level, it means you must think in an anime storytelling manner. This includes certain types of poses, moments of silence and confrontation that cut back and forth between the two antagonists, certain types of shots (for example, ultra-close-up on eyes), and other such poses and characteristics that you can absorb only by watching a sufficient amount of anime.

On another level, there is a more fundamental difference in the nature of the stories the Japanese like to tell in anime. They tend to be more complex, sometimes sadder or grimmer or with a sense of doom, and approach the character's emotions and actions differently than a Western writer tends to do. For some reason, this aspect of anime hasn't had the same level of influence on Western writing. When someone says, "Write this in an anime style," what they mean most of the time is to mimic the visual storytelling style, not the plot, dramatic structure, or thematic style.

Alternate Forms of Animation

Exciting developments have made it possible for creators to make animated projects on a more independent basis. These innovations allow homegrown talent to develop outside the realm of the media megacorporations.

Flash software makes it possible to create animation for the Web, and has advanced to the point where Flash animation has been used in animated TV series. Though it's a limited form of animation, Flash nonetheless provides the means for individuals to create original projects of good enough quality to demonstrate a creator's potential.

Machinima is animation created by using videogame technology, animation, and art assets, which are then edited, with voice, sound, and music added to create a virtual "film" using the videogame engine. Some of these Machinima have won awards at film festivals, two examples being *Hardly Workin'* and *Red vs. Blue*.

With the explosion of media being created for the mobile and wireless market, it's worth paying attention to ways in which animation might be created specifically for that use.

CHAPTER 2

Terminology

Most of the scriptwriting terms employed in animation scripts are the same as those employed in live-action scripts, with perhaps a few exceptions. Here are the terms you want to know before we move ahead to discuss script format.

They are followed by a further glossary of animation-related terms that will be useful to you.

Script Terms

ACTION

The ACTION, or description, paragraph occurs immediately below the SLUGLINE and is just what you think it is—a line or paragraph that serves any number of functions: to describe a setting or location, to describe what actions the character in the shot is taking, to set mood or tone, to indicate sounds, to give certain specific camera-movement directions, or whatever else is required to convey what the reader needs to know about that shot or for establishing a scene.

ANGLE ON, ANGLE -

A more generic way to call out an individual shot that indicates to the storyboard artist what to concentrate on for this shot, or simply who is in the shot.

```
ANGLE ON JACK

ANGLE ON JACK, DICK, AND JANE

ANGLE ON CORNER OF WEATHERED BUILDING

ANGLE - JACK

ANGLE - JACK, DICK, AND JANE

ANGLE - BARBARIAN HORDE
```

B.G. (BACKGROUND)

Used to indicate that some part of the action, an object, a character is to be set in the background of the shot. Or you could just be describing something that's in the b.g.

BEAT, A BEAT

This term, set inside parentheses, is used to indicate that you want the character to pause briefly between pieces of dialogue. It can convey hesitation, a moment of thought, a point of emphasis, or a moment of silence (where the character might be listening to someone on the other end of a phone conversation, but we don't hear the other side). (See other uses of the word "beat" under Other Animation Terms.)

```
ANGLE ON JACK AND JANE

She glares at him.

                    JANE
          You want me to leave? Fine,
          I'll leave.
               (a beat)
          When I'm good and ready!
```

```
ANGLE ON JANE

who answers the phone.

                    JANE
          Hello?
               (beat)
          He did what?
               (beat)
          Of all the stupid tricks. Where
          are you now?
               (beat)
          Stay put. I'm on my way.
```

CLOSE-UP, CLOSE ON

Used in a SLUGLINE to indicate to the storyboard artist that in this shot you want the camera to be very close on a person or thing, as indicated. You should have a solid reason for using a close-up rather than calling for it at random. Good reasons include wanting to emphasize a reaction, to call special attention to an important object, or to make sure the camera is close enough to clearly convey a significant piece of action.

```
CLOSE-UP ON JACK'S EYES

He squints against the painful glare of the sun that blinds
him.

CLOSE ON JACK'S HAND

as he secretly passes a datadisk to Jane.
```

CONT'D (CONTINUED)

It's used in three ways:

1. At the bottom of a page on a shooting script, to indicate that the script continues.

2. When dialogue is broken up across two pages, to indicate there is more dialogue on the following page. In this usage, it's centered in the middle of the dialogue column at the bottom of the page where the dialogue breaks.

3. After a character's name and placed in parentheses, to indicate the character is continuing a speech that was begun in another piece of dialogue, but was interrupted by a piece of action.

```
ANGLE FAVORING JACK

                      JACK
          I told you . . .

Jane reacts with surprise to his anger.

                 JACK (CONT'D)
          . . . I don't need your help!
```

CUT TO:

This is a TRANSITION that is used to indicate that this scene is ended and we are cutting to an entirely different scene in a different location. Visually, it means that the image on the screen is instantly gone and instantly replaced by the next image, with no time lag in between. CUT TO: is a general, all-purpose transition, though it's better to use a DISSOLVE TO: to convey a significant passage of time between scenes.

In a script, a transition is positioned along the right margin and is followed by a semicolon.

DIALOGUE

The DIALOGUE portion of a script consists of the character name and what the character says. There can be a parenthetical below the character name or within the body of the dialogue. There can be special instructions to the right of the character name, such as V.O., O.S., or CONT'D.

The reason for indenting and setting out the dialogue in this way is old and simple: to make it easy for actors to flip through a script and see what their lines are.

In animation, it also makes it easy to count the number of lines, as is sometimes required. NOTE: each individual "chunk" of dialogue is considered to be a "line" of dialogue. In the sample shown below, this would count as two lines of dialogue for Jack, one line of dialogue for Dick, one line of dialogue for Jane (even though all she has for a "line" is a burst of laughter), and one line for Jack's Dog—for a total of five lines. Jane's "line" and the Dog's whine still have to be recorded, and still take up time in the audio track, hence being counted as dialogue.

```
                          JACK
                    (annoyed - to Jane)
              Give me one good reason why I
              shouldn't drop-kick you from here
              to tomorrow? Well?

                       JACK'S DOG
                    (worried whine)

                          JANE
                    (burst of laughter)

                          JACK
              What's that supposed to mean?

                          DICK
              It means you're asking for a
              broken leg, Jack.
                       (a beat)
              Trust me, you want to stay on her
              good side.
```

DISSOLVE TO:

This is a TRANSITION that is used to indicate that this scene is ended and we are cutting to another scene with some amount of time intervening between the two. Visually, it indicates that the image on the screen will slowly dissolve, to be replaced by a new image. The time difference between the two scenes could be minutes, hours, days, years, past, or future. A DISSOLVE TO: is more about changing time than changing location. You might dissolve from Jack collapsing in bed in the morning to Jack waking up on the bed at night—same place, different time. It's a gradual transition on the screen rather than the instantaneous transition of a CUT TO:.

On occasion, a writer might also use RAPID DISSOLVE TO: (just a faster-than-usual dissolve to indicate a very short passage of time).

In a script, a transition is positioned along the right margin and is followed by a semicolon.

DURING:

This is a handy word to use to indicate that you want a piece of dialogue to occur while a certain piece of action takes place, without breaking away from the continuous movement of that shot or cutting it down into smaller shots. However, be careful not to use DURING: at times when you *should* break out those actions.

```
ANGLE ON JACK AND DICK

who enter the stairwell and work their way down the
stairs, tense, alert, weapons ready. DURING:

                    JACK
          They could be anywhere around
          here, kid. Don't get careless.
          And don't get nervous. And don't
          get in my way.
```

ECU, EXTREME CLOSE-UP

Just what it sounds like. Going very, very close on someone or something in a shot. It can be used in a slugline or used in a shot.

```
ECU ON JANE'S EYES

which brim with tears.

ON JACK'S EYES

Go to ECU to show that Jack is also at the point of tears.
```

ENTERS FRAME, EXITS FRAME

A command used in the action paragraph when you want to have one or more characters enter or leave the shot after you've established it.

```
INT. BUNGALOW - JACK AND DICK

look over the stolen documents. Jane ENTERS FRAME to join
them. Jack barely glances up at Jane.

                    JACK
          Good, you're here. Get me a glass
          of water.

Fuming, Jane EXITS FRAME. Dick grins and shakes his head.

                    DICK
          That was a baaaad idea.

Jane ENTERS FRAME and dumps a glass of water on Jack's
head.
```

EST., ESTABLISHING

Used in a SLUGLINE or ACTION PARAGRAPH when you're establishing where a scene is taking place before jumping into the interior action. This works best when the location has already been seen, and only a quick establishing shot is needed to alert the audience that the action is going back to that place. It's like seeing a quick establishing shot of a spaceship before jumping to the bridge or some other room inside the spaceship. Or an exterior shot to establish a well-known city, such as Los Angeles or New York, before jumping to another shot that is then assumed to be somewhere in that city. An establishing shot is usually a wide or long shot.

```
EXT. ESTABLISH OCEAN LINER - DAY

It plies a calm ocean.

EXT. HOLLYWOOD SIGN

just long enough TO ESTABLISH.

EXT. SPACESHIP - DEEP SPACE

Establishing shot.
```

EXT. (EXTERIOR)

EXT. is used at the beginning of a SLUGLINE to establish that this scene or shot is in an exterior location. Because you're establishing a scene, it's also vital to indicate whether it's DAY or NIGHT for the exterior location (with a couple of exceptions, such as space or the bottom of the ocean or someplace where day and night are irrelevant).

```
EXT. AIRPORT CONTROL TOWER - NIGHT

EXT. MEDICAL BUILDING - DAY

EXT. SPACESHIP - DEEP SPACE
```

FADE IN:, FADE OUT

FADE IN: is used to start the script and start each act; FADE OUT is used to end each act and end the script. Most commonly, FADE IN: is on the left margin, FADE OUT is on the right margin. For whatever mysterious reason, FADE IN is followed by a colon; FADE OUT isn't. FADE IN: should lead directly into the first SLUGLINE. Other information, such as TEASER or ACT ONE, comes before the FADE IN:. FADE OUT comes immediately after the final shot of that act or the script, followed by END OF TEASER, END OF ACT ONE, THE END, and so on.

FAVORING

One way to call out an individual shot in a script once the location or setting is established. This would be the start of a SLUGLINE, followed by the character, object, or whatever it is that you want the storyboard artist to emphasize in that shot. If there are a number of characters in the shot, FAVORING would most commonly be used to indicate that you want emphasis given to a particular character (or to more than one).

```
FAVORING JACK'S HAND

as he reaches out for the crystal skull.

ANGLE FAVORING THE SKULL

which reflects Jack's reaching hand. The glint of the
ring on Jack's hand creates the illusion of a glint in
the skull's eye.
```

F.G. (FOREGROUND)

Used to indicate that some part of the action, an object, a character is to be set in the foreground of the shot.

INT. (INTERIOR)

INT. is used at the beginning of a SLUGLINE to establish that this scene is in an interior location or set. Generally, you don't need to worry about establishing whether it's a DAY or NIGHT location for interiors unless you haven't established that information previously (such as going from an exterior shot of the same location to an interior shot), and there's some reason that you need to (an airport control tower, for example, where it would be important to indicate what can be seen from the windows).

```
INT. AIRPORT CONTROL TOWER - NIGHT

INT. SUBWAY STATION

INT. SPACESHIP COCKPIT
```

INTERCUT TO, INTERCUTTING TO

Another term that can be used when doing quick cuts back and forth between two ongoing lines of action, or a larger piece of action (such as a battle) — where there might be multiple fronts to deal with or multiple characters to follow, and where everything is happening more or less at the same time. Best used when it doesn't involve dialogue (see also QUICK CUT), but it can also be used when cutting back and forth between people engaged in a phone conversation.

```
INTERCUT TO:

    JACK hits the ground and readies his gun.

    JANE takes cover behind a metal container, her gun in
hand.

    DICK drops from the roof and takes up position outside
a window, a gun in one hand and smoke bomb in the other.
```

MATCH DISSOLVE TO:

This is a nice visual trick when called for, but don't overuse it. In a MATCH DISSOLVE TO:, some element in the scene that is ending will match up to an opening element in the next scene. Obviously, there should be a good thematic or story reason to tie the two elements together.

```
ANGLE ON JACK

who holds up the crystal skull to study it. MOVE IN on the
skull until it fills the screen.
                                        MATCH DISSOLVE TO:
CLOSE-UP ON CRYSTAL SKULL

except that this one is in a display case at the city museum,
labeled "Peruvian Quartz Skull."
```

MOVE IN

This tells the storyboard artist that you want a camera movement that moves in closer to something on the screen. Use in the ACTION (description) paragraph rather than in a SLUGLINE.

```
ANGLE ON WEATHERED BUILDING

A door <BANGS> crazily in the storm wind. MOVE IN on the
door as a hand suddenly grabs the door's edge.
```

(OC), (O.C.)

OFF CAMERA. Same as OFFSTAGE. See below.

(OS), (O.S.)

OFFSTAGE. It's used to the right of the character's name in dialogue to indicate that someone is speaking who is in the scene, but is not seen in that shot.

```
ANGLE FAVORING JACK

who stands by himself, staring moodily out a window.

                       JACK
               Guess I'm on my own.

                     JANE (O.S.)
               Not yet, you old grouch.

Jane ENTERS FRAME to stand next to him.
```

OTS

OVER THE SHOULDER. This tells the storyboard artist to draw the view of the scene as though the camera were seeing it over the shoulder of a particular character.

```
OTS ON JACK

facing Dick and Jane, who wait for him to speak.
```

PAN

Refers to a horizontal camera movement—either from right to left, or from left to right. It's used in the action paragraph and is especially useful when establishing a new location where you want to show more of it or linger over it for a few seconds more than you would with a quick establishing shot.

```
EXT. SURFACE OF THE MOON - SUNLIT SIDE

PAN ACROSS the stark beauty of sharp-edged craters until we
come to the moon base, a lonely haven on the airless
surface.
```

PARENTHETICALS

A PARENTHETICAL is extra information about the character who is speaking or making a sound. It's placed inside parentheses below the character's name in the dialogue. Parentheticals have three basic uses:

1. Indicating a specific tone, emotion, or inflection for the voice actor. This is discouraged in live-action scripts, but voice actors often receive only their own lines, and record their lines without interacting with the other voice actors. Consequently, parentheticals are more commonly used in animation scripts to clue in the voice actors to a tone or emotion they might otherwise miss.

2. Indicating that the voice needs special filtering or modification in editing (as in a voice coming through a communications device).

3. Describing a sound you want the voice actor to make, especially in the case of a nonspeaking character or creature. Even if you want a character only to laugh or scream, you need to cover it as a piece of dialogue by using a parenthetical. You would also use the parenthetical to indicate a whisper or low voice (sotto voce).

```
ANGLE FAVORING JACK
                    JACK
                 (sarcastic)
            Oh, that's just great.

                  JACK'S DOG
               (scolding barks)

                    JACK
               (with a snort)
            Everybody's got an opinion around
            here.
                  (laughter)
```

POV

POINT OF VIEW. In this type of shot, you're asking the storyboard artist to draw the scene from a specific character's point of view, to see the scene the way the character is seeing it.

```
JACK'S POV - THROUGH WINDOW

The thick glass distorts what he sees so that all he can
make out is the dark, indistinct shape of an unknown
person.

JANE'S POV - THROUGH SCOPE

The crosshairs in the scope focus on an enemy vehicle. The
scope's laser indicator LIGHTS UP.
```

PULL BACK, PULL BACK TO REVEAL

As with MOVE IN, this tells the storyboard artist that you want a camera movement that pulls the camera farther away from the shot or from something in the shot. See also WIDEN.

```
CLOSE ON CRYSTAL SKULL

held in a man's hand, but we PULL BACK TO REVEAL it's held
by Dick instead of Jack.
```

QUICK CUT

This is a method of intercutting (cutting back and forth) between quickly paced shots that may or may not be in the same location, but are occurring more or less instantaneously or in very quick sequence. It's especially useful in an action sequence, such as a battle, where you've already established where the characters are and basically what's going on, but you need to jump around a lot. It saves having to use space-eating CUT TO: transitions where they aren't really needed.

```
ANGLE ON JACK

settled into position. Satisfied everything's ready, he
talks into his commlink.
                         JACK
                  (into commlink)
             This is it. Countdown!
```

```
QUICK CUT - JANE

                              JANE
                       (into commlink)
                   Three!

QUICK CUT - DICK

                              DICK
                       (into commlink)
                   Two!

QUICK CUT BACK TO JACK

                              JACK
                       (into commlink)
                   One! Hit it!

He charges forward!
```

SCENE HEADING (SEE SLUGLINE)

(SFX:)

SOUND EFFECTS. This method of specifically notating a sound effect using (SFX:) was more prevalent in animation scripts earlier than it is now. What has become common is to call attention to a specific sound by putting the sound in CAPS. Depending on the preferences of the story editor, some scripts will make the sound effects **bold** or will add carets around the sound: <CAPS>. Adding the carets helps draw attention to the sound.

The original intent of using (SFX:) was to make it easier for a sound editor to find the sounds he or she needed to know about. I've dropped the use of (SFX:) in favor of the other two methods. Here are examples of three ways to indicate sound effects:

```
WIDE SHOT ON ENEMY TANK

It's hit by Jane's laser beam and <EXPLODES MASSIVELY>!

or

WIDE SHOT ON ENEMY TANK

It's hit by Jane's laser beam and EXPLODES MASSIVELY!

or

WIDE SHOT ON ENEMY TANK

It's hit by Jane's laser beam and explodes! (SFX: massive
metallic explosion)
```

SLUGLINE

A slugline is always typed in CAPS. The slugline immediately informs the reader that this is a new scene or a new shot. In animation, every individual shot needs to be set up with a slugline. A slugline should never be more than a few words, only the bare minimum necessary to establish where, what, or who. Anytime a script transitions to a different scene or location, the slugline needs to begin with an EXT. or INT. In some current scriptwriting software, SLUGLINE is instead called SCENE HEADING.

SOTTO VOCE

Latin for "low voice." Nowadays, many writers simply write "low voice" or "under his breath" instead. It means just what it says, that the character should speak in a low-volume voice as though not wanting to be overheard — which is different from speaking in a whisper. This falls into the category of being a parenthetical, which is voice direction for the actor.

```
                          JACK
                     (sotto voce)
              Do you think she heard us?
```

TRACK WITH

This is used in the action paragraph when you want to have a shot that follows a particular character, vehicle, or object while in motion.

```
INSIDE MEDICAL LAB - JACK

enters stealthily. TRACK WITH HIM as he moves silently
across the lab to a table of virus samples.
```

TRANSITIONS

Transitions are a way of telling the reader and the editor — and ultimately, the viewer — that the story is shifting from one time or place to another. The three most common transitions are CUT TO:, DISSOLVE TO:, and WIPE TO:. A show can have specialized transitions. *X-Men: Evolution* had an X-WIPE TO:. Why? Just for fun, really. There are endless variations on transitions — such as DISSOLVE THRU TO: (as in moving through a wall to see what's inside), RIPPLE DISSOLVE: (in which a ripple effect is used), RAPID DISSOLVE TO: (just a faster-than-usual dissolve to indicate a very short passage of time), FLASH CUT TO:, INTERCUT TO:, and on occasion, I've seen a writer invent weird and meaningless transitions simply to mess with the artists' heads. I prefer to keep it simple. CUT, DISSOLVE, and WIPE work just fine 99 percent of the time.

Over the years, I've seen a trend in animation scripts toward doing away with transitions almost completely. The main reason for this is to save the three lines that would be used for a transition so that those lines are available for the other parts of the script. In other words, it's a space-saving cheat. I don't recommend using this cheat for spec scripts or when first breaking in, but I also don't recommend going overboard with excessive transitions. Use them only when really needed for a major scene or location shift.

In a script, transitions are positioned along the right margin and are followed by a semicolon.

TWO-SHOT, 2SHOT, 2S

Used in a SLUGLINE to indicate a medium shot, meaning the camera moves in close enough to frame two characters fairly tightly. It's more commonly used in live-action scripts than in animation. I include it mainly in case you run across it somewhere.

(VO), (V.O.)

VOICE-OVER. This is placed to the right of the character's name in dialogue to indicate that the voice being heard is coming from some other location, and that the character is not present in the scene or the shot—such as a voice coming over a phone or communications device. One exception to the rule of the character not being in the scene would be narration where you want to hear the character narrating a piece of the story rather than speaking in dialogue. The narration could be done with the character relating the story as a flashback, or it might be done with the viewer hearing the character's thoughts.

```
EXT. CITY STREET - NIGHT

Rain drenches the desolate street. Jack comes into view
under a streetlamp, a long figure hunched inside a dripping
wet coat. He looks thoroughly miserable.

                    JACK (V.O.)
                 (narrating)
            It began on one of the most
            miserable nights of my life.

A cell phone <BEEPS> in his pocket. With no great
enthusiasm, he pulls it out and flips it open.

                    JACK
                 (into phone)
            Yeah?

                    JANE (V.O.)
                 (via phone)
            If this is Jack, I have an offer
            for you.
```

WALLA

An old script term to indicate general crowd or background voice noise. Typical walla would be the murmur of a crowd before the concert begins, the angry noises of a mob, background chatter at a party. It's never used for individual dialogue. It's written as a parenthetical.

```
                    MOB
                 (angry walla)

                    CONCERT AUDIENCE
                 (walla)
```

WIDE SHOT

Used in a SLUGLINE. Pretty much self-explanatory. Use it when the shot requires seeing a wider view of what's going on.

```
WIDE SHOT - A LINE OF ENEMY TANKS

<RUMBLES> toward the camera.
```

WIDEN, WIDEN TO INCLUDE

This is used in the action paragraph to indicate to the storyboard artist a camera move to widen the frame of the shot to include something else. It's similar to a PULL BACK, but usually indicates widening the frame to the left or right, rather than overall.

```
ANGLE ON JACK

who kneels to examine prints on the dusty floor. WIDEN TO
INCLUDE JANE as she kneels down beside him.
```

WIPE TO:

A transition that is used to convey a change in location, but not time. Use a WIPE TO: when the new scene could be taking place concurrently with the scene that just ended, or immediately after it. The visual swiping effect of a WIPE TO: suggests immediacy, rather than a passage of time between scenes. It says to the eye that "we've whipped from here to there." In a script, a transition is positioned along the right margin and is followed by a semicolon.

Other Animation Terms

2-D, 3-D (CG)

2-D = two-dimensional—traditional cel animation that is drawn or painted. 3-D = three-dimensional, also called CGI (computer-generated images), or CG for short. This is animation created using computer software. Besides the fully 3-D look, CG can be modified to superficially look like 2-D cel animation, while retaining the capability of making 3-D movements.

ACT BREAK

The point in the script where you end the act to provide for commercials.

BACKGROUNDS

In 2-D, the background is a drawing or painting that is used behind the animated characters as the shot requires. It's important to understand that a background is different from a location. For example, let's say that in the script, you've asked for a location that is the interior of a bus terminal. In your mind, you might think *INT. BUS TERMINAL = one background*. That depends on what action you've written for that bus terminal. If your character enters, walks past a wall lined with seats, buys a ticket at the ticket window, then looks out a window while waiting for the bus to pull up, you've created at least four backgrounds: (1) entrance to terminal, (2) wall of seats, (3) ticket window, and (4) window to the outside. The number of backgrounds that need to be designed and created affects both schedule and cost.

In 3-D, the bus terminal is constructed in the computer, but the CG artist might construct only whatever part of it is necessary. If a full 3-D effect is wanted (as in being able to move around the room in any direction), then the entire location will be constructed, which again affects the schedule and the cost.

BACKSTORY

A term for the story that takes place before the time your script or series begins. It could be an origin story, a series of events leading up to the opening of the series, an epic history, a personal biography—whatever leads up to the current moment of the story you're telling. The backstory may or may not ever be related within the series or the movie, but you need to know the backstories of your world, your characters, and your current story in order to have the richness and depth a good story requires.

BEATS

A "beat" within a script relates specifically to a pause in dialogue, but there are many other uses of a beat or beats in the writing process, especially during the outline stage, where you're establishing the structure of the story. If you imagine that you're working out the structure of your story on three-by-five-inch index cards, then each card would have a notation for a key scene to cover your major plot points, your major action moments, your important emotional moments, and so forth. Each index card is a beat, and the sequential beats are the structure of your story. I will often work out the beats of my story using pen and paper, simply because that method somehow feels more comfortable. Then I go to the computer to put the flesh on the bones until I have an outline.

BIBLE

The show bible—or series bible, or just "the bible"—refers to the development document that was written before the show went into production. A bible contains all the information about the concept, character biographies, character relationships, setting, vehicles, weapons, what a story editor does or doesn't want to have pitched, or any other details that a writer needs to know in order to write for the show. Ideally, a bible is added to and updated throughout the course of a series. For details on creating a bible, see Chapter 4.

BUMPERS

These are very short pieces of animation, only a few seconds long, that are inserted at the end of acts and at the beginning of acts to create a distinct transition between the show and the commercials. Their purpose, supposedly, is to make it obvious to the kids that the show is stopping at this point and starting at this other point, and that whatever comes in between isn't part of the show. At one time, there were advocacy groups complaining that kids had trouble discerning the difference between the show and the commercials, hence the bumpers.

You as the writer do not have to be concerned about bumpers or include indications for them in your scripts. It's strictly a production element.

CEL

Short for cellulose acetate. Each cel is a clear plastic sheet of acetate (an average size being twelve and a half inches by ten and a half inches) on which the characters or objects to be animated are painted. The cel is then laid over a background and photographed to complete a single frame of film. One cel = one frame. In full animation, twenty-four frames = one second of animation.

CHARACTER ARC

This is a common term used when talking about how a character will begin, develop, and change over the course of time. That time could be one episode, one movie, or an entire series. It's easier to create a strong character arc for a character in a feature, which runs longer and is usually self-contained (unless it's a trilogy or series). It's trickier to come up with good character arcs over the course of a continuing, episodic series. If your character never changes at all, never has insights or losses or gains, you have a boring character. But a character who reaches the end of his or her arc before a series ends can cause you all sorts of other problems. If his or her arc is resolved, where do you take the character next? Is there a new arc? Is the character played out and no longer useful to the series?

Obviously, this isn't much of an issue for comedy shows. You don't really expect Bart Simpson to have a character arc. He is what he is, and his inherent nature drives the gags. Character arc applies to shows that rely on some level of continuity in the stories.

- Example
  Jack begins as a loner, unwilling to make friends. During the course of the series, he is forced to ally himself with Dick and Jane in order to achieve his goals. He is indifferent toward them at first, but as they face danger and adventures together, Jack comes to realize the importance of friendship. At the climax, Jack is willing to put his own life on the line to save his friends.

HIGH CONCEPT

This term is commonly used throughout the film and television industry. It means that the underlying concept that is being pitched is strong enough or quirky enough or has a good enough hook that it can be summed up in one sentence that sells the idea. Here are some examples of high concept:

- A man trapped in a high-rise office building must single-handedly defeat a group of terrorists to save his wife.

- A little boy who can see dead people gets help from a doctor who doesn't realize that he himself is a ghost.

- An ogre becomes human to win back the princess he loves, only to find that she prefers the ogre.

LIMITED ANIMATION

Animation produced using fewer than twenty-four frames per second, or other production shortcuts. See "SHOT ON THREES," "SHOT ON TWOS" for more details.

MODELS ("ON MODEL")

Refers to the drawings that are done of the characters, locations, or major props to pin down exactly how they should look consistently from show to show. If a character that should be short is suddenly tall, the character is no longer "on model."

"SHOT ON THREES," "SHOT ON TWOS"

The standard frame rate for anything that is shot on film is twenty-four frames per second (fps) because this is the rate that tricks the eye into seeing twenty-four still shots as being in fluid motion when run at the proper rate of speed. In digital, the higher-caliber cameras emulate twenty-four fps. In 2-D animation, the only way to achieve truly comparable, fluid motion is to use twenty-four fps, but this is expensive and time-consuming because one has to create twenty-four unique cels of animation for each second of the show. To cut budget and production time, lesser-quality animation may use twelve fps or only eight fps. This is achieved by using the same cel for two frames instead of one, or using the same cel for three frames instead of one. It can go even higher than that, but the quality of the animation suffers drastically. Anime is commonly shot on threes.

SIDES

"Sides" is a term that refers to sample dialogue (a hefty paragraph's worth) for characters that need to be cast. The dialogue should capture the personality and speech patterns of the characters. Sides are then given to the actors who are auditioning for those roles.

SPEC SCRIPT

This is a script written on speculation, not for money or on an assignment. For more details on spec scripts, see Chapter 4.

STORY ARC

Story arc is another way of laying out the beginning, middle, and end of your story, but in episodic television, it can apply to the overall story thread that runs through a group of episodes. Arcs can encompass anything from a single episode to any number of seasons. It's difficult to lay in a big story arc for a kids' animated series because the general preference in this field is to have "stand-alone" stories that don't have to be aired in any particular sequence. This makes it easier to strip the show for syndication (meaning the episodes air each day of the week at the same time, a "strip" of syndication).

STORYBOARDS

An artist's rendering in pencil or pen (usually black-and-white, rarely in color) onto a series of panels to approximate what the composition, angle, and movement within the frame will be for each shot of animation. The storyboard shows what the visual sequence of the entire episode or movie will be. Dialogue and sound effects from the script are placed beneath the shots where the dialogue and sound should occur. The storyboard is used as the guide for all further artwork and production in creating that piece of animation, as well as providing an early indication of whether the script is too long or too short.

TAG

A short scene that is used to wrap up the end of a TV episode. It occurs after the final set of commercials and before the closing credits.

TEASER

A short scene that opens a TV episode in some exciting way that snags the viewers' attention so they'll return to watch the rest of the show after the opening credits and first set of commercials.

CHAPTER 3

The Basics

This section covers the fundamentals of how animation is created; the format of a premise, an outline, and an animation script for television; and information about feature-film animation writing. After that, we get into "Beyond the Basics," where I give additional tips, tricks, and advice.

The Animation Process

Many books have been written that cover the animation process from beginning to end. Unless you work up to a position of producer, most of these steps don't have much effect on writing the script. To be thorough, here is a brief description of the process by which animation is created for television:

- DEVELOPMENT: The concept is born, whether it's an idea pitched by someone from the inside, developed by a producer on the inside, or adapted from an acquired property (such as a comic or game). Someone is hired to write the bible and a pilot episode. For details on writing an animation bible, see Chapter 4. Development can go on for a long time until the concept is either approved and moved into production, or killed.

- SCRIPT: A story editor is hired (unless the producer fills this role), who in turn hires writers and has scripts written.

- VOICE RECORDING: The scripts are sent to a voice director, and the dialogue is recorded. The storyboards and animation must be matched to these dialogue audio tracks.

- STORYBOARDS: The final, approved scripts are given to storyboard artists to break into storyboards, which become the primary template for the rest of the animation process. Directors time the storyboards to arrive at an estimate of running time.

- BACKGROUNDS AND CHARACTER DESIGN: Usually at the same time as storyboards are being done, a production designer or art director will be designing the look of the show, the major backgrounds, and the major characters, creating model sheets to be used as the template by all other artists and animators. Additional model sheets will be created for new characters, creatures, props, specialized effects, or what have you for the individual shows. Something called a Special Pose is a model sheet for an established character wearing an outfit that hasn't been seen on that character before.

- ANIMATIC: An animatic is a very roughly animated storyboard (sometimes also called a leica reel or a pencil test), edited with the vocal track, which is used to judge the timing and length of a show. It's also a good place to catch errors that need fixing before the animatic and other art is shipped overseas to complete the animation.

- ANIMATION PRODUCTION: For a 2-D show, this is the process of painting the backgrounds, inking the cels of the moving elements, painting the cels, and shooting the cels to create the moving animation. Virtually all 2-D animation for the United States is sent to studios in Canada, Japan, Korea, Australia, France, and elsewhere.
  For a 3-D show, it goes to the CG studio, where the background and all the elements are created on computers using 3-D software. Much of the CG work is being done in Canada, Hong Kong, and India.

- POSTPRODUCTION: The completed animation comes back so that the producer and directors can check for errors, do color correction, fix pacing or timing problems, and send problems or errors back to the animators for retakes (fixing the errors). Once the retakes are done, the dialogue, sound effects, music, titles, and other elements are edited together to create the completed show.

As you can see from this, there is only one step of the process where the writer is involved, and that's early on. You might, on occasion, get a chance to look at storyboards if you ask for them. Most production companies won't think of sending storyboards to writers, but anytime I've asked for them, the company has been willing to send them. By studying storyboards of your own scripts, you may be able to pick up on areas where you can improve your storytelling or writing skills.

The Script Process

The script process I'm covering here is for television. Feature-animation development would happen on a longer schedule, and the process will vary from studio to studio (see section on feature scripts (The Animated Feature Film) later in this chapter).

With a few rare exceptions, it all begins with the script. An animation script is usually created in a series of stages:

- Springboard (not as common)
- Premise
- Outline

- First draft
- Second draft
- Polish

I'm going to use as an example a produced half-hour script from *X-Men: Evolution*, cowritten with my partner, Randy Littlejohn. The episode was titled "Spykecam," and featured the skateboarding character Spyke.

The Springboard

A springboard should be no more than a few sentences with just a very basic concept for a story idea. If we had written a springboard for "Spykecam," it would have been something like this: "Spyke is given a class assignment to make a documentary about his family . . . just as Sabretooth decides to attack the X-Men."

When there are a lot of stories already pitched to a series, a story editor may ask for springboards. This keeps the writers from having to do too much development when the odds are high that an idea may already have been done. If the story editor sees something interesting that hasn't been done, he or she can then have the writer work it into a premise.

Note that all scriptwriting—including springboards, premises, and outlines—is written in present tense.

The Premise

A premise must contain the beginning, middle, and end of the story in concise form, but with enough detail to sell the idea. There are two different methods of developing premises: outside pitches or internal development.

OUTSIDE PITCHES: The first step, of course, is being invited to pitch. Story editors will not accept unsolicited pitches. On most shows, you'll receive the show bible and other material to work from. If it's a brand-new show, you should also get the pilot script. If the show's been on for a while, try to get a synopsis list of all the episodes approved or produced so far. This will save you from pitching something that has already been approved or done. Be very familiar with an established show before pitching for it.

Unless told otherwise, you should come up with three to six premises to submit. Try to keep it within that range. Fewer than three doesn't make much of an impression, but more than six is getting to be too much.

Submit the written pitches as quickly as you can (these days, usually by e-mail), because you're in competition with other writers, and inevitably more than one writer will submit similar or the same ideas. Being the first one to submit an idea gives you an edge, though a story editor may go with someone who came up with the best take on the idea, rather than whoever submitted the concept first.

INTERNAL DEVELOPMENT: On some series, it works out better for the producer, story editor, or others at the production company to come up with the story ideas first, then hand them out to writers. Most commonly, these will be springboards, and you'll be asked to develop them into a premise first.

LENGTH: For a half-hour show, a premise should consist of not much more than two double-spaced pages or one single-spaced page. The premise doesn't have to be broken into acts, but it's a good idea to do so if you're writing a longer, more detailed premise.

THE "A" STORY AND THE "B" STORY: The main plot is called the "A" story. Most of the time, you're expected to also have a "B" story. The "B" story is a smaller subplot that parallels and intersects with the "A" story. It usually involves characters different from those used in the "A" story (because those characters are busy dealing with the main plotline), and often tends to reinforce the theme of the "A" story. For example: X character is wrongly put in jail. X's friends try to prove his innocence (the "A" story). Meanwhile, X might have an encounter in the jail (the "B" story) that gives him an insight regarding his situation.

Or you might start with all your characters involved in the "A" story and need to spin off a couple of them into a "B" story. For example, a team of heroes needs to attack a stronghold. The main attack is the "A" story, but two of the heroes (the "B" story) are separated during the action and face a different danger that tests their loyalty to the rest of the team.

The "B" story can directly tie into the "A" story or have a more indirect effect. Sometimes the "B" story provides a complication or obstacle for some part of the "A" story. For example, your hero learns that his car is wired to explode and he has one hour to defuse it (the "A" story), but a car thief makes off with the car (the "B" story). The main story is the hero having to find the car in time, while your subplot revolves around the unlucky thief who is unaware he's driving a ticking bomb.

Once in a while, you might even insert a third thread, a "C" story. This can be tricky when you have only twenty-two minutes to tell a story, but it can be done if the plot threads are simple enough.

Here is the premise for "Spykecam":

X-MEN: EVOLUTION
Spykecam
(PREMISE)
by Christy Marx & Randy Littlejohn

Mr. Vandermeer is at his wit's end trying to get Evan to do an actual book report; that is, one based on the *book*, not the movie version of the book (no, there are no musical numbers in the original version of *Les Misérables*). Claiming he wants to put Evan's media mania to good use, Mr. Vandermeer arranges for Evan to participate in an NPR-style "day in the life" visual journal. Evan gets a cool, hi-tech camcorder, and is told to record every aspect of his life for a few days for a TV show on today's American teenagers. A new Spielberg is born!

Evan thinks this is the coolest thing ever, but his constant in-your-face camera is driving his teammates and friends crazy. He's following them around the halls of the school, recording every little deed and misdeed . . . with the exception of the Toad, who desperately wants to be on film and is edited out constantly. The Toad threatens to get even. Mystique doesn't miss any of this action either. In a disguised form, she gives Evan encouragement and reminds him to get plenty of tape of his home life as well, to "balance" things out.

At the Xavier Mansion, Evan rolls tape with abandon: not only does he tape normal stuff, like Institute defense drills and Xavier operating Cerebro, but Kitty and Rogue have a mutant-style tiff over their musical differences, and Evan gets it all. Kurt stages some swashbuckling action and teleports himself and Scott into the Danger Room for the "action sequence," but Scott loses his shades, making the sequence a bit too hairy for their taste. Jean is caught using her powers to do an extra-fast cleanup in the kitchen, and when she realizes Evan is taping her—CRASH!!! She lets her power lapse, and half the kitchenware is in pieces.

The kids, all annoyed, chase Evan outside, planning to make him eat his blasted camera. But this is what Mystique's crew has been waiting for. Leaping onto the grounds, they attack our heroes in a spectacular frenzy that is actually a diversion—in the ruckus, Toad manages to switch Evan's camera with a duplicate before the villains flee.

Prof. X is concerned and has a heart-to-heart with Evan. The boy glumly admits he knows he can't use any of his cool footage . . . but he has to turn in SOMETHING. Maybe some judicious editing . . . but when he hits "playback," there's just footage of the Toad having what he thinks is that last laugh. Mystique's crew has made off with a videotape detailing some of the Institute's most closely guarded secrets! The X-Men must rush to track down Toad and the others and recover the videotape before Mystique gets information that could seriously endanger them all!

The Outline

With luck, the premise is approved, though there may be notes and changes as required by the story editor or producer. It would be extremely unusual to rewrite a premise. Instead, you'll take the notes into account when you write the outline.

An outline is usually a beat-by-beat description of the script, broken into the necessary number of acts, with the major sluglines (interiors and exteriors) indicated. I say *usually*, because you will write the outline according to what the story editor wants, and I know at least one story editor who hates the beat-by-beat format. Instead, you may be instructed to write it as straight descriptive prose without EXT. or INT. sluglines.

Either way, the outline should convey enough information for the story editor and production people to know how many locations there are, how many locations are new (requiring new background art), and other production items that may need to be taken into account even before getting to script.

A half-hour script that has a teaser and two or three acts should be broken out as "Teaser," "Act 1," "Act 2," "Act 3," and so on, but you don't need to include fade-ins or fade-outs or transitions.

An outline is written single-spaced in most instances (unless a story editor specifies otherwise). The length of an outline will vary. An outline for a half-hour episode normally runs around five to eight pages, depending on how detailed you get. I've done outlines as short as two to three pages (single-spaced), and up to eighteen (when they wanted it double-spaced). If you're working on a series, the story editor should give you some guidelines for the length of the outline. If not, ask the editor what length he or she would like to see, or get some already-completed outlines to look at.

A good outline should cover everything that will be in the script in quick descriptive passages, minus actual dialogue. It's all right to indicate joke lines or even to include one or two actual lines of dialogue within the body of the outline (not broken out in dialogue format, as you would do in a script), but generally speaking, you should not put actual dialogue into an outline.

You need to be sure you cover all the action beats, the essence of what the characters are saying to one another, the humor beats (if any), the emotional beats, and whatever else is crucial to conveying what will be in the script.

In the live-action world, the word *treatment* is used instead of outline. A treatment can be anything from a detailed outline to a shorter summary of the story.

You should be allowed a week to write an outline. If the schedule is very tight, you may be asked to turn an outline around in as little as three days.

In the outline for "Spykecam" that we already had one large change from the premise — instead of having Mystique as the villain, we have Sabretooth. The "A" story remains the same — Spyke has to make a video about family. The "B" story is Sabretooth stalking Spyke to get at Logan. And we also had a "C" story, the rivalry between Kitty and Rogue. The "B" story intersects with the "A" story, but doesn't resolve it. The "C" story is resolved by the "A" story. You will find this outline at www.christymarx.info.

The next step will be to get notes on the outline. The story editor might let you go directly to script, or might ask you to rewrite the outline before giving you the go-ahead to write the script. That will depend on the nature of the notes, how comfortable the story editor is with your ability, and what his or her schedule allows. A story editor on a very tight schedule might even present you with his or her rewrite of the outline and have you go to script from that, simply because it can be faster for the editor to do the rewrite than to give you notes.

One rewrite of an outline is perfectly reasonable; a second rewrite would be unusual but O.K. Multiple requests for outline rewrites are not reasonable, unless you're very, very new and the story editor is doing you a favor by mentoring you. In that case, do the rewrites.

If you make it past the outline stage, you go to script.

The Script Format

There are significant differences between an animation script and a live-action script. I have also written in "hybrid" formats that are somewhere halfway between animation and live action (more on this under Difference No. 1). There is no one single, absolute, unvarying script format for either animation or live action. However, there are some basic rules. The key things you need to know are how to lay out the page (margins, spacing, indents) and how to use the five basic elements from which every script is built:

    SLUGLINES / SCENE HEADINGS
    ACTION DESCRIPTION
    DIALOGUE
    PARENTHETICALS
    TRANSITIONS

It's rather like someone handing you a set of five tools from which you can build anything from a five-minute skit to an epic three-hour movie. What makes you stand out as a writer is how you use those tools to create an exciting, evocative read that conveys the images and emotions you want the reader to experience.

Too often, I see newer writers obsess over the tools of a script. Know the basic rules, but then make them serve your purpose. The script must look professional, but ultimately the quality of the script is what gets you a sale, not how prettily your slugline or action or dialogue is arranged on the page.

If you don't know how the tools work, read the previous chapter on script terms for definitions and examples.

The Basic Layout

As far as margins, spacing, indents, and font, animation and live-action scripts are basically the same.

A standard layout for a script page is:

SPACING: Double-spaced for everything except the dialogue and action description.

FONT: 12-point Courier font. For emphasis on a word, use either CAPS or underlining. Don't use *italics* or **bold.**

MARGINS: One and a half inches for the left margin (the extra half inch allows room for the binding). One inch for the right, top, and bottom margins.

INDENTS:

> SLUGLINES, ACTION are on the left margin.
>
> CHARACTER NAME is two inches from the left margin, one inch from the right margin.
>
> PARENTHETICAL is one and a half inches from the left margin, two inches from the right margin.
>
> DIALOGUE is one inch from the left margin, one and a half inches from the right margin.
>
> TRANSITIONS are aligned to the right margin (or four inches from the left margin).

NUMBERING: Page number in the upper right corner, except on the cover page. You can leave it off the first page of the script as well.

ACT BREAKS: Begin each act on a new page.

You won't get into trouble using this basic layout. You may encounter a company or a story editor who has a specific template that he or she wants you to use. In that case, the editor will have to provide you with the template or give you the specific parameters. These vary only slightly from the format given above (maybe half an inch this way or that), but the layout on the page will look the same. Obviously, you use whatever parameters you're told to use.

Otherwise, use the parameters given here. If you're using scriptwriting software, it will set the standard parameters for you.

The Title Page

If this is a spec script, your title page should contain the name of the series, below that the title of the script, below that "written by Your Name." This should be centered and in the upper one-third of the page. At the bottom of the page, aligned to the right, put the name and contact info for your agent (if you have one), or your own contact info. I do not recommend putting a copyright notice or WGA registration info on the title page of a spec script. Many people consider that the mark of an insecure amateur.

If you're working on a show, you'll see an example of what information the company wants, but generally that's going to be the name of the series, title of the episode, the episode production number, your name—centered and placed as described above. The company may want a date, and usually they'll want the copyright and the company's name centered along the bottom. You don't need to put contact info on this type of script, because you're already doing it under a contract.

COVERS: Most of the time when hired to work on a show, you'll be turning in an electronic version of the script. For a spec script, put on covers (front and back) mainly to keep the script intact, and fasten it with two brass brads (that way, if the script needs to be taken apart and photocopied, there are only two brads to deal with rather than three). Avoid ridiculous colors or patterns or outlandish finish for the covers, and don't go any heavier than 20-lb. stock (many readers like to fold over the pages as they read, and you don't want a cover that is an obstacle). Bizarre covers won't do you any good or garner special attention (except maybe to look silly). What matters is what's *between* the covers.

The Differences

That's how live-action and television animation scripts are the same. Now let's get into how they're different.

Difference No. 1: Calling Out the Shots

A live-action script uses "master scenes." This means that a slugline establishes the location, but the rest of the action and dialogue is laid out without specifying the individual shots. In fact, that's strongly discouraged in a live-action script, because deciding on the shots and angles is the turf of the director. It's the live-action director who translates the script into the final visuals.

A television animation script is exactly the opposite. The person who interprets your script and turns it into visual form is the storyboard artist. As an animation writer, you are expected to call out (specify) *every single shot*. You're storyboarding as you write. You decide how to open each scene and what is in every shot in the scene in order to convey your action and dialogue. You decide the pacing. You decide what the visuals will be. A good storyboard artist may tweak what you've done, but it's still up to you to call out every shot.

An animation writer must be able to clearly visualize the script *as animation*. This is where watching a lot of animation becomes valuable. Some things that you can do in a fully animated feature you can't do in a half-hour TV series episode, due to time and budget constraints for TV. You need to be familiar with the look and techniques of the type of animation for which you're writing. Some things that you can do with 3-D (such as swooping around in a 360-degree circle) you can't do in 2-D. Many of the techniques developed for anime have less to do with creating a style than with finding ways to do animation on a tight budget, such as the "speed lines" background to indicate movement rather than showing a background speeding past. You need to study and be aware of how a story is visually told shot by shot in animation before you can re-create that in a script.

I developed and was story editor on a half-hour kids' series called *Hypernauts*, which was primarily live action, but featured a substantial amount of CG. We wrote the live-action parts in live-action format, and the CG portions in animation format, which led to scripts that were slightly longer than the live-action people were accustomed to seeing. Because I was familiar with how both formats paced in airtime, I was able to arrive by instinct at a correct page length for that hybrid style of script, which came out to about twenty-four to twenty-six pages for twenty-two minutes of airtime.

Here are two examples of the same scene: as it would be laid out for a live-action script, and then as it would be broken out for an animation script. First, live action:

INT. JACK'S HOUSE

Jack stands with folded arms watching as Dick and Jane take in his shabby surroundings.

                    JACK
          You said you have a proposition.
          Start talking.

Jane notices something unusual and goes over to it. It's a CRYSTAL SKULL. She picks it up and looks at it with wonder.

                    JANE
          How did you get this?

                    JACK
          Long story.

                    DICK
          If I didn't know better, I'd say
          it was stolen.

Jack scowls at him. He goes over to Jane and takes the skull away from her. He plunks it back down where it was.

                    JACK
          Well, you don't know better. You
          don't know Jack, as the saying
          goes. You're wasting my time, and
          I don't like people who waste my
          time.

                    JANE
          I think you don't like people,
          period.

                    JACK
          Perceptive, aren't you?

Now an example of how this would be done in an animation script format:

INT. JACK'S HOUSE

Jack's living room has peeling wallpaper; an old, patched
sofa; a rickety table and one chair; a bare lightbulb hanging
from the ceiling instead of a fixture. Any windows we see are
covered with shabby, but very opaque, curtains. Off to one
side (not seen in this shot) is an old bookshelf holding only
a few ragged books and a CRYSTAL SKULL.

Jack stands with folded arms watching as Dick and Jane take in
his shabby surroundings.

> JACK
> (irritated)
> You said you have a proposition.
> Start talking.

ANGLE ON JANE

who reacts with curiosity and heads toward the bookshelf.

ANGLE FAVORING THE CRYSTAL SKULL IN F.G.

as Jane picks it up and looks at it with wonder, her face partially distorted by being seen through the crystal.

> JANE
> (amazed)
> How did you get this?

ANGLE ON JACK

> JACK
> Long story.

ON DICK

who lounges on the old sofa.

> DICK
> If I didn't know better, I'd say it
> was stolen.

ANGLE FAVORING JACK

Jack scowls at Dick. TRACK WITH Jack as he moves across the
room toward Jane.

> JACK
> Well, you don't know better. You
> don't know Jack, as the saying goes.

```
ANGLE ON JANE

holding the skull. Jack ENTERS FRAME, takes the skull away from
her, and <PLUNKS> it back onto the shelf.

                         JACK
             You're wasting my time, and I don't
             like people who waste my time.

CLOSER ON JANE

                         JANE
             I think you don't like people, period.

CLOSE ON JACK

who narrows his eyes at her.

                         JACK
                      (sarcastic)
             Perceptive, aren't you?
```

In a live-action script, you can get away with less detail about the surroundings, which will be filled in by the director in conjunction with a production designer, art designer, set designer, prop master, and so forth.

In animation, the artist knows what to draw only if you tell him. You aren't trying to keep the storyboard artist in suspense, so if you need something specific (such as a crystal skull) in the setting that he has to create, let him know up front. Sometimes an important prop will be designed in detail by the prop artist, and that design will be given to the storyboard artist. Either way, the artists need to know that the prop requires special attention. Keep your description as concise and to the point as you can. Animation scripts must be written to a specific length, and you can't afford to waste a single line on superfluous description.

If you're using backgrounds that already exist, don't worry about description, unless you need to add something new to it.

Notice that you don't necessarily need to have an action/description line underneath every slugline, particularly when all you're doing is cutting to a character so he can speak a line.

You can leave most of the choice of angles up to the storyboard artist, and specify only certain angles (high, low) or type of shot (wide, close, pan) where needed.

HYBRID ANIMATION FORMAT: A new format has been used more frequently of late, and may be on its way to being the norm. In this format, the writer is still required to call out every shot, but without using a separate line for the sluglines. Instead, you would begin a new shot with elements of a slugline, but continue directly into the action description without dropping down to a new paragraph. It would look like this:

INT. JACK'S HOUSE

Jack's living room has peeling wallpaper; an old, patched
sofa; a rickety table and one chair; a bare lightbulb
hanging from the ceiling instead of a fixture. Any windows
we see are covered with shabby, but very opaque, curtains.
Off to one side (not seen in this shot) is an old bookshelf
holding only a few ragged books and a CRYSTAL SKULL.

Jack stands with folded arms, watching as Dick and Jane
take in his shabby surroundings.

                         JACK
                    (irritated)
             You said you have a proposition.
             Start talking.

ANGLE ON JANE who reacts with curiosity and heads toward the
bookshelf.

ANGLE FAVORING THE CRYSTAL SKULL IN F.G. - Jane picks it up
and looks at it with wonder, her face partially distorted
by being seen through the crystal.

                         JANE
                    (amazed)
             How did you get this?

JACK grows more irritated.

                         JACK
             Long story.

ON DICK who lounges on the old sofa.

                         DICK
             If I didn't know better, I'd say
             it was stolen.

JACK scowls at Dick. TRACK WITH Jack as he moves across the
room toward Jane.

                         JACK
             Well, you don't know better. You
             don't know Jack, as the saying goes.

ANGLE ON JANE - holding the skull. Jack ENTERS FRAME, takes the
skull away from her, and <PLUNKS> it back onto the shelf.

                         JACK
             You're wasting my time, and I
             don't like people who waste my
             time.

```
CLOSER ON JANE who reacts to him.

                        JANE
            I think you don't like people,
            period.

CLOSE ON JACK who narrows his eyes at her.

                        JACK
                    (sarcastic)
            Perceptive, aren't you?
```

This format allows the writers to pack more story into a shorter script (around twenty-four to thirty-three pages), but retains the underlying structure of an animation script and makes for a smoother read. As long you understand that it still gets down to using the five basic tools, in one form or another, you should have no problem with this.

Difference No. 2: Dialogue and the Lip-Synch Factor

Another major difference between live action and animation is the nature of the dialogue. In live action, you can do long passages of dialogue because you have a real person delivering the lines. The director decides how to move the camera or break up the delivery of the dialogue into shots, but no matter how it's shot, you have the reality of that live actor on-screen to carry the dialogue using eyes, facial muscles, body language, and a host of subtle factors.

Full animation in an animated feature can come closer to this at a greater cost in artist hours, but it won't equal what a live actor can do. In the limited animation of television, the last thing you want to have sitting on the screen delivering long speeches is a flat animated face with minimal expression. First, because it's not very interesting. Second, because lip-synching takes time (and time = money).

Some anime takes a shortcut around this by not bothering with a realistic mouth, so no lip-synch is necessary. You'll find that the requirements of short dialogue still apply, perhaps even more so *because* there's no lip-synch and it looks funky when it goes on for too long. The same has been true for CG. As CG-animation techniques improve, lip-synching will become less of a factor, but if you look at the early CG shows for TV, you'll notice how often they tried to design characters wearing full-face helmets or masks in order to trim down the lip-synching work as much as possible.

Dialogue in animation is expected to be minimal, pithy, concise, strong, and punchy. Each piece of dialogue should be kept down to one or two fairly short sentences at most. In the examples I gave under Difference No. 1, notice how I took one of Jack's longer speeches in the live-action format, split it into two shorter pieces, and spread it across two shots in the animation sample.

You might be wondering what I mean by "strong and punchy." When I wrote my first animation scripts, I had no mentor, no guidance, and no one to tell me anything about the craft.

It was learn-as-you-go. After I'd done one script, I was able to show it to someone who at the time was one of the major animation producers in the business. When I asked for feedback, he told me, "Your dialogue is too soft." I was baffled. I had no idea what he meant by that. When I asked him to clarify, he couldn't. The producer knew what he meant, but he wasn't able to explain it to me. "Soft" was just "soft," that's all. My dialogue was short, and there were no wasted words in the actual lines. My guess all these years later is that he meant I used too much back-and-forth dialogue to get to the point. My characters would use twenty pieces of dialogue to do what should have been boiled down to maybe five pieces of dialogue or less. Having pages of characters trading one-liners is as much of a mistake as having long pieces of dialogue.

When you craft a story and set up a scene for animation, you need to boil down your dialogue to the bare minimum and make that dialogue have the maximum impact, utilizing visuals in place of dialogue as much as you can. Avoid exposition like the plague. If your character absolutely must say several things in a row, break it up across a number of shots and make those shots interesting. Either give your character something to do (what's called "business," as in "give this character some piece of business here"), or have some other action going on.

Difference No. 3: Script Length

One of the other things you should notice from these samples is that calling out the shots for animation makes for a longer script.

Scripts became codified in their present form of font and layout for numerous reasons, but one of the big reasons is to write scripts that are the right length for specific periods of time, especially when it comes to television.

There's an old formula for how much time = one page of script.

> LIVE ACTION: one minute = one page.
> ANIMATION: one minute = one and a half pages.

Theoretically, then, a twenty-two-minute live-action script would be twenty-two pages. A twenty-two-minute animation script would be thirty-three pages.

This is why the "standard" length for a live-action movie script is 90 pages to a maximum of 120 pages, because most movies are expected to run between 90 and 120 minutes in length.

To fit their airtimes, television programs require scripts written to fairly precise lengths, but even here you run into exceptions. Some live-action shows that are heavy in dialogue exchanges without a lot of action might run to fifty-five or sixty pages for an hour show. This is because dialogue alone eats up a lot more pages than heavy action or a combo of action plus dialogue, but dialogue usually takes up less airtime.

When I first began writing animation scripts, we were doing fifty-five- and sixty-page scripts for a half-hour action show, and most of it ended up on the screen, in contradiction to the formula given above. Over the years, I've watched the length of half-hour animation scripts shrink to forty-five pages, then to thirty-eight pages, and now to around thirty-two to thirty-three pages.

There are a couple of reasons for this. For one, the actual airtime of these shows has shrunk. The granddaddy of half-hour animation, *The Flintstones*, had twenty-seven minutes of airtime. Over the years, more and more commercials and breaks have been added, so that the current half hour of animation is about twenty-one to twenty-two minutes. For now.

The other reason for today's shorter scripts is that less actual animation per minute is being done (being shot on twos or shot on threes), due to shrinking budgets. Stories by necessity have become simpler, and the pacing slower, to accommodate the shorter script length.

Writing to Length

Getting back to television, when a story editor says that the length of the script should be no more than, say, thirty-three pages, you must take that seriously. You should turn in a script that is between thirty-two and thirty-three pages. TV writing is precision writing. If the script is too long, it simply means that pages are cut—and you may not have any control over what gets cut. Naturally, your script shouldn't be too short either—at the risk of annoying the story editor, who will then need material added and may have to do it herself if she's in a rush.

The overall length is one issue. The other issue is act breaks.

Working Out Act Breaks

If you're writing a script for a show that's already on the air, you'll get the act structure from watching the show. Otherwise, you'll get the info from the show bible or from the story editor. A very common structure is a teaser and three acts, or a teaser and two acts. An alternative is a teaser, two acts, and a tag (rarely seen these days). One-hour animation is extremely rare, but a live-action one-hour show commonly has a teaser and five acts—some do without a teaser; some add a tag. For a ninety-minute animated TV movie, there are usually eight acts.

You might occasionally encounter a show that does individual eleven-minute segments (two per show), rather than one half-hour story. Those are generally written as one act without teasers or other breaks.

The acts must be roughly equal in length. You might observe that in some one-hour or two-hour live-action dramas, they will let the first act run extremely long in order to make sure they've hooked the audience before cutting to the first set of commercials. With a longer form, such as a ninety-minute animated TV movie, you can also get away with a longer first act.

In half-hour animation, you have the option to make the first act a little longer, but not by any more than one or two pages. Assuming a thirty-three-page script, you should strive for a formula that is as close as possible to eleven/eleven/eleven (eleven pages per act). If you have a teaser, you have to carve out a couple of pages for that, so your formula might be two/eleven/ten/ten, or two/ten/eleven/ten, and so on depending on the demands of the story and the best place to put an act break. You can probably get away with two/twelve/ten/nine or similar variation.

What you absolutely don't want to do is let any one act get out of control. If you turn in a script that breaks out as nine/six/seventeen, you can count on your story editor wondering what on earth you were thinking, and telling you to fix the act breaks. There's room to be somewhat flexible, but no more than a couple of pages in any one direction.

Act breaks provide an extra challenge in working out the pacing and dramatic three-act structure of your story. By dramatic three-act structure, I refer to the triad of exposition-conflict-resolution that is the blueprint of your beginning, middle, and end. Exposition-conflict-resolution applies equally to a three-minute comedy short or to a ninety-minute epic adventure. Keep that dramatic structure in mind when you're crafting the overall story, without tying it to any specific act in the script. It might seem easy to divide up the dramatic triad to a three-act script, but do you really want to spend the entire third act solely on resolution? It's more likely that the resolution will take place halfway through the third act of the script, especially given the compressed nature of animation stories.

So we'll assume you have a grasp of your dramatic three-act structure as it applies overall to your story. Now you have to figure out how to build to a critical act break that takes place at approximately so many pages into the script. Your act breaks must be gripping, exciting, and dramatic. If you don't have your viewers totally hooked, you'll lose them during the commercial break. The purpose of a cliff-hanger act break is to keep the audience in enough suspense to stick around. The act break doesn't have to be a cliff-hanger based on physical peril. It could be a moment of suspense or mystery, or it could be a moment of emotional confrontation.

Which means that each act must have its own internal momentum that brings it to that critical point at the right time. In a ninety-minute animated film, this means finding seven points at which you can break the story with either a physical or emotional cliff-hanger . . . while not making it look contrived.

This is where having a solid outline is so important. Most of your scenes are going to run somewhere around two to three pages. Simple math tells us that trying to fit, say, ten scenes into an eleven-page act isn't going to work, unless you have an insanely frenetic story. This is where you need good instincts to estimate how many pages you will actually need for a scene vs. how many scenes you can realistically fit into a single act. As you work out your major story beats, you can reasonably estimate being able to fit three to four major story beats into an eleven-page act. You might be able to squeeze in five scenes if one is really short. By the time you take into account dialogue and breaking out all the shots, you'll find that three to four beats, or scenes, will easily fill eleven pages. You might have an instance where you're cutting back and forth between two major story beats rather than having separate scenes, and you'll need to estimate how many pages that will eat.

The best way to become good at this is practice. Write lots of sample outlines and sample scripts.

In the past, it was common to allow two weeks to write a half-hour animation script. These days, it isn't unusual to be given only one week to turn in a half-hour script.

You will find the "Spykecam" script available to read at www.christymarx.info.

The 3-D Script vs. the 2-D Script

I find myself being cautious in what advice I give about writing for CG (3-D) vs. traditional cel animation (2-D) because the field of animation is in a state of flux as CG continues to develop, transplanting 2-D in some areas of the business, but not others.

At the time I write this, the major animation-movie companies have abandoned 2-D entirely in favor of 3-D. This is a function of CG getting better and better, combined with dramatic successes in 3-D features. At first, CG elements were incorporated cautiously into 2-D films such as Disney's *Beauty and the Beast* and *Aladdin*. The steamroller began with Pixar's wonderful *Toy Story* and subsequent successes with *Monsters, Inc.* and *Finding Nemo*, along with the great success of DreamWorks SKG's *Shrek* and *Shrek 2*. At the same time, some expensive 2-D films didn't perform well, and turned into large losses for the studios.

What some of these companies forget is that the best visuals in the universe—whether they are 2-D or 3-D—won't save a weak story or weak script. Disney's *Treasure Planet* had spectacular CG, but a story that didn't quite work.

Consequently, it's hard to say at this point whether CG will remain the flavor of the decade, or whether 2-D will make a comeback in features. There will likely always be smaller studios that continue to produce 2-D features or direct-to-video features.

Meanwhile, in TV, there were some superb CG shows made early on (such as *ReBoot* and *Shadow Raiders*), but they were expensive, and it was tricky to churn them out on a tight TV production schedule. TV animation is trending toward more-stylized 2-D work, Flash animation, and whatever else will grab eyeballs to the small screen while keeping the budgets low. There is also a style in which 3-D is rendered to look like 2-D while retaining the ability to move in 3-D. MTV's version of *Spider-Man* is an example of this.

I wrote for some of the early CG TV series, all for the same production company. At the time, we wrote the scripts in a live-action format using master scenes, rather than an animation-script format. This was due largely to that particular company's method of parceling out the art tasks without using storyboards.

In most TV animation, one artist is given one act of a script to storyboard, so you can end up with three artists drawing storyboards for a half-hour show with three acts. Those three artists determine the look and flow of the visuals.

This company instead assigned a CG artist to handle particular characters, and the artist would create the animation for the scenes containing those characters. Essentially, the artist took the place of the storyboard artist on a rather piecemeal basis, but with a director to pull the various pieces together.

However, the last time I met with someone from that company, I was told they had gone to doing storyboards. Note that even scripts that are written in a live-action format have to adhere to other animation "rules," such as keeping dialogue short.

When it comes to something that is evolving, as CG is, each company or studio will likely have its own approach to how it wants the scripts done. Your best bet is to be familiar with both live-action and animation formats, as well as with the rules and requirements of each.

As for writing TV spec scripts, as you will certainly need to do, my advice is to write in an animation-script format regardless of which technology will be used to animate it. This shows that you know how to do it, and is more likely to be the right way to go. Just be sure that the visuals you create in your script will work for the technology you have in mind. If you're writing a feature-animation script that you intend for 3-D, your visuals should utilize the strengths of 3-D animation. If you're writing a 2-D series spec, your visuals must be in line with what can be done in 2-D.

What tends to be "expensive" in CG is creating the three-dimensional characters, especially when doing a TV series. This is because of the time it takes to create the wire frame of the body shape, then add texture, color, and all the other details to it. As the technology develops, this may change, but when I was writing for *Beast Wars*, we had a specific set of characters and a very strict rule against creating any new characters. I pitched a story idea that I thought got around the "no new characters" rule by calling for a new character that would be a conglomeration of parts from the other characters, so that existing components could be recombined rather than something new created. The story editor nearly didn't pitch it, but liked the idea enough that he went ahead. It became the episode "Transmutate," and the company liked the story enough that they went to the extra trouble of creating something entirely new for the Transmutate character.

Restrictions Breed Creativity

I've heard writers enthuse about doing animation because "you can do *anything* in animation!" This was usually said in comparing animation to live action. This was truer in the past than it is now, due to the increased use of CG elements in live action. It also highlights the difference between feature animation and TV animation.

Features have multimillion-dollar budgets and a long development period. They can afford to pull out the stops. They need to because they have a big investment to recoup.

TV animation is about doing the best you can within the limitations of shrinking production budgets and tight production schedules.

Here are some examples of the type of restrictions I've run up against in animation. These restrictions called for adaptation and creative thinking.

THE CROWD SCENE RULE: One big example is crowd scenes. Movies can afford to use sophisticated programs to generate and control huge crowds of 3-D animated characters on the screen (look, a zillion CG orcs are storming the Hornburg!). For a TV episode, you need to avoid crowd scenes. When you need to have a crowd scene for some reason, you find ways to cheat around it. You stick to close shots, or pick shots that show as few random people as possible (such as a few feet rushing by at ground level). In short, you get creative. You also want to avoid lots and lots of small objects flying around. Asking a TV animation artist to draw a hundred Ping-Pong balls bouncing around in a scene could be dangerous to your health.

LIMITED BACKGROUNDS: One show had a very tight budget that prohibited more than a few new backgrounds per show. Remember my example of how quickly one location can eat up several backgrounds? The challenge with that show was to use the maximum number of already-existing backgrounds from episodes in production, and to sharply curtail how many new backgrounds were in the script. It's also helpful to have generic backgrounds such as "jungle" or "rock wall."

LIMITED VOICES: Another show would allow me to use only a relatively low number of voices. Let's say it was ten voices. The trick here is that the cast I was required to use took up eight of the voices. The challenge was to come up with stories that stayed tightly focused on those characters with almost no outside characters.

LIMITED DIALOGUE: Besides limiting voices, I've had shows where I could have only so many lines of dialogue per episode. It was a matter of going through the script and counting the lines. If there were too many lines, I had to either find places to trim out dialogue, or else rewrite the speeches to be more condensed.

TOO MANY PROPS OR MODELS: Shows with a very tight budget might also prohibit the writer from asking for too many new characters that have to be designed, or even for new props that have to be designed. Once again, it's a matter of finding a way to work around the restrictions by changing the scene or altering the story. Whatever it takes.

Other Things You May Be Expected to Do

Once you're given a script assignment, you should be told what additional info you will be expected to provide along with the script. The most common ones are as follows:

- LOGLINE AND/OR SYNOPSIS: The logline is one sentence of the type you'd see in *TV Guide* to give the gist of the episode. The synopsis is about three short paragraphs.

This type of synopsis should be crafted to give other writers enough detail to gain a quick knowledge of what's in your script, so they can avoid having situations or scenes that are too similar to yours.

- CAST LIST: For established characters, you need to give only the name. Characters should be listed in order of importance. For any new, secondary, or incidental characters, you will need to give the character name, indicate whether it's a speaking part (if a speaking part, you should give an indication of how many lines), and give a description of the character (usually the same description you put into the script).

- SET LIST: This would be a list of your major INTERIOR and EXTERIOR backgrounds. If it's a new background, include full description.

- PROPS LIST: This isn't as commonly asked for these days, but it would be a list of special or unusual props that would have to be designed for your episode, such as a handheld GPS that transforms into a laser gun, a type of vehicle not used before, or something that is more than just a background object (such as the crystal skull I used in my script examples).

Scriptwriting Software

More and more companies, especially with TV series, are requiring writers who work on their shows to use scriptwriting software. The two main pieces of software currently on the market are Final Draft and Movie Magic Screenwriter. So far, every company that has required me to use scriptwriting software has used Final Draft, whether it was a live-action show or an animated show. Final Draft is now very prevalent on live-action shows, and has rapidly become prevalent in animation, including theatrical features.

This doesn't mean you should run out and buy a copy of Final Draft. That depends on your budget. If you have plenty of money to spare, go for it. However, it is perfectly legitimate to ask the company to loan you a copy of the software if they're requiring you to use it. The advantages to already having the software are that it sounds more professional to say you have it (and less hassle for the story editor to get it to you), and that you'll have a chance to become familiar with it ahead of time, thus not having to deal with a learning curve while trying to get a script done under deadline.

Scriptwriting software has its good points and bad points. The software automates much of the process and gives you handy shortcuts. Some of those automated shortcuts have been known to drive me mad. I have to live with that, and you can make some adjustments to how you want the software to work. I haven't had much luck importing previously written scripts into the software, or exporting scripts to a plain Word format from the software. Both actions left me having to do a lot of editing to fix the odd quirks that happened in the process. Because you can print a Final Draft formatted script only from Final Draft itself, you will either need to have the program in order to print out a copy later (for example, for samples of your work), or you will need to have an exported version in Word format or in Rich Text Format (RTF).

Final Draft Viewer is free software that will let you read and print Final Draft documents without having the full version of the scriptwriting software.

The Animated Feature Film

The animation-development process is different for theatrical projects. Writing actual scripts for theatrical animation is a recent development, beginning mainly when Michael Eisner (as head of Disney) mandated that for *The Little Mermaid,* the script be done before any animation work. This created a major shift in how feature animation was developed. However, it's a far more collaborative process than in television.

On features, usually more writers are hired, sometimes one writer or one team of writers after another. Often, writers are hired as "story consultants" to give their input.

The writers go back and forth in a more fluid process with the animators—with script influencing storyboards, and storyboards influencing script. Big meetings are held in which everyone involved goes over storyboards in detail. Unspoken etiquette dictates that the directors get to comment first, after which everyone else in the room can give an opinion.

Storyboards are turned into "story reels," which are carefully evaluated to get a sense of how the story is working, especially in a visual sense. At its most effective, a feature animation film should convey just about everything the viewer needs to know when viewed without sound or dialogue, as though it were a silent movie. After input on the story reels, there is more rewriting. The rewriting is a constant back-and-forth process.

One of the big differences is the time span of the development and production, which typically runs four to five years. In April 2005, Jeffrey Katzenberg, head of DreamWorks Animation SKG, commented that DreamWorks spends three to four years in production, with budgets of around $125 million per picture. That's a huge commitment.

I should mention that direct-to-video features are developed in a fashion more like television animation, and have the same kind of tight, short schedules of a television series.

I consulted with Terry Rossio, who, with his partner Ted Elliott, has written or worked on numerous feature-animation projects—including *Aladdin*, *Small Soldiers*, *The Road to El Dorado*, *Treasure Planet*, *Shrek,* and *Shrek 2.* Terry generously shared his experience in this area.

A feature-animation script runs about eighty to eighty-five pages (and no more than eighty-five), containing around twenty sequences. In this sense, sequences would be similar to beats. This refers to the major story beats, events, or action, or a series of events that are grouped together because they are related. Terry said, "[Jeffrey] Katzenberg (Dreamworks SKG) will speak of a five/ten/five-act breakdown of sequences (meaning five sequences in Act 1, ten in Act 2, and five in Act 3), but that's very loose and informal. We tend to think of animated movies as having a two-act play structure. In the end, just about any structure fits a good story."

The emphasis in features is on simple story, but complex characters. The focus is on the characters and on the underlying theme, not the plot. Having a clear theme is also at the heart of creating an animated feature. That theme should have a simple, strong core, such as "family is important" or "if you love someone, you must be willing to let them go."

Because of the fluid process I described earlier of the writers working more closely in collaboration with the artists, the studios don't want the writers to break their scripts out shot by shot. Instead, they're written in a live-action script format, which keeps the scripts much shorter and leaves the scene and shot layouts to the animators.

Another reason for using the live-action format is that the first people to read the scripts are studio executives, who are more accustomed to reading live-action scripts. These scripts are shorter than the norm because animated features are (mostly) designed for a young audience with a shorter attention span, so they tend to be shorter movies.

I asked Terry about the inclusion of music, because it often plays a significant role in animation features. Terry said, "If music is important to the film, then it gets included in the screenplay, exactly as it is intended to be in the final cut. A musical sequence can be a montage, or we prefer 'series of shots.' But it can also be a single scene designed to move the story forward, or anything in between."

Aside from these major differences between television and feature-animation scripts, a couple of the rules for television should still apply. You will want to keep your dialogue short and pithy. You will want to remember that you're working with animated actors, and not live actors, when it comes to calling for subtle emotion.

Beyond the Basics (Advice, tips, and tricks)

Now we'll assume that you're actually working on a show. Here's a grab bag of additional advice, tips, and tricks.

Keep Your Story Editor Happy

There are certain things you should never, ever do to your story editor:

- Never turn in a script late, unless there's a very good reason and your story editor has approved an extension.

- Never fail to return phone calls or e-mail as a way of avoiding having to give your story editor bad news or an excuse. Avoidance is a bad, bad idea—as I learned the hard way. Be honest and stay in communication with your story editor or producer.

- Never cheat on the format. If you're using a program such as Final Draft, this is moot, because the program will set standard margins. But if you're using Word or some other program, never deviate from the template or guidelines set by the story editor. Adding one extra line per page can add one entire extra page to the script. Don't try to cheat the margins or use a smaller font or anything else that will provide the story editor with a headache later having to reformat your script. You only hurt yourself in the end, because when the script is properly formatted and comes out too long, it will have to be cut. Make it the right length the first time around. After all, the reason standard formatting came about was to provide a reasonably accurate way to judge how many minutes of airtime will result from a script of a given length.

- Do not argue excessively with your story editor. This is something I encountered with new writers doing their first scripts. They wanted to argue about *every single note* I gave them. I'm not talking about asking for clarification on a note—I'm talking about a stubborn resistance to changing anything. Not only is this irritating on a personal level, but it takes a lot of time that most story editors don't have. This gets down to two things: (1) if you don't have the temperament to get notes from ten different people whose sometimes contradictory notes must be reconciled, then don't even think about getting into scriptwriting; and (2) *learn to pick your battles.* I can't emphasize this second point enough. To put it another way, don't sweat the small stuff. Make the changes. When it comes to something that you truly consider significant to the story, don't argue it—*discuss* it. This is a fine point of semantics, but an important one. What you really want to do is get at the precise reason for the change, to present your reasoning in a nonconfrontational manner, and—if you can't win your point—look for a compromise. Often, if you listen carefully, you can defuse the change by coming up with an alternate way to do basically the same thing. Then both sides win. But the minute you get the sense that this isn't a battle you can win, make the best of it with good grace and find a way to make it work for you, rather than risk never working for that story editor again.

Needless to say (I hope), never flatly refuse to change something. That's the kiss of death. If the notes are really that bad, your only remaining course of action is to give up the job and walk away, regardless of the consequences.

Be Kind to the Storyboard Artist

Don't keep secrets from the artists. If there is an important prop that will be used in a room in a later scene, be sure to include that prop in the *first* description of the room, so that it can be taken into account when that background is being designed and created. Likewise, if you need some special feature in a location, such as a hidden trapdoor, give some indication of it in the first place you describe the location. Capitalizing the prop is a good idea. Even though the door may not be revealed until Act 3, the artist will need to design the room to account for it when working on Act 1. The same rule applies to characters. Don't suddenly mention that your character has a scar on his right cheek several scenes after you have already introduced the character. When you first introduce or describe the character, make sure all the significant information is there.

Be consistent in how you refer to a character, prop, or place. Remember that there can be a different storyboard artist working on each act. You don't want to confuse them by saying "trapdoor" in one act and "flip-up hidden door" in another act, or by referring to an "Aztec temple" one time and an "ancient Mexican temple" another time.

Present Tense and "-ing" Words

All scripts are written in the present tense in third person. If you're not accustomed to writing in present tense, check your scripts afterward to make sure you didn't slip into past tense here or there. Although it's not absolutely forbidden to use something other than third person (such as "we see Jack at work"), you'd better be very good at it, or you may turn off a reader who is expecting standard third person. When ending an act or script, there is one fairly common usage of "we." It looks like this:

```
CLOSE ON JACK

pinned down by <GUNFIRE> from both sides! And as Jack
desperately hunches behind a flimsy wall, we . . .

                                        FADE OUT
```

This is a stylistic choice. Some people like it; some don't.

It's also a good idea to avoid writing passive sentences or words ending in "-ing." For example, avoid "Jack is looking at Jane." It reads better as "Jack looks at Jane." It's shorter and more dynamic. Make sure your characters "walk" instead of "are walking," "run" instead of "are running," "talk" instead of "are talking," and so on. This is a not 100 percent rule, and there may be times you want an "-ing" word, but for the most part, go for shorter and stronger in your language. This holds true for dialogue as well.

Verboten Words

Have you ever wondered why the villains in a Saturday-morning cartoon will cry, "Destroy them!" or "Annihilate them!" In children's animation, certain words are considered forbidden, with very rare exceptions. Words that are commonly forbidden include "death," "die," and "kill."

I've also been told not to use supposedly offensive terms such as "idiot," "moron," and "cretin." Sometimes it's a personal quirk of the producer or story editor, such as one exec who hated the use of the slang word "idjit."

Employ common sense when writing a script for kids. Avoid the forbidden words noted here, as well as swear words or words with explicit sexual meanings.

Everybody Gets Out Alive

You may have also noticed in most action-adventure cartoons, that no matter how big the explosion, anybody inside or riding the exploding vehicle/building/object will get out safely. As with the forbidden words, having anyone (good or bad) die on the screen in children's animation is strictly taboo. There have been some rare exceptions, depending on the type of show, but generally you should take it for granted that you need to *show* good guys or bad guys escaping from explosive or destructive situations. This makes it clear that they didn't die.

Imitatable Behavior

The following "rules" do not apply to full-on comedy, such as squash-and-stretch cartoons (for example, the Looney Tunes characters Road Runner and Wile E. Coyote), where the action is obviously not real. The rules apply to action or adventure shows or to anything that isn't pure comedy.

"Imitatable behavior" refers to any TV show's physical action that a child could imitate—action that would do damage or cause injury to that child or to another living thing (especially to other kids). This is something that anyone producing visual works for kids worries about, and it governs much of what is considered acceptable or unacceptable in a script.

A prime example of this is the use of fire. One of the reasons there was no Johnny Storm the Human Torch in the early *Fantastic Four* series is that the producers worried about kids trying to imitate him by setting themselves on fire. In scriptwriting for kids, use of fire in a way that could lead to imitatable behavior is strongly frowned upon.

Other forbidden behaviors include poking anything into eyes, punching, hitting, kicking, choking around the neck, and so forth. It means no guns, no knives, no weapons that kids could manage to obtain (which is why you see a lot of beam or laser or other unreal weapons).

There are exceptions, of course. Shows geared for an older audience might allow a careful use of weapons, but the show would specifically have to allow that. For a series that has martial-arts characters, the producers or the story editor will lay down guidelines about what type of martial-arts moves are acceptable and where on the body the blows can land.

Then we have something such as *Teenage Mutant Ninja Turtles*, in which the heroes carry martial-arts weapons. When I wrote for *TMNT*, the unwritten rule of indirect use of force applied. By indirect use of force, I mean that the Turtles couldn't use their weapons directly against an opponent. Instead, they would have to use the weapon against some inanimate object, which would then in turn have some impact on the enemy. For example, if the Turtles are in a store, the weapon is used to knock down a pile of canned goods. The cans then fall on the villain or trip him up. Or if the villain is standing under a tree branch, you have the Turtles cut off the branch so it falls onto the villain.

I have seen this go so far that on another show, I wasn't allowed to have a character throw a cream pie directly into the face of another character! Instead, the pie had to levitate out of the character's hand and *then* be thrown.

This rule about indirect use of force applies to a lot of shows, but a truly classic example was when I was asked to develop Robert E. Howard's Conan character into an animated series. Conan is a barbarian. He uses a sword. He isn't squeamish about using a sword. But I couldn't let him kill anyone, not even the villains, or use a sword directly against them. This was a challenge, to say the least.

I began by researching the source material. I pulled an element from one of Howard's original stories, then bent it to my own use. I gave Conan not an ordinary sword, but a "magic" sword. In this case, it was made of star-metal that had fallen from the sky. Any weapon made with this star-metal (and all of Conan's regular companions ended up with some type of weapon made of star-metal) had the ability to reveal and vanquish Conan's main enemies. These enemies were the lizard-men, who could assume a human disguise. Merely getting close to Conan's sword made them revert to lizard-man form, and the merest touch of the sword sent the lizard-men POOF! into an alternate lizard-man dimension, where they couldn't get back to Earth. The end result: Conan gets to "use" his sword (sort of) and get rid of his enemies, but nobody dies. Not even lizard-men.

And of course, any *other* use of Conan's sword against a living foe had to follow the indirect-use-of-force rule.

Or you can have the villains be robots, machines, or rock monsters, or something else far enough removed from humanlike that the rule can be ignored.

One other factor is having an increasing influence on what level of action can be used in animation series. Many shows are being financed as foreign coproductions. Studios in France, Canada, Germany, Britain, and elsewhere help finance the production in exchange for having the rights to the series in their own country. However, Britain and other European countries have a lower threshold of acceptability in physical action (some people call it "violence," but I draw the line at calling any kind of action "violence"). These sensibilities will affect what is allowed in a show. In general terms, Europeans want their kids' shows to be less "violent" than American shows. When writing your physical action, you need to have a good mind for coming up with clever alternatives.

And if you think all this sounds extreme, writing children's live-action shows is even *more* restrictive.

Subtle Emotion

Don't write lines such as "There is deep sadness in her eyes." Or "Standing stone still, he radiates cold anger." Most animation, and especially the limited animation of television, can't adequately convey subtle emotion. Flat, animated eyes can't communicate the level of emotion that we can read from human eyes. This has to be done with broader facial movement and body language, as well as emotion in dialogue.

Slang and Fantasy Language

Using contemporary slang will make you sound hip, but will also quickly date the show (or, for that matter, a comic or a videogame). Many clever writers get around this by inventing slang that doesn't really exist, but sounds appropriate for the show. This is even more useful when dealing with a futuristic or science-fiction show where you don't want modern slang to sound out of place or archaic . . . unless that's by deliberate intent.

If you're going to use foreign slang, *do your homework*! It's embarrassing to read slang for, say, a contemporary Australian that hasn't been used for twenty years except as a joke.

Then there's fantasy. It's easy to forget how modern some of our phrases are when writing a pure fantasy show. "Fast as lightning" is fine, but "faster than a bullet" is a problem if your characters use only swords. You never want to hear Conan say, "Wow, cool." Be careful to avoid anachronistic slang.

I came up with the Marx Fantasy Dialogue Scale to differentiate the various ways in which fantasy dialogue could be spoken, ranging from colloquial/modern (No. 1) to High Epic/Poetic (No. 5). Here's an example:

1. He doesn't know what he's doing.

2. He does not know what he is doing.

3. He does not know what he does.

4. He knows not what he does.

5. He knows not what his purpose is, for confusion lies heavy upon him.

You would rarely want to use No. 5, because it's wordy and sounds least natural to modern ears. Using purely colloquial language can sound jarring in some fantasy settings. Creating the right fantasy dialogue depends a great deal on how you use contractions, on your word arrangement and sentence structure, and on the vocabulary you employ.

Dialect

Let's say you have a character who is Russian and speaks with a heavy Russian accent, or a character who is Irish or Romanian or whatever. How do you express that in dialogue?

Mainly, just indicate the character's nationality when you describe the character, and then leave it to the actor. Don't try to write in dialect unless you're very, very good at it—and then only if it doesn't distract from giving the actors readable dialogue. You might want to play around with grammatical structure in a way that's appropriate to that dialect, or toss in verbal quirks, but make sure you get it right.

If you want a piece of dialogue spoken in a foreign language, but you're unable to come up with a translation yourself, I would recommend this:

```
                         JANE
                  (spoken in French)
           What do you know about the crystal
           skull?
```

This throws the responsibility onto the casting or voice director to find an actor who can speak French. Which raises another point: if you create a major, recurring character who needs to speak another language, make sure you include this in the character description *before* the casting takes place.

The Other Translation Problem

As I've mentioned, nearly all television animation these days is done overseas. This means that the scripts have to be translated into Japanese, Korean, French, German, and so on for non-English-speaking animation-production houses.

This can create some quite funny glitches, particularly when it comes to the use of English idioms. A friend of mine likes to tell the story of a *G.I. Joe* script he wrote in which his characters were in a desert location having an argument. He used the idiom "X decides to stick his oar in the water," meaning X character decides to give his opinion.

When the animation came back, his characters suddenly went from standing in the desert to sitting in a rowboat with oars in water that suddenly appears out of nowhere!

It has become necessary to avoid using English idioms in animation scripts that will go overseas for production. This can also apply to using references that are too obscurely American and might mean nothing to an overseas animator. An overseas animator might understand something as internationally known as "he had ears like Mickey Mouse," but a phrase such as "he had hair like Don King" will probably leave them mystified.

Getting Around the Lip-Synch Problem

As I mentioned earlier, lip-synching is expensive, and anytime you can come up with a useful way to have dialogue without requiring lip-synch, it helps the schedule and the budget. Here are a few tips:

- Have dialogue begin during your EXT. establishing shot (as V.O. dialogue). Partway through the dialogue, cut to the interior shot with the character completing the speech. Or vice versa, have the character begin a speech about something, then cut to the location or object under discussion and complete the dialogue as V.O. or O.S.

- A variation on this first tip would be to start the character's dialogue during a long pan when the character is O.S. at the beginning of the pan, and then finish the speech when the camera brings the character into view.

- Have the character turned away from camera in a way that hides most of the face (such as an OTS or POV shot).

- If it fits the story, have something else (helmet, scarf, mask) obscure the face. In CG shows, they often create secondary characters with helmets or face masks for exactly this reason.

- Go to an ECU on the eyes so the mouth doesn't show. I wouldn't recommend this for more than one very short speech, because of what I said about the lack of emotive power in animated eyes.

- Self-reflective dialogue (such as the character's inner thoughts) can be done as a narrative V.O. rather than having the character talking out loud to himself. However, whether or not this method of hearing inner thoughts is appropriate in your script depends on whether it's been established in the show already. You wouldn't want to suddenly have a character's inner dialogue be heard when that technique hasn't been used in the series previously—unless the story editor or producer says it's O.K.

Capitalizing Character Names

It's a common practice to put the name of a character IN CAPS the first time that character appears in the script, but not afterward. This refers only to naming the character in the action description paragraph—not to sluglines or dialogue, where the character name is always in caps.

Be a Good Net Citizen

Animation writing became one of the first sectors of writing to get wired. I attribute much of this to Steve Gerber, who in the 1980s required writers on *G.I. Joe* to do their scripts on a computer, to communicate via his bulletin-board system (BBS), and to send scripts by modem. That was what propelled me abruptly into the world of computers.

Since then, animation and television in general have become very wired. In animation, the majority of pitches, outlines, scripts, and notes are exchanged via e-mail. Sometimes artwork for a series is posted on hidden Web pages for the writers. In addition to having a good handle on using e-mail and browsers, it's very important to have good antivirus protection in place so that you don't become the pariah who spreads an infection to the story editor or other writers. Or conversely, so you don't get hit by someone else who's being careless.

The "Spykecam" Outline and Script

You will find the outline and the full script of the "Spykecam" episode of *X-Men: Evolution* (available to read and study by going to www.christymarx.info). If you happen to see the finished episode, you'll notice differences between our script and the finished version after rewrites by the story editor. For example, we used a Shakespearean play in our version, not realizing that another writer had already used a Shakespearean play as a key element in her script. Rather than be repetitive, the story editor changed our script to accommodate using a different play. Noting such changes can be instructive when studying scripts vs. finished episodes.

CHAPTER 4

Breaking and Entering

There is no one way to break into writing, especially in television or film. There is no magic way to go about it, no secrets that will guarantee getting a break, but there are ways to improve the odds. Because it's one of the things everyone asks, I'll relate how I broke in.

I was living in Los Angeles and had managed to sell a couple of stories to Marvel Comics editor Roy Thomas, who had recently moved to L.A. One of the stories I sold was about *The Fantastic Four*. I began attending the monthly meetings of a group of professional comic book writers and artists. I got to know people and made friends in that circle.

One day, one of the writers I'd gotten to know passed me a tip that an animation studio called DePatie-Freleng Productions was looking for writers, especially writers who had worked on *The Fantastic Four*, because they were doing an animated version of the FF.

On the basis of the one comic book story, I was able to get a meeting with one of the founders of the studio, David DePatie. He was a small, dapper man with a huge antique desk and two nice, but absolutely enormous, dogs. As I sat across from him, the dogs pressed up to me, and I spent the meeting book ended between them, doing my best to get a job. Apparently, I passed the test. DePatie asked me if I knew what an animation script looked like. I said no. He tossed a script across to me to use as a template, and off I went to work on "The Diamond of Doom." I studied and studied that script, though I was completely clueless about what the terms meant or how to create a TV script. Somehow I managed, and that led to more work with DePatie-Freleng.

Nowadays, you would certainly be expected to know what an animation script is and to have a very good spec script already written. Back then, animation scripts were so new, it was perfectly understandable to not know. Though it would be hard to re-create this type of break given today's competitive field, my experience does contain one of the most important steps: networking.

Breaking into Television Animation

If you're a writer who already has credits in another field, such as comics or games, you should have an easier time making a lateral move into animation writing. You likely have contacts that can get you in the door, and you probably won't have much trouble getting a meeting at an animation studio based on your other work. I would still recommend that you have one or two sample animation scripts that will show that you know how to handle the format, but it may not be necessary if your other credits are impressive enough.

If you're brand-new, you should consider the words of Louis Pasteur: "Chance favors only the prepared mind." No matter how much raw talent you may have, it won't do you much good unless you are prepared to take full advantage of whatever piece of luck or opportunity comes your way. This means knowing the animation field, being familiar with what shows are on, and having some strong animation spec scripts as samples of your work for a studio exec or story editor to read when that opportunity comes along.

Spec Scripts

A script is called "spec," or "speculative," because you don't actually expect to sell it. The purpose of a spec script is to show your writing chops and your ability to "get" the show you're writing for. Remember that your primary goal is to be hired to write, whether it's for that show or another one. Actually selling a spec script would be the cherry on the whipped cream.

There are two schools of thought about writing a spec script for a show and submitting the script to that show's story editor or producer. One school of thought favors it because there is always at least the slim chance they could buy your script. A more predominant school of thought is that it's a bad idea because unless your script is absolutely, positively spot-on in every respect, it's more likely to fail. The reasoning is that the story editor or producer is judging the spec script by more-exacting standards because it's their show and they know the characters so well. I would go with the shows you feel the most compelled to write, rather than worrying about this choice.

Choose a show that's been on the air more than one year, is going strong, and is well known. Don't pick a show that is so obscure that no one will know what it is. Write to your interests or strengths, meaning write spec scripts based on the genre of animation that you most want to write for. If you're great at light humor, pick that type of show. If you're great at hard action, pick one of those. If you're crazy about the anime-style shows, pick an anime series. If you're versatile, do one of each. If you write a spec script for a show that goes off the air, set it aside and write something new.

Avoid the three prime mistakes many newcomers make:

Mistake No. 1: Don't write a story that is clearly contradicted by something that happened in the series or contradicts how the characters normally behave. Obviously, you must be *very* familiar with the show's characters, tone, themes, and everything that is unique to that show. If you haven't seen every episode, go to Internet fan sites and research the story lines.

Mistake No. 2: Don't write a story that causes a significant change or life upheaval for one or more of the major characters, or an event that would turn the series upside down (such as killing off a major character). Only a story editor or producer gets to write those kinds of shows. You want to write a really great, but *typical* stand-alone episode of the series, something that wouldn't feel out of place if it were aired in the middle of the series' other episodes.

Mistake No. 3: Don't introduce a new, unknown character and build the story around that character. Stay focused on the central characters of the series. You *can* take a secondary character that already exists in the series and do something interesting with him or her, but make sure you have plenty of action focused on the central characters as well.

Do your best to get hold of copies of scripts for that show: *(a)* because it's helpful to see what format that series uses; and *(b)* because sometimes the story editor or producer has some special quirk related specifically to that show. For example, in *X-Men: Evolution*, they used a special X-Men graphic they called the "X-Wipe" in place of a generic wipe. Not that it's critical to know that, but it can't hurt either.

Getting hold of animation scripts isn't easy. They're not commonly put out for sale. I would try a few different methods:

- Contact the production company or studio that makes the show, explain that you want to write a spec script, and ask them if they will send you the bible and/or sample scripts. This is iffy, but worth a shot.

- Do a search on the story editor and writers of the show to see if they have Web sites with a way to contact them. Ask to buy scripts from the show for the purpose of writing a spec script. Do NOT at this point ask these people to read your script when it's done. Asking for that kind of favor might prevent them from answering you at all.

- If you live in L.A., go to the Writers Guild Foundation Shavelson-Webb Library (formerly the James R. Webb Memorial Library). This will allow you to at least read scripts, though you won't be able to take them with you or photocopy them. I would recommend calling the WGA library first (323-782-4544) and inquire whether they have animation scripts for that show. The library is working to obtain more animation scripts. Unfortunately, not many animation writers think of donating their scripts to the library. The odds of finding the most current scripts are slim, but the library has both series and feature scripts that are worth studying.

- Try the shops and Web sites I list in the resources chapter to see if they have animation scripts for sale or for downloading.

Networking

You've done your research, studied animation, written your terrific spec scripts . . . now you network. This is the single most important activity you must engage in if you want to get the lucky break that, because you are prepared, you will be able to use to your advantage.

Animation, as with any area of scriptwriting, is a people business, so a great deal of succeeding at networking is having good social skills, strong communication skills, knowing how to interact with people, how to make a good impression, how to be witty and chatty without coming across like a sycophant, all the while subtly conveying that you're a professional who would be fun to work with. Even if you're not a professional yet, you want to put forth a professional attitude consisting of awareness of the business, self-confidence, enthusiasm, and pragmatism. Easy.

It's way beyond the bounds of this book to teach you those skills, but you need to have them.

Networking is about making the business contacts any way you can, but in a way that leaves a positive impression. You must walk that fine line between putting yourself forward and being obnoxious.

Ways to Network

Don't restrict yourself to these methods. Be creative. Consider these as starting points, but do it any way you can.

- Use the Internet: You may, stress *may*, be able to strike up a relationship with a story editor or producer via Web forums or e-mail. Most pros are frankly too busy to carry on an extended e-mail exchange. Forums exist here and there where you might be able to bump into some pros. I don't consider this to be a highly effective route, but I wouldn't rule it out. The Net will probably be more useful as a research tool to learn about the animation business and about people in the business.

- Media Conventions: The mother of all conventions is Comic-Con International, which is held every summer in San Diego. Comic-Con began decades ago as a little comic book convention. It is now a massive monster convention that covers comics, animation, anime, TV, and film with almost equal fervor. Lately, computer games have also been making an appearance. Hundreds of pros show up. Some are there to promote new projects, some do panels and lectures, some do signings at the big company booths, and some show up just to have fun. The WGA Animation Writers Caucus does a panel every year.

  This is *not* a place to shove your résumé or spec script in someone's face. That's the last thing a speaker wants to deal with during a busy convention, though a business card is always acceptable. However, it gives you a chance to at least meet pros and then follow up afterward in the hope they'll remember you. Plus, the panels and lectures can be extremely informative.

- Trade Shows/Conferences: There are writing-craft conferences you can attend such as Words Into Pictures, which is put on by the WGA Foundation. Although this conference isn't specifically about animation, there is sometimes overlap with people who write for animation (for example, I have been a panelist at their event). You need to search out other such conferences, lectures, or panels that might touch upon animation writing or feature-animation writers, story editors, or producers. Again, the point is to make some sort of contact and attempt to follow up on it later.

- Join animation-related organizations: Professional groups out there have a variety of members, but may have writers and story editors among them. Any way you can get to know people is worth it. Women in Animation requires professional credentials to join (and men are welcome), but they also have a student membership, if you qualify. ASIFA (Association International du Film d'Animation, or International Animated Film Associaton) is an international group dedicated to animation. Contact information is given in the resources chapter.

- Get an entry-level job: This is an old, standard method of breaking in. You get any kind of entry-level job you can at an animation studio or production house, learn the ropes, meet people, make a good impression, and try to leverage your way into a writing job. Getting a writing job may not happen while you're working at that particular place, but could happen later if you maintain contact with the right people.

- Parties: It may sound humorous, but one of the all-time best ways to make contacts is to get invited to parties where the pros hang out. I can't tell you how to do this, other than meeting or knowing someone who can invite you. Animation writers are not, in general, big party animals, so it's going to take some luck to go this route.

- Schools and classes: There aren't a lot of formal courses for teaching animation writing, but if you can find one that's taught by someone who is actually working in the business, find a way to take the course.

Writing Contests and Other Outlets

In the world of live-action writing and feature writing, there are many contests that can prove an extremely good way to gain entry-level attention if you can win or place highly. Unfortunately, there's nothing comparable in the world of animation writing. Here are some possibilities:

- Scriptapalooza: This television-writing contest is held twice a year, with the current deadlines for submissions being May 15 and November 15, with the winners announced three months later. It has three categories for scripts: existing one-hour spec scripts, existing half-hour spec scripts, and pilots. The contest welcomes writers from around the world.

    Although Scriptapalooza is not specifically for animation writing, at least two writers won Emmy Awards for writing animated programs after having used the Scriptapalooza TV competition to get their breaks into the industry. For more information, visit http://www.scriptapaloozaTV.com, e-mail info@scriptapalooza.com, or call 323-654-5809.

- Nickelodeon Productions has begun a Writing Fellowship Program for both live action and animation, though one can never predict how long such programs will last. According to their Web site, "Nickelodeon Productions is continuing its search for new creative talent and is looking for writers to work full-time developing their craft at Nickelodeon. This program stems from Nickelodeon's commitment to encouraging meaningful participation from culturally and ethnically diverse new writers." At this time, however, they are accepting applications only from American writers. For more information, go to: http://www.nick.com/all_nick/fellowshipprogram/.

    Or contact them via:

    Nickelodeon Productions
    Writing Fellowship Program
    231 West Olive Avenue
    Burbank, CA 91502
    Attn: Karen Horne
    818-736-3663 hotline

You may also want to consider online sites such as InkTip.com (http://www.inktip.com), an Internet database of scripts that are made available for reading by registered, legitimate producers, production companies, or studios. You pay a fee to upload your script to the site. You also receive a regular newsletter in which producers or production companies indicate specific types of scripts they're looking for. Every once in a while, a producer will look for an animation script. Because we're talking about feature scripts with this particular type of site, any live-action-style script you've written that fits the requirements could be considered as a feature-animation script.

Learning about the Business

It's also extremely important to learn as much as you can about the business in general. You need to know who produces animation, which channels air animation shows, what type of shows each channel puts on the air, and how the overseas producers of animation and the overseas market are affecting animation in the United States.

I recommend these sources:

- *Animation Magazine* (http://www.animationmagazine.net). It covers not only television and film animation, but also increasingly the world of games. It does a good job of covering overseas animation and anime. The magazine comes out once a month, and your subscription will also give you access to their daily Internet newsletter, which will give you news more quickly than the monthly magazine (but the magazine is a lovely thing to hold in your hand and have for reference).

- Animation World Network (http://www.awn.com/index.php). This is a highly useful Internet site bursting with information about the world of animation, along with forums, festivals, and a place to post your résumé. It also features job listings, though you need to be wary of the people who want you to work for free. You should also subscribe to their informative e-mail newsletter, *Animation Flash* (http://www.awn.com/flash).

- *Cynopsis: Kids.* This is a compact but useful e-mail newsletter that arrives every weekday morning. The original *Cynopsis* newsletter is described as "a free daily early morning trade news composite featuring pertinent updates from the entertainment business, with just a dash of editorial." *Cynopsis* deals with television and film data, including ratings and box-office results, with a slant more toward the marketing and sales end of the business. *Cynopsis: Kids* focuses on the entire kids' market, including games. Subscribe to either or both by going to: http://www.cynopsis.com.

- The Trades: By "the trades," I mean the two major trade papers that deal with the entertainment business: *Variety* (http://www.variety.com) and the *Hollywood Reporter* (http://www.hollywoodreporter.com/thr/index.jsp). They cover all aspects of the business, but once or twice a year (mainly around Oscar time), each one also puts out a special issue covering animation. Because the trades are quite expensive, it might be worth trying to pick up only those issues dealing with animation. You can also get an online subscription, rather than a paper subscription, which might be more useful for doing searches related to animation. This is also pricey, however. It's a matter of what you can afford.

Breaking into Feature Animation

Terry Rossio put it rather succinctly: "There is no strategy that doesn't fail over 99 percent of the time, and no strategy that is far more effective than any other. I would say it makes more sense to write a live-action screenplay, because there actually is a market for live-action screenplays!"

From everything I've gathered, landing a job writing an animation feature is the ultimate crapshoot. The trend is toward big-name feature writers, or someone who happens to be hot in the live-action-feature realm, or someone who already has a feature-development deal with a studio and is tapped for an animated feature under that deal (in other words, the studio is already committed to paying them to write a feature, so they may as well write an animation feature).

The studios are not open to an unknown walking through the door to pitch an idea for an animation feature. The exception to that would be that you've created or own the rights to a property that the studio is dying to have. A highly successful children's book (preferably a series of them), for example. This is still no guarantee that you would be offered the chance to write the script, unless you have a strong script sample or other credits that would convince them.

Selling an Animation-Series Concept

Far too often, I'm asked by someone with no credits or experience how to sell a series. It's hard enough for established pros to sell a series. However, there are some general guidelines and things you need to know if you want to attempt to sell a series or property at some stage in your career.

First, you will need to create a pitch bible.

The Animation Bible

Every series has a bible. In reality, there are actually two different kinds of bibles, and they serve two different purposes. Though their purposes are different, the bibles contain the same basic elements. Those two kinds of bibles are the PITCH BIBLE and the SHOW BIBLE (or series bible, or writers' bible).

THE PITCH BIBLE: This is a short version of the bible, no more than maybe ten to twelve double-spaced pages, often with large type and lots of white space, and often with sample artwork—in other words, designed to be a very quick and exciting read with the purpose of *selling* the series idea. A pitch bible must be written entirely with one thing in mind—that you are selling how exciting and fresh and fantastic your idea is.

THE SHOW BIBLE: If you're being hired to develop a bible for a show that is a definite go, the bible will be intended primarily for the writers who will work on the show. When I do that kind of bible, I use single-spacing, I get into detail, and I don't worry so much about length. It still needs to be a good read, of course, but your purpose in this case is to make sure the writers have enough information about the show to go off and write the appropriate scripts.

I've also heard mention of the so-called MINIBIBLE, which usually just means they want to pay you half the price to write a smaller version of a regular bible. Be wary of someone asking for a "minibible." Clarify what they really want, and don't let shortness be an excuse for cheapness.

It's not unusual for the pitch bible to end up being the show bible/writers' bible, with perhaps a few extra pages of info added. Those extra pages are usually from the story editor, dealing with production details (such as "keep the length to between thirty-three and thirty-four pages"), or giving specific guidelines about the show (such as "we don't want time-travel stories" or "it's a fantasy show, so don't use modern slang"), or whatever else the writers need to know that might not have been covered by the pitch bible.

It's also not unusual for a show bible on a new series to be rewritten even while you're in the middle of doing a script. There can be a lot of last-minute and ongoing adjustments to a show that's in development. You need to be flexible and go with the changes.

In the live-action world, a bible or a proposal for a series is called a *format*. This is due to the specific language used in the WGA's Minimum Basic Agreement.

What Goes into an Animation Bible

A more or less standard format has developed that calls for these elements:

- TITLE PAGE

- CONCEPT/HOOK: The opening pages must immediately convey what the show is. It must tell in a quick and exciting way what the concept is, what the hook is, who the significant characters are, what the show is about, where it's set. For a pitch bible, it must draw the reader in and make that reader want to know more. For a show bible, it must also convey necessary information.

- THE SETTING: If there's something special about where the series is set, you might want to do a section about that, especially if you're doing a science-fiction or fantasy series. Or you may be dealing with a special time period (past, future, alternative time line), and need to go into more detail in order to convey that aspect of the series.

- CHARACTER BIOS: For a pitch bible, these would be short, exciting descriptions of each major character (heroes, villains, important pets/creatures). For a show bible, these are hopefully more detailed, and accompanied by a section describing character interactions or relationships—meaning how does Jack, for example, get along (or not) with Jane and Dick; how does Jane relate to Jack and Dick; how does Dick interact with Jane and Jack. This section can be put under each character's bio, or off in a section by itself, depending on what seems to work better for your bible or style. A short paragraph for each interaction should suffice. You would want to touch on character relationships in a pitch bible, but perhaps not at this level of detail.

- SPECIAL ELEMENTS: Depending on the nature of the show, you might want to add sections that deal with weapons or vehicles or other unique elements. In a pitch bible, this is a good place to show what sort of toy-property potential your show has (if that's appropriate). For science-fiction/fantasy shows, it can be helpful in establishing more detail about how this series will handle these special elements. If the show is set in a future world, for example, how has the technology evolved, or have we gone backward and are living a more primitive life, or are the characters using alien technology, and so on. Some of this would be covered earlier under your opening-concept pages or your pages about the setting. These special elements would be specific additions to that, and only if really needed.

- STORY/SPRINGBOARDS: In some bibles, I've seen the entire pilot episode laid out—told in an exciting story form, but with enough detail that you have everything you need for an outline. This can come earlier and can be a part of your concept/hook pages, if that works in setting up the series. But toward the end of the bible, it's a good idea to include anywhere from five to twelve story ideas, done as springboards, to indicate that you have lots of good ideas and the series has plenty of potential.

Bear in mind that these are only guidelines. The basic elements should be present in the bible, but how you present them and how it's all put together can vary tremendously. Each writer who creates a bible will develop a personal style and approach. Some writers like to use larger type and bold emphasis on certain passages or words to make them stand out. Some writers like to get into a lot of story description; others stick with generalities. The main thing in a pitch bible is to have plenty of white space (no pages crammed with tight rows of text) and a fast, engrossing read.

You will find an example of a pitch bible at www.christymarx.info.

Using Artwork in a Pitch Bible

This issue gets a lot of debate among writers, and there is no easy answer. Many people will swear that having artwork is a must. Having a hot, popular artist do the artwork might be an asset if you aren't that well known yourself. On the other hand, I've heard a studio executive tell me that he'd rather not see artwork—because if he doesn't like the art, it might turn him off to the whole idea. On the other, other hand, I've encountered studio executives who had no interest in the written work and wanted to see only images. It's the luck of the draw, and there's no way to predict it.

It might be that you have a truly special approach to the *look* of the show, and showing what the look will be might be vital to selling your idea.

Or, if you're working from an established property, you may have art that is already associated with that property. This is ideal.

One thing is certain: if it isn't good, professional-grade, quality art, *don't use it*. Far better to have no art at all than to have poor or obviously amateur art. You'd better study enough animation art to know the difference.

Finding an artist is another issue. Can you afford to pay someone? Or would you have to find someone who would be willing to work for free? Free generally implies someone young, such as an art student, who is willing to do the art in order to get exposure.

You could attend comic book conventions, where both professional and aspiring artists abound. You could go to local colleges or art schools that have illustration or graphic-design classes and connect with students there. You could contact schools that specialize in teaching comic book art, such as The Joe Kubert School of Cartoon and Graphic Art, Inc.(http://www.kubertsworld.com/kubertschool/KubertSchool.htm). You could go to your local comic book store and inquire about *really good* local artists. (See also, in the Comics section of this book, my advice about looking for artists.)

If you're paying a professional artist, have a signed, written agreement that specifies that you retain all rights to your work. You should also at least offer to use your best efforts to get the artist work on the show if it should sell.

If you have someone working for free, definitely have a signed, written agreement that clearly states that you retain all rights to your work (but not to the artist's work), and that you have free use of the artwork. However, you should work out a payment for the artist if the show should sell, as well as offering to use your best efforts to get the artist work on the show.

You can't make hard and fast guarantees to get an artist work on a show (that would usually not be under your control), so be careful to phrase it as "best efforts" or a similar term.

What Will Sell and Why

The most difficult thing to sell in today's market is an original concept. You have a better shot at selling an established property—whether it's a published children's book, a comic book, a computer game, or a toy. Marv Wolfman and Craig Miller (jointly as Wolfmill Productions) produced an animation show based on a line of popular sculptures, *The Pocket Dragons*.

However, you can do this *only* if you have legally obtained the rights from the creator or owner of the property to make this adaptation. I've encountered far too many people who want to write a script based on some big property, thinking they can somehow magically sell it and then somehow equally magically get the rights. Put this notion entirely out of your head. With a very big IP (intellectual property), something major such as *Batman* or *G.I. Joe*, the studio or company that owns the rights will want to have it developed and written by well-known people with strong credits and status in the field. They won't turn over such an important property to an unknown.

But let's say it's something not as well known that has potential. You have to option the property first. This means a signed contract that clearly spells out what rights are being granted, what you're paying or offering in return, and the time period allowed for you to sell the idea. You would want to have an option for at least two years. These things take more time than you might think.

The trick with optioning an established property is *(a)* beating out people with bigger reps, more power, and more money than you; and *(b)* having the means to buy an option and pay a lawyer to draw up an option agreement. If you're very lucky, you might be able to work out a deal that doesn't involve money up front, but you can't shortcut having a professional written agreement. To do it on the cheap, you could try to find a sample option agreement on the Net, but you'd better know a lot about intellectual-property law, copyright law, and trademark law first. Otherwise, you need to use an attorney who specializes in intellectual-property and/or copyright law. Sometimes they're called entertainment attorneys.

Alternatively, you can take your original concept and try to get it made in some other format first, such as putting out a comic book, or putting it on the Internet as a Web comic or Flash animation. To protect yourself, first register your copyright with the U.S. Copyright Office (see information under Resources at the end of this chapter).

Whatever you decide to pitch, it will need to be so extraordinary, so unique, so special that it can grab the attention of studio or production executives who have hundreds, if not thousands, of ideas pitched at them year in and year out. Believe me, they've heard it all. You will need to be good at delivering a quick, coherent, cohesive and interesting verbal pitch of your idea. You must be thoroughly prepared for any question they might throw at you, which means having your concept fleshed out enough to cover anything they could want to know about it, possibly beyond what is in the pitch bible. If the exec expresses interest, you can leave them a written version (often referred to as a "leave-behind").

Then, if the gods smile upon you, you may get a development deal and be paid money to continue working toward developing your idea into a full-fledged series. This is often known as "development hell." Bear in mind that studios develop many more projects than they actually make. They might develop dozens of ideas for only a handful of series openings.

Getting in the Door

There is the obstacle of even getting in the door to pitch an idea to someone. Your strongest chance lies in having a list of animation credits to your name, and an agent who can make the call to set the pitch meeting.

If you have strong credits in a related field—such as comics, games, or children's books— or if you have an established property, you might still be able to pitch your concept, but you may not be considered as a candidate to write the show if you don't have animation-writing credits. One alternative is to write the pilot episode or a sample episode as part of your presentation in order to show that have a grasp on writing an animation script. Of course, your sample had better be a very good script, or it could have the opposite effect. It's still likely they'll want to pair you up with an experienced animation producer and story editor whom they trust.

Without an agent or someone with connections to do it for you, you would have to make a cold call to the studio, network, or company to ask for a meeting. Your first step is to watch a lot of animation to determine which studio/network/channel is producing the type of animated show you want to pitch. In today's market, that narrows it down to only a few places such as Kids' WB!, Disney, Nickelodeon, ABC Family, Fox, and the Cartoon Network. Research them on the Net, find out where they're located, and try to get the names of their development executives. The title will be something along the lines of Director of Development, VP of Development, VP Creative Affairs, Senior VP Original Programming, and so on. If you want to pitch comedy, you want to make sure you get to the development executive who handles comedy rather than action-adventure, because these jobs are sometimes divided into genres.

If you make the call yourself and ask for the executive's office, you will end up dealing with an assistant. The assistant's job is to be the gatekeeper—to weed out unwanted calls and make sure any calls that get through are valid business. The best thing you can do is *win the goodwill* of this assistant, who is very important to you in getting anywhere. Be unfailingly polite and professional. Have a clear and concise explanation of who you are and what you want. If the assistant deems you worth consideration, the odds are high that you will first be requested to send a query letter and material for evaluation. Be prepared to do that, and confirm that you have the proper mailing address. If they request you to sign a release form, do so. It's a standard legal method of protecting themselves.

Keep your query letter short and to the point. Remind them that you spoke by phone and that the material was requested, so they don't think it's an unsolicited submission. Don't waste a lot of time in a query letter trying to describe the property or do a big sales job. Give just enough to get a taste of who you are and what you're offering, and let the material speak for itself. If you want your material back, include a stamped, self-addressed envelope. Otherwise, indicate that the material doesn't need to be returned.

Wait three to four weeks for a reply. If you don't hear anything, place a very polite follow-up phone call to inquire. This will take patience, because it could take a long time for the exec (usually surrounded by reading material up to their eyebrows) to get to your material. If you hit the bull's-eye, then you might be invited to come in and have a face-to-face meeting. It's a long shot, but my attitude is: the worst they can do is say no.

Getting an Agent

One of the frequent questions about animation is "Do I need an agent?" Although I wouldn't say it's absolutely necessary for animation in the way it is to write for live action, I strongly recommend getting an agent. An agent gives you legitimacy. It immediately says to a potential employer that you've gotten through a significant gate that separates the amateur from the professional.

Having an agent also allows you to keep clear of the negotiating and money end of things, which is what you want. Let the agent run interference for any problems that come up, so that you remain above the fray.

Back when I started out, I had no animation agent for the simple reason that television and film agents dealt only with live-action and either had no awareness of animation or didn't consider it worth the effort.

Then Candace Monteiro, who formed what is now the Monteiro Rose Dravis Agency, had the brilliant idea to gather up all those loose animation writers for representation. For a long time, this resulted in Candace's repping the majority of animation writers. Gradually, other agents and agencies realized there was something to be had here, but the overall pool of agents who specifically handle animation today is still rather small.

Probably the best way to determine who the current agents are is via the online database set up by the WGA's Department of Organizing. Go to http://www.wga.org, click on *services*, click on *find a writer*, and enter the names of an animation writer whose credits you've seen on the screen. If that writer is listed in the WGA database, it will show his or her agent and contact information. Do that for enough writers, and you will begin to see the same agent names showing up consistently. This will give you a good place to start.

Also, there is a general list of agents at wga.org. Click on *services*, then click on *find an agent.* It's a good idea to double-check an agent here. Plus, each entry indicates whether the agent is open to new writers or has special requirements.

Getting an agent to read your spec script is the next hurdle. Do not send an unsolicited script to an agent. It will most likely be returned unread. Many of these agents have as many clients as they feel comfortable handling, and may not be open to taking on a new person. The task is to find one who will be open to at least reading your spec. Never pay a fee to have an agent read your script. Anyone who asks for a reading fee is not someone you want to deal with.

Your best bet is to get a personal recommendation, either from someone already represented by that agent, or from someone (such as a producer, director, or story editor) who has read your script and liked it enough to recommend you to an agent. This gets back to the value of networking and personal connections. A personal connection of some sort will get you the agent's attention more effectively than coming in cold.

If you don't have that sort of personal connection, your first step is to send a query letter or e-mail. As with any query, keep it short, simple, and to the point. Agents have highly attuned b.s. detectors, so keep it factual. Explain who you are, list any pertinent accomplishments (college degree, work in other media, winning contests, and so on), and ask whether the agent would be kind enough to read one of your spec scripts. Be patient. After a few weeks, follow up with a polite inquiry. If you never get an answer back, strike that one off your list and keep going.

A standard script agent's commission is 10 percent Avoid anyone who wants more. If you happen upon someone calling himself a manager, check carefully into his credentials. Whom else does he manage? What has he accomplished for his clients? Managers are not held to the same licensing standards as agents, and they can charge whatever commission they want. Anything over 15 percent, however, should make you turn and run.

If you want to or choose to proceed without an agent, consider using an entertainment attorney when you need a deal negotiated or a contract finalized. You're going to pay at least $200 to $250 an hour, so be prepared for that. Those hours can pile up quickly. Work out ahead of time *exactly* what you can afford. State that very clearly to the lawyer, and stick to it. In some instances, a lawyer *might* consider handling you for a commission instead, but usually only if that lawyer considers you a good prospect to be a long-term, high-earning client.

Once You Have an Agent

The worst mistake any writer can make is to think, "Great, I've got an agent. Now I can kick back, relax, let the agent get the jobs, and wait for the phone to ring." Certainly, a good agent will be putting your name out and scouting for work, but you must continue to network, promote, get scripts out there, and do everything you can to bring in the work.

Agents are not the magic answer to success. An agent is a calling card, a confidant, an adviser, a negotiator, and a money collector. But *you* must bring in the work, using any and all techniques that you would utilize without an agent.

Be positive and honest in your dealings with your agent. It's a professional partnership that needs to be nurtured from both sides. Remember that you are not your agent's sole client. Your agent won't be calling you every day or every week, maybe not even every month. You should stay in touch regularly with little reminders that you exist. That doesn't mean pestering your agent every day, but once every couple of weeks is a good idea. Having new material or bits of good news will help keep your agent excited about repping you, and gives the agent something to work with when putting your name out.

Getting Paid

Ideally, you will have an agent who will handle all negotiations, contractual affairs, and payments. If you're new to the business and perhaps have just gotten an agent, I will share the primary rule that my first agent quickly drummed into my head with a sledgehammer: never, never, NEVER talk money. Always let your agent handle the money discussions. The agent's job is to get you the best money possible. Your job is to do the writing. Keep those things separate.

If you don't have an agent, consider using an entertainment lawyer, as mentioned earlier, and let the lawyer talk money. If you insist on doing it yourself, it will be up to you to handle the contract; to find out from the company to whom, when, and how you send an invoice; and to follow up on getting paid.

Don't expect to get rich writing animation. There are exceptions (as in any business), those exceptions being people covered by a WGA agreement or who have the clout to command large money.

The dirty secret of the majority of television-series animation is that animation writers are making about the same fees as they made in the 1980s. There has been virtually no improvement; in fact, and in some cases, it's gotten worse. Back in the mid-1980s, getting $6,000 for a half-hour script was considered terrific money. But how many people do you know whose income has barely budged in twenty years? Two decades later, some shows pay only $5,000 per half hour. Anything less than that (for a half-hour show) should be considered completely unacceptable.

What a company or studio pays depends on how big or how successful they are and what market they operate in. The smaller, independent studios, foreign coproduction, or the company doing syndicated animation can't afford to pay as well as a major studio, network, or big cable channel.

For half-hour fees, the average low end is between $5,000 and $6,000; the average high end is between $7,000 and $8,000. Writing a pilot can earn you anywhere from $10,000 to $15,000. Some writers with sufficient clout have gotten more, but that was the general range as of the time this book was written.

There will also be no residuals (additional payments for repeat airings of the episode) and no royalties from VHS or DVD sales or anything else unless the show is covered by the WGA. Which means it's time to talk about unions.

Unions and Organizations

There are two labor organizations that deal with animation writers: the Writers Guild of America (WGA), and IATSE Local 839 (The Animation Guild). This is an especially tricky and complicated topic, due to the history of animation development and the quirks of federal labor law governing unions.

As you may recall in my brief opening chapter on animation history, actual scriptwriters entered the process very late when the needs of television required writers in addition to storyboard artists, or "gagmen." Consequently, there were no writers taken into account by the two unions involved until very much after the fact, by which time the animation business was set in its ways and had no interest in seeing animation writers get the benefits of union protection.

Without the protection of a union, animation writers were (and are) subject to a great many abuses. Typical abuses include the following:

- Getting writers to work for unacceptably low amounts of money or to do ridiculous amounts of work for one payment.

- "Cattle calls," in which dozens of writers were called together at once to pitch for a series that had only a limited number of scripts available. Writers would generate pitch after pitch with no guarantee of getting a job, against the dozens of other writers doing the same. This practice has been pretty much stamped out by animation writers taking a stand, but there is nothing to prevent it from happening again.

- Giving writers only a gang credit or no credit at all. A gang credit would be one long list of every writer who worked on a series, ganged together in the end credits so that it was impossible to know who had written which episode. Although most shows now do a much better job of giving a writer a proper credit up front, there is nothing to guarantee this except the goodwill of the company or studio.

- Writers have no right to sell their scripts (copies of the script itself) as WGA writers can do.

- No residuals or other participation (for VHS, DVD, and so on).

- No health insurance or pension.

- No arbitration over disputes, nor anyone to help a writer with a dispute.

Along with many of my fellow writers, I have been part of a fight going on for more than twenty years to achieve WGA union protection for animation writers. We are finally making inroads in this tough battle, but we still have a long way to go.

The WGAw and the Animation Writers Caucus

The Screen Writers Guild was formed in 1933, reorganized into the Writers Guild of America, west and Writers Guild of America, East in 1954 (members living west of the Mississippi River belong to the WGAw, and members living east of that boundary belong to the WGAE). The early union was focused on the only game in town at the time—live-action movies. Because animation of the time was created by artists, it was excluded from later bargaining negotiations. Coverage for television was included much later.

The document that lays out every detail concerning how scriptwriters are paid and treated is the MBA (Minimum Basic Agreement). The MBA covers what the minimum payment will be to the writer. Minimum payment is known as scale (example: "My agent negotiated a deal that was scale plus 10 percent"). The minimum payments for any project are based on several factors, such as:

- Whether it's a theatrical feature, TV feature, series, or whatever
- The project's budget (mainly for theatrical features)
- The time length (mainly for TV)
- For TV, the time slot in which the show will air (daytime vs. primetime, and so on)

The MBA also covers how writing credits are determined, what the residuals will be (a residual is a payment that is made each time a TV show is rerun), rules on how writers have to be treated, provisions for arbitration in case a credit is disputed, payments to cover health and pension, and a myriad of other details designed to protect the rights and interests of writers. The MBA is renegotiated every three years.

When a studio or company signs the MBA, they become signatories to that agreement, meaning they are legally bound to abide by these rules in every detail. Although the company must pay no less than the *minimum* amount set out in the MBA, it's up to your agent, lawyer, or you to negotiate a higher price, if you can. There is no upper limit to how much you can be paid.

Most movie and television production entities that produce live action are signatories to the MBA, but until fairly recently there were among the signatories few studios or companies that produced exclusively animation. Because scriptwriters became a serious factor in the animation process only in the 1960s, it wasn't until around the 1980s that we began the first serious efforts to be covered by the WGAw. I won't go into the tedious details (which is a book in itself), but we found ourselves up against two major obstacles. One was the tangled complications of federal labor law that governs how guilds and unions can operate. The other—no surprise—was (and is) stiff resistance by the animation companies and studios.

In the early 1990s, I joined the Steering Committee of the newly established Animation Writers Caucus. The WGAw formed this caucus as a means for organizing and representing animation writers under the guild. For a minimal fee (waived if you already belong to the WGA), anyone who has written the equivalent of a half hour of produced animation can join the AWC. A member of the AWC is considered an associate member of the WGAw, which provides certain benefits that include receiving *Written By* magazine, all guild mailings, the AWC newsletter, access to the credit union, reduced member rate for registering scripts, joining the WGA Film Society, and access to an alternative health plan. The AWC arranges panels, awards, and other events.

Most importantly, the AWC, under the auspices of the WGAw, works to bring animation writers fully into the WGAw by having studios or companies sign the MBA.

I had the pleasure to work on the first animation series covered by a WGA agreement, *Pocket Dragon Adventures*, in 1997. The first show fully covered by the MBA was the prime-time animated series *The PJs* in 1998. Since then, more shows have been organized and have become signatories to the MBA, though nearly all of them are prime-time series. This is because of what I said earlier about prime-time animation shows being written mostly by sitcom and live-action writers who are accustomed to writing as WGA members and expect to have those rights, benefits, and protections.

In 2004, an agreement was put into place between the WGA, IATSE Local 839 (see below), and eight companies: Adelaide Productions, Cartoon Network Studios, DreamWorks SKG, Fox Television Animation, Sony Pictures Animation, Universal Cartoon Studios, Walt Disney Pictures and Walt Disney Television Animation, and Warner Bros. Animation. The eight companies/studios have agreed that they must give notice to writers with their first monetary proposal as to which union (WGA or 839) will cover the writing work. The writer can then request that her work be covered by a WGA agreement, or, at the very least, receive WGA equivalent benefits (meaning payments to health and pension, credit arbitration, residuals, and so forth).

If you are hired by a company or studio that is not one of these eight, you need to request WGA coverage yourself. Don't be afraid to ask!

The important thing to know about all of this is that should you ever find yourself in a position of power or have the necessary clout, you should fight to have your show done as a signatory to the WGA. To get help in doing this, contact the WGAw Organizing Department at 323-782-4511.

Having worked in live action as a WGA writer and in animation without the benefit of the WGA, I cannot emphasize enough how important this struggle is. The WGA is the right home for animation writers. We must make that happen.

IATSE Local 839 (a.k.a. The Animation Guild)

The cartoonists union began as the Commercial Artists and Designers Union, which won their first contract after a courageous strike in 1937. This was followed by a Screen Cartoonists Guild in Hollywood and numerous battles to organize the artists and animators at major studios such as Disney and Warner Bros.

In 1951, the animators voted to join the International Alliance of Theatrical Stage Employees (IATSE), and a year later they became Local 839 under IATSE. More recently, Local 839 has renamed itself The Animation Guild (TAG).

Local 839 covers layout artists, ink and paint artists, 2-D and 3-D animators, storyboard artists, and other related categories. Because there were no actual scriptwriters early on, the people who came up with story were simply called "story men." And by the odd manner in which writing developed in animation, the people writing animation fell under this category of "story men" (later "story persons"). Thus, rather by accident, Local 839 has ended up with scriptwriters (now at least referred to as "animation writers") within the body of union members who are otherwise working in the art end of the business.

If you get a job to write for a show that is covered by Local 839 and you are unable to get WGA representation instead, you will need to pay an initiation fee and dues to Local 839. Depending on what you earn, you may also be eligible for health insurance, and there will be payments made to a pension and welfare plan. There are, however, no individually paid residuals in the manner of the WGA.

Location, Location, Location

In the United States, if you want to break into animation writing in a serious way, you need to be in Los Angeles. That is still where the bulk of animation development is done, where the major studios are, and where most of the work originates. This is also where you need to be to meet the people who hire writers and to do personal networking.

There are some animation companies in San Francisco and New York City, and those would be other possibilities to explore, provided those companies actually hire writers. In many cases, the animation company provides the art while the scripts come from somewhere else—for example, L.A.

There is independent animation production being done elsewhere, such as in Florida, but the trick once again is to find places that hire writers. If you're in Canada, you need to go to the major centers of animation production—Vancouver or Toronto.

Finally, there is the overseas factor. More and more animation is being done using coproduction financing from studios in France, Britain, Ireland, Australia, Korea, Japan, China, India, Taiwan, and elsewhere. There's no easy, straightforward way for an American to get work for those companies. It would once again be a matter of networking. If you live overseas, however, you would be advised to find out where the largest producers of animation are in your country, and then move to that location. Your goal would be to meet people at that company who can hire you, and you need to be close enough physically to do that.

Comic Books

CHAPTER 5

History/Evolution of the Comic Book

My belief is that the storytelling form we know today as "comic books" goes back tens of thousands of years to the paintings of animals, hunters, and shamans on cave walls. After all, they are visual depictions "framed" by their setting, and no one can authoritatively say they weren't intended to tell a pictorial story. I suspect that the urge to tell a story through images is as old as human consciousness.

Egyptian artwork qualifies, with scenes sometimes set out in strips or panels, accompanied by "text" in the form of hieroglyphs. The Greeks told visual stories by wrapping them around vases, or around the friezes of their temples. Comic books are referred to as one of the true American-generated art forms (along with jazz), but I think the truth is more universal. However, because this section deals with writing for the modern form, I should define it. Essentially, what I'm talking about is sequential storytelling conveyed by a combination of pictures and text. From a modern viewpoint, the evolution of comic books goes back to the invention of the printing press and the development of the newspaper. The *Smithsonian Collection of Newspaper Comics* defines newspaper strip comics as ". . . a serially published, episodic, open-ended dramatic narrative or series of linked anecdotes about recurrent, identified characters, told in successive drawings regularly enclosing ballooned dialogue or its equivalent and minimized narrative text."

Prior to that form, however, there were political and social satirical single-panel cartoons dating back to the early 1800s. Beginning in 1867, the British magazine *Judy* had a long-running serial character called Ally Sloper, whose misadventures were told with illustrations accompanied by text captions beneath the image. The disreputable Ally Sloper was an illustrated superstar of his time, appearing on a wide range of merchandise from pocket watches to ashtrays to cast-iron doorstops.

A key turning point in the evolution of comics came on October 18, 1896, with the publication of a strip called the *Yellow Kid*, drawn by Richard Felton Outcault and published in William Randolph Hearst's *American Humorist*, a weekly comic supplement that came with his *New York Journal.*

In this six-panel cartoon strip, a young boy (the Yellow Kid of the series) has an exchange with a parrot. The dialogue for the Yellow Kid himself is printed on the Kid's long, blank garment, but the dialogue for the parrot appears in a rough balloon form. The action is dynamic and very directly sequential, each panel leading from one second of action to the next.

The success of the *Yellow Kid* led to the continued development of integrating dialogue with images from the late 1800s into the 1900s, expanding upon the use of word balloons. The early newspaper strips were humorous or fantastic, such as the beautiful whimsy of *Little Nemo in Slumberland*. A next step in the early 1900s was introducing continuing story lines and weekly comic strips. In 1912, the *New York Journal* again broke ground with the first full daily comic page. Soon other papers followed suit, and the popularity of the comic strip took off.

From the 1920s into the 1940s, there was an explosion of serious storytelling and continued stories, leading to such enduring series as *Little Orphan Annie*, *Terry and the Pirates*, *Dick Tracy*, *The Phantom*, *Prince Valiant*, *Brenda Starr*, and the development of soap-opera strips such as *Mary Worth* and *Apartment 3-G*.

The first steps toward what we now think of as a comic book began when the early newspaper strips were reprinted in a magazine/book format. The *Yellow Kid*, like his predecessor *Ally Sloper*, was republished in a book format and was heavily merchandised. The comic book really took shape with the publication of *Famous Funnies* in 1934. It was the inspiration of Maxwell Gaines, Harry Wildenberg, and George Janosik, who worked at Eastern Color Printing Company in Waterbury, Connecticut. Promotional one-off compilations of newspaper strips had done well, so the trio began a line of books featuring existing newspaper strips. The result was something slightly larger than today's comic books, but in the same basic format.

Famous Funnies was distributed to newsstands and sold for 10 cents, a price that would endure until 1961, when the price of a comic book went to 12 cents. George Delacorte of Dell Publishing got into publishing comic books in 1936 by creating Dell Comics. Maxwell Gaines went on to establish All-American Comics (later a part of DC), and then EC Comics, which became infamous for its no-holds-barred horror stories.

Harry Donenfeld and J. S. Liebowitz began *Detective Comics* (which led to the company now known as DC Comics) in 1935. A few years later, in November 1939, a pulp publisher named Martin Goodman began publishing *Marvel Comics*. Goodman's company went through a number of name changes, such as Atlas Comics and Timely Comics, before settling down to Marvel Comics in 1963. DC and Marvel have dominated comic book publishing ever since.

It was the work of two young men in Cleveland, Ohio, that brought about the next key turning point in the evolution of comics. Jerry Siegel and Joe Shuster created an entirely new kind of character—an alien transported to Earth, with superhuman powers and a secret identity. They called him Superman. Although the concept of a secret identity wasn't new (having been seen in novels such as *The Scarlet Pimpernel* and in pulp fiction with *Zorro*), the concept of a being with superpowers was quite new.

Siegel and Shuster spent four years trying to sell their new hero as a newspaper strip. They finally sold him to editor Vin Sullivan at DC. Superman made his first appearance in *Action Comics* #1 in 1938. The superhero genre was born.

Though its main character was not technically a superhero, one cannot overlook the creation of *The Batman* by Bob Kane and Bill Finger. Batman first appeared in *Detective Comics* #27 in 1939. Other long-lasting superheroes followed throughout the 1940s—such as the Flash, Green Lantern, Wonder Woman, and Hawkman.

The point at which comic books were created using new and original characters, rather than relying upon newspaper strips, is also the point where the writer became a separate entity from the single writer/artist of the strips. This was a function largely of the need for more material than a single person could produce. Siegel was the writer, Shuster the artist in the Superman team. Bob Kane the artist credited Bill Finger the writer as his partner in the creation of the Batman.

The success of Superman and Batman spawned a host of copycats, most of which are long forgotten. Marvel Comics created some memorable characters such as the Human Torch (the original being an android rather than a human being), Sub-Mariner, and Captain America.

From Superman, comics gained the archetype of the suspicious girlfriend trying to ferret out the hero's true identity. The creation of Robin spawned a horde of teenage sidekicks, forever imprinting that archetype upon the field.

Comics hit their first major stumbling block and went into a steep decline due primarily to one man, a psychiatrist named Fredric Wertham. In the 1940s, Wertham linked crimes by juvenile delinquents with the fact that many of them read comic books. He published his first anticomics article in 1947, beginning a crusade to ban comics that culminated with the publication in 1953 of his book *Seduction of the Innocent*. Wertham was the first in a long line of authoritarian figures who blamed crime and acts of violence on some form of media, as we've seen since with similar blame laid on television, toys, and videogames. I won't debate the merits of Wertham's arguments, but the outcome was to cripple comics publishing.

Publishers defended themselves by establishing the Comics Code Authority (CCA) in 1954. A comic book that wanted to stay on the newsstands needed the CCA stamp on the cover of the book. The code directed how crime and criminals could be portrayed; how legal authorities had to be portrayed (always in a positive light); that good had to triumph over evil; that gore was forbidden; that the use of the words "crime," "horror," and "terror" were greatly restricted; and that vampires, cannibals, and zombies were forbidden. There were restrictions on how comics could deal with topics such as religion, marriage, and sex. There were regulations on what sort of advertising could be accepted. It boiled down to making comics into a bland, wholesome medium considered safe for children—and children were considered to be the only readership.

As a result, sales plummeted. Superheroes took a nosedive. Comics floundered. There was still variety in comics—covering genres of war, Westerns, and romance, along with humor books—but horror comics almost ceased to exist. Eventually, at the end of the 1950s, DC revived and updated a number of superhero characters and had success doing so. Superheroes were about to explode into the limelight once more.

The next big step in the evolution of comics and comic writing came in the form of one prolific, longtime comics writer, Stan Lee, and his dynamic creative partnerships with artists such as Jack Kirby and Steve Ditko. In 1961, Lee and Kirby created *The Fantastic Four*, an entirely new way of portraying comic book superheroes. The FF had no secret identities, had family relationships, argued and carried on like real people, and had none of the usual superhero stereotypes. The success of *The Fantastic Four* was followed by the creation of *Spider-Man*, *The Hulk*, *The X-Men*, *Thor*, *Dr. Strange*, *The Avengers* and many more that rejuvenated the comics medium. Heroes from the '40s, such as Captain America and Sub-Mariner, reappeared in new forms.

Counterculture latched on to comics. In 1968, what is considered the first "underground" comic was published—*Zap* #1 by R. Crumb. Other great underground comics followed, such as *Mr. Natural*, *The Fabulous Furry Freak Brothers*, and *Air Pirates Funnies*. Being filled with sex and violence—plus political, cultural, and religious satire—they operated well outside of the mainstream.

Then, in 1971, came *Spider-Man* issues #96 to #98, in which Stan Lee wrote a three-part antidrug storyline. This doesn't sound groundbreaking, but even mentioning drug use meant that the books had to be published without the approval stamp of the Comics Code Authority. And so they were—with no ramifications whatsoever. These *Spider-Man* issues weren't picketed by angry mobs, or sued, or confiscated by the government. They just sold, like any other comic, but without that little CCA stamp.

By the 1980s, the CCA was defunct. Underground publishers ignored it, and gradually the mainstream publishers stopped worrying about it.

Soon DC began publishing more "relevant" stories, and creators everywhere rebelled against the narrow strictures of the code. In 1974, Mike Friedrich published a line of "aboveground" black-and-white comics called *Star Reach*. The *Star Reach* books used professional comic book writers and artists, but didn't go through the CCA because they were sold only by direct sale, meaning to comic book stores rather than on the newsstands. It was the first attempt at creating alternative comics.

In 1979, Wendy and Richard Pini began the publication of their long-running, highly successful, independently published series *Elfquest*. Numerous alternative comics publishers have come and gone: Pacific Comics, Eclipse Comics, First Comics, and CrossGen. Others, such as Dark Horse Comics, have managed to stay in the business and have moved beyond pure comics publishing into other media, such as movies.

As those of us who grew up reading comics became adults who wrote and drew comics, we wanted comics to grow up with us. Marvel and DC both have special lines of "mature" comics for an over-18 audience. With the creation of the direct-sale market and comic books stores (replacing newsstand distribution), it was possible for comics publishing to reach an older audience. Innovative alternative comics such as *Love & Rockets* by Gilbert and Jaime Hernandez, *Concrete* by Paul Chadwick, and *Strangers in Paradise* by Terry Moore prove that comics can be a mature, challenging, and intelligent medium for adults. It's not just for kids anymore.

Whatever the content, comics are also a business, and one that has been in decline as far as the numbers are concerned. The big publishers turn to gimmicks (special covers, multiple covers for a single issue, the "death" of a major character) to pump up sales, or they totally reinvent old characters in an attempt to connect with a new audience. While comic book stores struggle to stay afloat, comics have become less a medium unto themselves, and more a medium that is used to generate other, more-profitable product, especially movies. Comics are now used as a launching platform for films, television series, toys, licensed merchandise, and videogames. DC is part of the Time Warner entertainment juggernaut. Marvel has established a special division strictly to deal with turning their characters into movies and other media. Platinum Studios was formed specifically to publish comics and graphic novels that could be turned into movies/TV, *Men in Black* being one of their successes. Movie-production companies are being formed specifically for the purpose of turning comic books into films. And it's common to see a popular movie or television series generate a subsequent line of comics, along with the requisite media novel tie-in or videogame or what have you.

Big-name TV/movie writers such as Joss Whedon (*Buffy the Vampire Slayer, Angel, Firefly*) and J. Michael Straczynski (*Babylon 5*) write comics, while numerous comic book writers (for example, Stan Lee, Len Wein, Marv Wolfman, Gerry Conway, Howard Chaykin) have moved into writing for film, TV, and animation.

Genres and Categories

What you decide to do as a writer for comics depends a great deal on your personal goals and what you want to accomplish. You can be a purist, creating a comic book purely for the sake of telling a story in that medium; or you can go to work for a large publisher, hoping for regular work and big bucks; or you can create a book specifically aimed at the comics-to-film market. The difference between now and a few decades ago is that you have that choice.

Although a large segment of the population continues to mistakenly believe that comics are "kid stuff," that is no longer true. If anything, there's a shortage of good comics for younger kids, with the bulk of books out there aimed at teenagers and adults.

That's a function of the marketing, not the form itself. Like any other art form, it can be inspired and inspiring, or it can be insipid.

Publishing Options

Here are your major outlets for publishing a comic:

- Work for hire for a major publisher—Marvel or DC. This means writing for one of their established books in which you have no rights or ownership.

- Creator-owned work for a major publisher. If you can manage to sell an idea to one of Marvel's or DC's special publishing lines, you can have a chance of owning your work while being published under their imprint. There are not many of these outlets left.

- Write for an alternative publisher such as Dark Horse, Top Cow, or IDW. You're less likely to be working on an existing book, because they would be looking for new ideas from you, and more likely to have some ownership of your work. Image Comics was formed in 1992 by a number of comics creators for the purpose of publishing work in which they kept ownership. It was a smart idea, and one that made Todd McFarlane (creator of *Spawn*) quite rich.

- Publish your own book. This is a tough road to walk, and works best if you are both a writer and an artist (otherwise you need to form a partnership with an artist), but it gives you the maximum control and ownership of your work.

- Publish on the Internet. This is certainly a viable alternative, though it's hard to make money doing it, unless you're discovered by a publisher or producer or someone who can finance your dream.

Comics will be best served by having a variety of genres and types. Here's a listing of possible categories:

- Superhero—certainly one of the predominant genres, ranging from individuals (*Superman, Batman, Spider-Man, Hulk*), to teams (*X-Men, Fantastic Four, Justice League, Teen Titans*), to the offbeat (*Astro City*)

- Anthropomorphic animals—ranging from "funny animals" (*Donald Duck*), to serious books (*Usagi Yojimbo*), to *Teenage Mutant Ninja Turtles*

- Family fare (*Archie, Scooby-Doo,* Disney)

- Media tie-ins (*Buffy the Vampire Slayer, Star Wars, The Powerpuff Girls, The Incredibles, Alien, Predator, The Simpsons*)

- SF/fantasy (*Star Wars, A Distant Soil, Elfquest, Bone, Love & Rockets, Hellboy, Spawn*)

- Contemporary (*Sin City, 100 Bullets, Strangers in Paradise*)

- Autobiographical (*American Splendor*)

- Manga (Japanese comics)

- Erotica

- Miscellaneous genres—war stories, Westerns, horror, romances (genres that are scarce in the current market, but a few titles can be found here and there)

- Political/modern events such as 9/11

- Fumetti—extremely rare, these are comics using photos in the panels instead of illustrations, complete with word balloons like a regular comic ("fumetti" means "smoke," taken from the idea that the word balloons look like clouds of smoke coming out of the characters' mouths)

CHAPTER 6

What Is a Comic Book?

Make mistakes. Make great mistakes, make wonderful mistakes, make glorious mistakes. Better to make a hundred mistakes than to stare at a blank piece of paper too scared to do anything wrong, too scared to do anything.

— Neil Gaiman

Before getting into terminology, which is minimal, let's examine the standard formats in which "comic books" appear:

- MONTHLY COMIC BOOK: the best-known format, fairly standardized (at the moment) at six and a half inches by ten inches, center stapled. Quality can vary, but paper and coloring are vastly better now than in the old newsprint, four-color days of comics. Story content in the mainstream book runs around twenty-two to twenty-three pages, though the actual length of a book can be longer depending on how many ads it contains. The number of pages in a monthly book, or any comic format, is also determined by the number of pages that are printed per sheet. For example, a standard figure is four pages to a printing sheet. Therefore, a book that is twenty-four pages long is printed on six large sheets of paper, which are then cut and folded to make the book. To print one less sheet would give you a book with twenty pages; add a sheet, and you get twenty-eight pages. The printing requirements determine the overall length of a book.

    Books from alternative publishers can vary. The various comics put out by the Hernandez brothers (*Love & Rockets* spin-offs) run around fifty to fifty-two pages of story in black and white, for example. Stan Sakai's *Usagi Yojimbo* has twenty-four pages of story, also in black and white.

- GRAPHIC NOVEL/TRADE PAPERBACK: A graphic novel or trade paperback can vary in size and length, but it tends to be roughly the same length and height dimensions as a monthly book (six and a half inches by ten inches). They are perfect-bound rather than stapled, meaning they have a square spine and the pages are glued to the spine, with a thick stock for the cover. The story might run a hundred pages or so. Usually they have high-quality paper, coloring, and printing because they are higher priced and treated more like a book than a magazine. Unlike a monthly book, which lasts on the shelves or on a newsstand for only a month, a graphic novel/trade paperback can occupy a bookshelf indefinitely because it is usually a stand-alone item.

- HARDCOVER GRAPHIC NOVEL: rarer, but when we printed *The Sisterhood of Steel* graphic novel, we also did a limited-edition run of hardcovers that were signed and numbered and sold for a higher price. They're treated even more like a "real" book.

- MINISERIES, LIMITED SERIES: These might run anywhere from three issues on up (I've seen something billed as a two-issue miniseries, but I think that's pushing the concept a bit far), and might be printed in the same format and same length as a monthly book, or in a graphic-novel form, though usually fewer pages than a stand-alone graphic novel. A miniseries might also later be collected and published as one or more graphic novels.

- MANGA: As Japanese comics, called manga, have gained in popularity, American publishers are jumping on the bandwagon to produce manga-size books (fig. 6.1). The format size is usually five inches by seven and a half inches, softcover, perfect-bound, in black and white. They are thicker than the typical book, and page length can vary a lot. I've seen them with anywhere between 61 and 110 pages of story.

Just to confuse things, there are people publishing actual manga from Japanese creators. True Japanese manga are read back to front, right to left—the total opposite of how we in the Western world read comics or books. This makes reprinting them for a Western market trickier than it sounds, because rearranging the pages disrupts the flow of the artwork. Some manga published in the American market have dealt with this by keeping the right-to-left arrangement of art and balloons, requiring Western readers to learn that method of reading.

It isn't just American comics publishers grabbing on to the manga format. Regular book publishers are seeing a potential market—ranging from educational publishers wanting to reach out to younger readers, to publishers of romance novels seeking to expand their audience by converting prose romance novels into manga.

One final comment about manga: if done right, manga are about much more than a mere size-and-shape format. There is, of course, the unique visual look of manga, represented by a number of styles. In terms of content, manga focus heavily upon the characters, character angst, and character interactions over plot or action. They are more introspective about the characters' thoughts and feelings. Manga reach a broader audience in Japan, and increasingly here in the States, in particular hitting a female market in ways that most American comics have all but abandoned. I think this is entirely for the good, and I hope this distinction doesn't become lost in the rush to mine a hot new target audience.

- ASHCAN: This term refers to a small-size (usually around four by five inches), short booklet form of comic, done in black and white. Basically, these are quick, inexpensive do-it-yourself comics produced by the original creators. They don't generally receive regular distribution, and are sold via mail, Internet, at conventions, and so on. The original purpose of ashcans was for the creator who couldn't afford to do a full-production book to at least have something he could hand out to show off his work, to give out to editors or publishers in an attempt to sell the idea or get work, and to establish copyright ownership. I've since seen professionals who sell ashcans as promotional pieces.

Figure 6.1
This *Elfquest* graphic novel *(left)* was also published in a manga format and size, seen on the right for comparison.

This covers only American comics and doesn't touch upon the other formats you might find in Europe and elsewhere. But size, shape, and thickness of the book, while relevant, are secondary considerations. They set the parameters for how much can go into a story, without determining in any way how you will tell that story or what the story will be.

Web Comics

Then we have comics that go beyond the paper versions. Web comics use the same characteristics and elements of a traditional comic, but can push into entirely new territory. There are striplike Web comics that look and feel like reading a comic strip from a newspaper, either as continued stories or stand-alone jokes. Scott McCloud took some of his published *Zot!* comics and relaid the panels in a clever, lengthwise design that took advantage of how

Web pages read best on a computer screen (see http://www.scottmccloud.com/comics/zot/index.html). Or there is Charley Parker's Web comic *Argon Zark!*, which is done in comic book panels, but with interactive elements (see http://www.zark.com/front/hub.html) and links to additional humorous material. At the far end of the spectrum, there are fully moving comics done with Flash, a cross between the comic format and animation.

Newspaper Comic Strips

Creating a comic strip for newspaper distribution is a highly specialized field. Although I've been hired to create two newspaper-strip presentations (several weeks' worth of strips), I don't know enough overall about newspaper strips to offer advice.

Instead, I'll point you to an excellent and detailed book, *Your Career in the Comics* by Lee Nordling. It covers every aspect of the art and business of a newspaper comic strip, and includes advice from many top professionals. I will point out that the vast majority of newspaper strips are created by one person who is both the writer and the artist—so if you are strictly a writer, you are at a disadvantage. For more about finding an artist partner for a comics project, see Chapter 7.

The Production Process

A comic can be an expensive, full-color graphic novel or a tiny, independent black-and-white effort. Unless the comic is being done by an artist who writes as he goes, there will always be a need for a script first.

Comic book production has changed dramatically with the rise of computer-graphics programs. A book might be entirely penciled, inked, colored, and lettered digitally and never see a piece of paper until it's printed. Coloring especially has come a long way with the advent of computer-graphics systems.

Here are the traditional steps of comic book production, outside the computer realm:

- The writer creates the script. At a large company, the script goes to the editor for revisions or approval. In other circumstances, it might go directly to your artist.

- The primary artist is the penciller, who breaks out the penciled art of the story from the script. A penciller usually works on art board that is about twice the final printed size of the page.

- If the script was done only in outline form, the penciled pages should go back to the writer, who can complete the script by writing the final dialogue and captions to fit the art. Sometimes a writer is also expected to indicate where the balloons and captions should go in each panel.

- The penciled pages go to an inker, who inks the pencils.

- If it's a color book, some version of the inked pages (paper or digital) goes to the colorist to add the color work.

  Blue line refers to a comic book page in which the black-line art (penciling and inking) has been reproduced in blue lines instead of black. These pages are usually twice as large as the printed size will be. Blue lines are printed onto art paper so that the colorists or painter can paint directly onto this art paper. The black lines are a separate production element printed onto a clear overlay, so that when the final page is reproduced, it will have the black lines on top of the colored or painted page.

- A letterer adds the balloons, dialogue, captions, and sound effects, usually on a clear overlay, rather than onto the original art.

With the advance of digital technology, any of the steps after the script goes to the artist could be produced solely on a computer. The artist could produce pencils digitally, ink it that way, add the color, lettering, and so on.

Terminology

BALLOONS

The visual unit that conveys dialogue, either spoken or thought. Balloons have developed into a more-or-less oval shape, with a pointer or tail to indicate to which character they belong. There are many specialized forms of balloons, either traditional or invented. Pretty much anything goes, as long as the balloon serves its function the examples are taken from my series, *The Sisterhood of Steel*. Some of the standard balloon types are as follows:

Figure 6.2
SPEECH BALLOON: the usual rounded oval shape and pointer tail to indicate normal speech.

Figure 6.3
THOUGHT BALLOON: cloudlike scalloped edges with the pointer tail replaced by dots of decreasing size.

Figure 6.4
WHISPER BALLOON: like a speech balloon, but drawn with a dotted outline rather than solid.

Figure 6.5
JAGGY BALLOON: a speech balloon drawn with pointy "barbs" all around to indicate yelling, extreme emotion, or anything way beyond normal speech.

CAPTION

A caption can have a number of uses, but mainly it's a square or rectangle that sits by itself on the panel, not visually connected to anything in the panel (fig. 6.6). A caption is used mostly to convey narrative information, such as time or place, or to set a mood, perhaps to convey additional nonvisual information such as a sound or smell.

Another use has developed in which the caption takes the place of a thought balloon (fig. 6.7). It allows the reader to have the insight into what a character is thinking, while keeping the effect of those thoughts distanced from the image—as though the character were narrating to the reader, rather than the reader looking into the character's thoughts.

A caption doesn't absolutely have to be enclosed by a border (fig. 6.8). It can sit as floating text inside a panel, but for the purposes of a script, you would still indicate it as a caption.

GUTTER

The space between panels. In the old days, this was simple white space. The appearance and usage of gutters has also changed tremendously. In many current comics, panels are laid onto panels without actual gutters. However, the conceptual purpose of a "gutter" remains unchanged. It is more than a simple graphic element to separate panels. Fundamentally, the gutter encompasses everything that happens *between* what happens in the panels. More on this later, too.

Figure 6.6
A regular caption. Sample from *The Sisterhood of Steel*.

Figure 6.7
A narrative caption. Sample from *The Sisterhood of Steel*.

NEGATIVE SPACE

This refers to the amount of space allowed in a panel or on a page to accommodate the nonvisual elements of balloons and captions. The artist needs to make sure there's enough negative space so that vital sections of the artwork aren't obscured by the text elements. Negative space can also be used purely for visual effect (Will Eisner, creator of *The Spirit*, was a master of this).

Figure 6.8
A borderless caption. Sample from *The Sisterhood of Steel*.

PANEL

A "frame" around one image that is a component of telling the story. There are endless ways of creating panels. The most common panel is a square or rectangle bounded by a black line, but a panel can be any size or any shape as long as it creates a cohesive visual unit of storytelling. More about this later.

SFX (SOUND EFFECTS)

Used in a comic book script where the writer is telling the letterer when the panel needs a sound effect and what that sound effect should be.

SPEED LINES, ACTION LINES

These are lines the artist uses to convey that someone or something is moving swiftly through the space of the panel. They might be the lines that describe the arc of Thor's hammer through the air, or the lines behind a character to indicate he's moving at extremely fast speed. These are one of the artist's tools, and not something you need to worry about as a writer, but it doesn't hurt to know what they're called.

SPLASH PAGE

Traditionally, this referred to an opening page that consisted entirely of one large panel, containing whatever image led into the story, plus the credits for writing, art, lettering, coloring, editing, and so on. Nowadays, there often isn't a splash page, or it occurs some number of pages into the story, or it might be a double-page spread. There is no requirement to use a splash page; it's more a tradition than anything else.

The Comic Book Script

The most important thing to know is that there is no one way to create a comic book script. You will see about as many variations on comic book scripts as there are writers. There is a basic, somewhat standard format, and these variations usually fall within the parameters of that format.

When I first learned to write comic book scripts, I was taught that there were two main "styles"—the DC style and the Marvel style. Marv Wolfman refers to them as script style (DC) vs. plot style (Marvel).

In brief, they can be defined this way:

- DC STYLE (script style): This is a fully detailed script in which all the pages are broken down into panel descriptions, with the dialogue and captions written, and the sound effects indicated. All elements of the script are complete.

- MARVEL STYLE (plot style): In this approach, an outline or descriptive version of the story is written, allowing the artist more freedom to decide how to break out the visuals. The final writing of dialogue and captions is done after the pencils are finished. The outline can be written like a set of instructions or like a short story. This is up to you, your editor, and your artist.

Although referring to these styles may become obsolete, it's good to understand the basic approach of each one. You may find yourself using an approach that's halfway between the two, for example.

You may be lucky enough to choose which approach you want to take, but other factors may determine how you'll be required to write the script. For example, I wrote some manga-style books for an educational publisher who was sending the scripts overseas to artists in the Philippines. I was required to use a very specific script format because it was a format these artists were familiar with. It wasn't a format that was easy to use or that I especially liked, but that was the requirement, so that was what I used.

With that in mind, let's examine the pros and cons of the two styles before getting into the layout of a sample script.

DC Style/Script Style

By writing a full script with every single element specified, you as the writer have more control over the finished book. You will have determined the page breaks and the number of panels per page. You are more in control of the pacing and layout. The artist will know exactly how much lettering has to fit in each panel, and can take that into account when doing the art. However, using this style also ends your creative input pretty much at the writing stage, unless the editor or publisher includes you again after the art is done.

For an editor or publisher on a tight schedule, this is a faster method. If you're not in close contact with the artist, it may be necessary (such as when using artists who are overseas). Depending on how stringently the artist is required to follow your script, this style does take away from the artist's freedom to come up with different, possibly more interesting ways to break out a page—ways that may not have occurred to you.

If you're a new, untried writer in this format, the editor may want this type of script to see how well you understand the medium. For submitting a spec script, this is the only way to go.

Marvel Style/Plot Style

Writing an outline as the first step opens more of the creative decision-making process to the artist. You can still indicate thoughts about how the page might be broken out. For example, you might call for a single-panel page when you want to create special emphasis for that instant of action. You can break your outline into pages, with a rough idea of what you want to fit on each page, or you can leave out any page breaks at all and leave it entirely up to the artist.

This works best when you fully trust the artist and feel confident that you'll get the results you want. If you aren't including dialogue in your outline, you should at least give the artist as much indication of dialogue as you can. To lay out a page, the two big things an artist needs to know are how much visual material she has to pack into it, and how much negative space she has to leave for the balloons and captions.

Once the pencils are done, they would come back to you so that you can write the rest of the script, meaning the specific dialogue and other text, to go with the art you receive. You may have the freedom to indicate where you want the balloons placed, or that may be left up to the letterer to determine. That brings up the weakness of this method—you are stuck with the artwork you get, and if it doesn't quite provide you with the layout or arrangement of characters that you wanted, you'll have to work around it. You might be able to have changes made to the art, but that would depend entirely on your working relationship with the artist, publisher, or editor, plus considerations of scheduling and cost.

Although this method gives the artist more creative freedom, it can, in the worst cases, lead to sloppy writing. There's a story that's probably apocryphal, but it is nonetheless a good illustration of lazy writing. The story goes that the writer set up the action, then simply wrote, "And they fight for the next twenty pages."

The Script Format

As I said, there's no standardized format for a comic book script, and every writer can have her own way of laying it out. I've seen some writers use a format that looks very much like a film or TV script.

What I'm showing here is a format that is commonly used. Some writers like to do their description paragraph IN ALL CAPS. Some might use bold or have other quirks. But in general, this format will look familiar to an editor or artist. You indicate:

- The comic book page number at the top
- Below that, the panel number
- Below that, your description for the images and action of the panel
- Finally, you write your captions, dialogue, and sound effects (if any).

If you have a panel that is visual only, with no text at all, it's helpful to indicate "No dialogue" below the description area to ensure that the artist and letterer have no doubts about missing dialogue.

Some companies may ask you to number the captions and balloons. The numbering is sequential for each comic book page (1 to whatever), then starts the numbering over again from 1 on the next page. This makes it easier to refer to a specific piece of dialogue when communicating with the editor, artist, and letterer. When indicating where captions or balloons are placed on a page, the captions and balloons can also be numbered to indicate to the letterer which piece of numbered text belongs inside which caption or balloon.

If your script for a single comic book page goes longer than a page of printed document, be sure to indicate the comic book page number at the top of the additional script pages, and indicate that the comic book page is continued on that script page. That way, if the script pages should get separated or mixed up, the editor or artist or letterer will know which comic book page belongs to which script pages.

I also recommend putting a hard page break at the end of the script pages for each comic book page. This makes it easier for the artist. If your script for page 1 of the comic runs to two script pages, the artist can easily separate out those two pages and refer to them as he designs page 1, without having to worry about pieces of another comic book page being on the same script page.

You should put a header at the top of each page to identify the book, the issue (if applicable), and the writer.

Here's an example of a full script style, as though broken into two script pages.

```
THE CRYSTAL SKULL #1—Christy Marx

PAGE 1

PANEL 1

Panel should occupy the top half of the page.

JACK is a scruffy, dissolute man in his 40s, a man who looks like
he has a lot more mileage on him than that. He's in a run-down,
rural Mexican hacienda that, like him, has seen better days. We
can glimpse the ocean and bit of beach through the open door. The
furnishings are crude and devoid of personality. There are no
special objects in the room that would give a hint about the
owner's background . . . with one exception—a crystal skull sit-
ting in the middle of a battered wooden kitchen table.

Also in the room is JANE, an attractive young woman in jeans,
T-shirt, and black leather jacket (in spite of the heat). She has
black hair cut short. Her companion, DICK, looks like a frat boy
in a Hawaiian camp shirt. They're an odd pair.

In the panel, the three of them stand at the table, where Dick,
on the left, gazes at the skull in awe. Jack, in the middle
between them, is sardonic. Jane, to the right, is self-contained,
giving away little.

CAPTION:    Somewhere in Mexico . . .

DICK:       It's awesome.

JANE:       Where did you find it, Jack?
                                                        (cont'd)
```

```
THE CRYSTAL SKULL #1—Christy Marx

PAGE 1 (continued)

PANEL 2

Closer on Jack, who comes across like a smart aleck.

JACK:       Found it in a thrift shop. Salvation Army, I think.
            Somewhere in Cleveland.

PANEL 3

Jane, cold as ice, has smoothly pulled a revolver and placed it
against Jack's cheek with the trigger cocked. Jack is as cool as
ever, not the least bit worried.

SFX:        Klikk!

JANE:       Let's try the truth this time, shall we?

JACK:       O.K., it was Nepal. A Salvation Army thrift store in
            Nepal.

JACK (thought balloon): Joke's on you, babe. It really was in
                        Cleveland.
```

Several things to think about:

Note that I gave only a general description of Jack's appearance. If you wanted to have Jack wearing a specific type of clothing or have a certain haircut or other details, you would need to include that in the description for the artist. If you don't specify something, you leave it up to the artist to fill in the blanks. That's a matter of comfort level between you and the artist.

Note that in the first two panels, the characters are laid out so that Jack is to the left of Jane, but in panel 3, in order to fit the flow of dialogue, Jane will need to be to the left of Jack. This requires the artist to reverse the angle at which he's been laying out the flow of action so far. Otherwise the artist will have to come up with another way of arranging the characters in the panel so that the balloons can still be placed in the correct reading sequence. You have to think about whether that will help or hinder the visual flow of the page.

Notice how much action happens between panels 2 and 3: she has gone from standing next to Jack without a gun, to having a gun in Jack's face and cocking the trigger. See more about the significance of what happens "in the gutter" in the Beyond the Basics section below, Panels and Gutters.

Note also that in panel 3, the artist will have to leave room for two talking heads, a sound effect, two speech balloons, and a thought balloon, so it's best to keep the actual dialogue as short as possible.

The alternative is to break it out into a separate panel so that Jane makes her threat at the bottom right panel of page 1, and Jack gives his reply in the top left panel of page 2. Remember that the reader will have to flip the page before seeing Jack's reply, because page 1 is always a stand-alone page. As the writer, you need to decide which alternative feels better to you. Do you prefer the immediacy of Jack's reply right after Jane makes her threat, or do you mind that there's an implied beat of time between her threat and his reply in a separate panel on the next page?

You'll make countless such decisions throughout the script, if you're visualizing properly.

The Visual Elements

As with the other forms of writing covered in this book, writing for comics requires that you have a strong sense of visualization. Whether writing script style or plot style, you must have a clear mental image of each page so that your writing will be precise enough to convey that to the artist (and to other readers, such as the editor, but mostly the artist).

There are different trends of thought about how to visualize for comics. Some writers like the cinematic approach, to think of comics as a strip of film from which one selects individual frames to represent the action. If you were to take a movie and had to tell the story by selecting a few frames of action per scene, which frames would you choose? In this approach, you need to distill the action into those particular frozen moments that best capture the story, mood, theme, and pacing.

Although a chunk of action can be distilled down to one panel, it can be even more effective to show that action broken into a series of successive panels that simulate a cinematic flow. In other words, rather than reducing it to the one frame that represents the whole action, you would be using three or four frames. On the comics page, it comes out as three or four successive panels that convey a more dynamic sense of pacing and movement (fig. 6.9). This affects pacing by calling more attention to that piece of action. When an action is represented by a single panel, the brain processes it as happening in a split second. When the same action is told across three or four successive panels, the brain "reads" it as taking more time, even if the time is only another few split seconds.

Personally, I think the straight cinematic method ignores the full range of possibilities in the printed page. It's not a bad approach, and if it works for you, then go for it. I would consider it one method of storytelling that can be used, rather than the only one.

Figure 6.9
A cinematic flow of action. Sample from *The Sisterhood of Steel*.

My recommendation is to visualize a comic book page as a comic book page, not as any other medium. It is what it is. You can span all of space and time, you can be linear or nonlinear, staccato or static, realistic or abstract. The comic book page can be straightforward storytelling or a piece of conceptual art.

As a comic book storyteller, you must have mastery over telling your story with the images as much as with the words. The alchemy is in how you combine them to create a whole that is greater than the sum of its parts.

Script Length

A comic book script can be any length at all. Animation and live-action scripts use their particular format because each page roughly equals a certain amount of time; therefore, the page count has to relate to the number of minutes the film or TV show runs. A film or TV script centers the actors' dialogue the way it does to make it easy for the actors to flip through the script and pick out what they have to memorize.

Neither of those things applies to a comic book script. Your main reader is the artist, so most of what you write is for her benefit. The layout of the captions and dialogue in the script is mainly for the benefit of the letterer, who needs to know the sequence in which each element has to be placed in the panels, and also to make it quite clear to the letterer what is the text he's lettering (vs. description for the artist), and how many balloons or captions are required for it. For example, only one character may be speaking in the panel, but the writer can break up a chunk of dialogue into three pieces, requiring three connected balloons. I'll get into more detail on this below, under Panels and Text.

With comics, the actual script length is irrelevant, and you're writing to match the number of pages in the printed book. You need to have an instinctive sense of how much story will fit into those pages. Beyond that, you can write a sparse script that is minimal on details, or you can write a novel. The amount of detail you include depends mainly on your relationship with the artist and your own inclinations as a writer. Another factor is whether you're using established characters (who don't need description) or inventing new ones. It also depends on whether you're dealing with a known, familiar setting or with settings or situations that are newly invented, as in science fiction and fantasy. An artist can research "a typical middle-class kitchen from 1960." She can't research "the Magorgian Temple in the peaks of Zoenton."

It gets down to this—the purpose of the description is to tell the artist everything she needs to know in order to bring your mental vision to the page. No matter how poetic or epic you are in your descriptions, those descriptions don't reach the end reader. Only the images and the actual words on the page will have that impact.

Beyond the Basics (Advice, Tips, and Tricks)

The Page and Panels

One of the key decisions a writer must make, whether writing a full script broken into panels or an outline, is how many panels to have per page. Cramming too much onto a single page can make it hard for the reader to sort things out. The size of the page is important. For the smaller, manga-size pages, for example, I wouldn't recommend more than four or five panels per page, max. Otherwise everything becomes too small, and you defeat the purpose of using visual storytelling rather than prose.

Figure 6.10
A comics page is read top to bottom, left to right, in a zigzag pattern.

The comic book page is a visual unit that the eyes take in first as a whole, then as a sequence of visual elements flowing (generally) top to bottom, left to right (fig. 6.10). When you visualize a comic book page, you need to have that sense of the whole and the parts and how they work as a unit. Your page can be full of cinematic flow, or it can be a mosaic of separate but interrelated images happening anywhere at any time. The bottom line is, *does it work*? Do the words and images get across what you want the reader to know and feel?

You need to ask yourself whether it's such a big or dramatic moment that it calls for an entire page or an extra-large panel. Do you need to cram in a huge number of people or things (big panel)? Is it a good moment to go in ultraclose on someone's eyes for a single panel? Would a long horizontal panel (fig. 6.11) work better for what you want to convey, or would a tall, vertical panel work better?

Panels can be used for pacing. A page of characters talking can include a "silent" panel, in which the art focuses on the character's expression and omits words to create the sense of a pause in the conversation, of a moment in which the character thinks, emotes, or reacts rather than talks. A page of no text, such as a character carrying out an action in silence (fig. 6.12), can convey anything from loneliness to serene meditation to stealth. *Not* using text is another one of the tools in your storytelling toolbox.

I've seen this use of no-text panels carried to extremes. One book tried to tell an entire issue's worth of story with no text at all. I found that didn't work well. For me, the storytelling was out of balance. There are, conversely, times when you *want* the words.

Other experiments have included an entire issue of splash pages or an entire issue done sideways so that the reader had to flip through the book as though the pages were calendar pages. I found the latter especially annoying because it didn't accomplish anything useful and was a pain to hold and read. Beware of innovation for the sake of innovation. Do you *really* need to do that to tell your story effectively?

One of the most successful and interesting bits of panel-storytelling experimentation was done by Alan Moore and Dave Gibbons in their exceptional twelve-issue miniseries *Watchmen*. Each page was based upon a strict nine-panel grid, with each section of the grid the exact same size. Certain panels would be larger as needed, scattered throughout the book, but the underlying grid pattern remained firmly in place. Using this simple, highly structured page layout,

Figure 6.11
A horizontal panel spanning two pages, used for extra effect. From the *Elfquest: Wolfrider* graphic novel.

Figure 6.12
Panels of no text can convey silence or contemplation or—as in this example from *Usagi Yojimbo*—an unexpected moment of emotional connection between the characters.

the *Watchmen* series is some of the finest work ever done in comics, due to the tremendous strength of the writing and the superbly matched art. To my mind, this is a prime example of the perfect balance between writing and art that doesn't resort to visual gimmickry.

Be Kind to Your Artist

One final note about what you put into your panels. Be aware that what seems like a simple sentence to you can amount to a huge amount of work for your artist. You need to be aware when you're asking for something that is unusually difficult. There may be another way to do it that won't demand so much of the artist's time. Or it may be something you feel you must have for the effect. But at least think about it.

A classic example was the opening that I wrote for *The Sisterhood of Steel* #6. I wrote, "The army marches out of the city." Seven simple words. My artist, Mike Vosburg (a dear, sweet saint of a man) called me and gave me such a ribbing over that sentence. Seven words

Figure 6.13
Double splash pages from *The Sisterhood of Steel* #6, illustrated by Mike Vosburg.

that took me a split second to type meant hours of work for him, which never occurred to me when I wrote it. Being a clever artist, Mike found a way to reduce the work by rendering key characters up front (fig. 6.13), then quickly switching to an indistinct mass for the rest of army, but we're still talking about a huge amount of work. See for yourself.

Panels and Gutters

For a long time, the standard way of laying out panels was to have blank white space (the gutters) between them. As artists experimented, they tried layouts that eliminated gutters, with large background art that had smaller, floating panels laid on top of it. Or "open" (borderless) panels (fig. 6.14) that had no border lines to define their space, leaving the viewer's eye to decide where the panels began and ended. There's no end to the way panels can be laid out on the page, but no matter how it's done, the gutter is there—if not in fact, then in concept.

In his exceptional book *Understanding Comics*, writer/artist Scott McCloud writes, "Here in the limbo of the gutter, human imagination takes two separate images and transforms them into a single idea." Conceptually, the gutter encompasses everything that happens *between* the panels. That can be time, ranging from a nanosecond to eons. It can be space, moving from near to near, near to close, near to far, or it can range across the entire universe. The potential of the gutter is without limit. If you use the cinematic approach, the gutter is all of the other frames you've cut from the strip of film that connects one frame to the next one. They are gone, but they are implied. The eye and the mind fill in that gap, working out what the relationship is between the panels (and the images in those panels), what the action is, what the timing is, what happens between here and there.

Figure 6.14
A borderless panel from *The Sisterhood of Steel.*

The gutter is a mental negative space that is filled with everything that isn't in the panels. Even if your page is laid out without the traditional white space, the space is still there in essence and remains a crucial part of your storytelling.

Panels and Text

Beyond the layout and flow of the panels, the writer also has to think about the balance between both the amount of text and the placement of text on the page and in the panels. This is where the strengths and weaknesses of script style vs. plot style have a large effect.

When writing a full script, you have to be conscious of the amount of text (in captions and/or balloons or elsewhere) you're creating vs. how much art you want in the panel. There's certainly no hard-and-fast rule about word count (with the rare exception I'll give below), so it's very much a matter of getting an instinctive feel for what works.

When I was writing the educational manga books, which were geared toward achieving a specific reading level, I was given a word restriction of no less than seventy and no more than one hundred words per page, to be put into no more than five panels. Given the smaller size of the manga page, this feels like a good rule of thumb, but you'd be amazed at how quickly you can burn through one hundred words on a page.

With the larger size of the typical American comic book, you can obviously use more panels and have more text, but you still need to find a good balance between the two so that a page doesn't become cluttered and difficult to read by having too much packed into it.

The most useful exercise I was ever given to do was from Jim Shooter, during the time he was editor in chief of Marvel Comics. Epic Comics (Marvel's line of creator-owned books) was publishing my *The Sisterhood of Steel* series. Jim told me to get some large-size tracing paper and a pencil (mechanical pencil is a really good idea), lay the tracing paper over the finished pencils, and actually write the script onto the tracing paper, printing it within captions and balloons exactly as I would want them placed on the page. I went through a lot of pencil leads, but I gained an invaluable sense of how many words would fit on a page.

I've seen some writers who write such massive amounts of dialogue that their pages are overwhelmed by the text, which often has to be lettered at a smaller size to try and squeeze it in. Not only is this hard on the eyes, it's a poor balance between the images and words. This gets down to my personal opinion, but when it comes to a visual medium such as comics, I feel that the least amount of text you can use to achieve your ends is the best balance. For those times when you simply do need a large chunk of text, make sure you allow for it by using fewer panels or larger panels, and adjust your pacing to fit.

Creators can do a lot with the sheer visual possibilities of text, even to the point of using symbols rather than text. There was an issue of the *Grendel* series, created by Matt Wagner, in which symbols and icons were used inside the balloons to convey the emotion and ideas instead of words. Oddly enough, I found that this *did* work for me, at least for one issue. I wouldn't want a steady diet of it, but it was a fascinating way to look at how one can communicate the essence of a story.

Stan Sakai, in his *Usagi Yojimbo* series, always shows a little death's-head to indicate a character's death cry, rather than relying on text (fig. 6.15). It's a wonderful addition to the visual storytelling.

Perhaps the greatest master of combining visual elements of text and balloons with the storytelling is Dave Sim. In his long-running *Cerebus* series, he would use the shape of the balloons, the font of the text, size and layout of the text, symbols, and other tricks to make the text elements as much a part of the visual design as the images. Pick up any of his books from the latter half of the series, and study how much Sim experimented with conveying character and emotion through the visual quality of his text.

Figure 6.15
Panel from Stan Sakai's *Usagi Yojimbo*.

An old-fashioned style of storytelling goes back to the days of the *Flash Gordon* and *Prince Valiant* newspaper comic strips, in which there were no balloons at all. Each panel had an illustration that was free and clear of any text, and at the bottom of the panel was a chunk of prose, which was either descriptive or contained a dialogue quote from the character, as though excerpted from a novel. Although it's hard to see this form of storytelling working in a modern comic, it doesn't hurt to consider all of the possibilities of how text can be used. It might be applicable for a highly stylized graphic novel or another experimental form.

Another issue is the placement of speaking characters. If you have an experienced artist working from a full script, she will understand that the sequence of the dialogue you've written will dictate the placement of the balloons or captions, and she will design the placement of characters and visual elements to accommodate that placement. The first character to speak in a panel should be placed to the left with the second speaking character to the right of the first character, so that the flow of balloons can be read from left to right. This isn't an absolute rule, of course, but it's a useful guideline.

The first line of script will be the first balloon (or caption) that needs to be read in the panel, the second line of script will be the second balloon/caption, the third line of script will be the third balloon/caption, and so forth. Some writers will always put the SFX line at the bottom. There's no rule to govern this, because sound effects are placed separately from balloons or captions (fig. 6.16).

You can have back-and-forth conversation in a panel, where balloons are connected by stems to avoid having extra pointers, like pearls on a string (fig. 6.17). If you want to have character 1 speak, then character 2, then character 1 again, you would write your dialogue in that order as well. This takes more room, of course, and the artist has to allow for that, so it's better not to get carried away with too much back-and-forth dialogue in one panel. If you want a lot of back-and-forth for effect, keep the dialogue as short as possible.

Figure 6.16
Example of sound effects as part of the visual effect, from *The Sisterhood of Steel.*

The script for those balloons would look like this:

```
BORONWE:    So what's this place like?

DINDRA:     Dunno, one of the older girls said it was good.

BORONWE:    Who said so?

DINDRA:     Ferinda.

BORONWE:    She's only a year older and a slut besides!

DINDRA:     So? Want some rouge?

BORONWE:    It makes you look like a bargirl!

DINDRA:     So?

BOROWNE:    Are you taking a knife?
```

Figure 6.17
A string of balloons indicates quick back-and-forth patter between the characters. Sample from *The Sisterhood of Steel*.

Sometimes you can get a panel layout you didn't think of that you can use to your advantage. When I saw that my artist, Mike Vosburg, had done a vertical panel for the action of a falling flower (fig. 6.18), I laid out the captions and broke up the text to utilize the visual element to my advantage. I let the text work with the art to emphasize that sense of the flower fluttering from side to side as it reaches the ground.

One final comment regarding text and images. It may seem obvious, but I've seen it done, so it's worth mentioning. Avoid having your character say in dialogue what the reader can see the character is doing in the panel. As in, don't have a character say, "I'm jumping off the roof" when we can clearly see the character jumping off the roof.

Comic Book Script Samples

You will find sample comic book scripts to read at www.christymarx.info.

Figure 6.18
Vertical panel with captions used to reinforce the motion of the falling flower. Sample from *The Sisterhood of Steel.*

Here is a look at the "Marvel style," which I wrote The *Sisterhood of Steel* in. This is an excerpt from the outline for issue #2, entitled "The Ritual of Womanhood." In this issue, the lead character, Boronwë, has passed her cadet's training and is about to be sent out into the world as a full sister-warrior. First, she undergoes an ancient ritual designed to reinforce her bond with the Sisterhood. At the end of the ritual, she's confronted by her enemy, Vandalis, the powerful Princess of Swords. The scene is being watched by a Daughter of Death, a member of the secretive assassination arm of the Sisterhood.

The total length of the single-spaced outline was nine and a half pages. The following excerpt is what the artist received and had to interpret as pages and panels.

The bonfires diminish and the high euphoria of the drug wanes to a sense of peacefulness and calm. The Priestess tells them they may go out now and go where they will with whom they will, blessed in the heart of the Goddess who watches over them. Boronwë, basking in the warm afterglow of the fire, is content to be alone. Delani, on her way out of the stadium, stops to hug her, to show that all the hard feelings of the day have been removed.

As Delani leaves, another cup is thrust in front of Boronwë's face and a voice says, "Drink from my cup with me." The cup is unlike the ceremonial cups, being made of gold and embossed with mythological monsters. It is Vandalis. Boronwë's peace is shattered, replaced by wariness and confusion. What does Vandalis want of her? Is it poison?

Easily guessing her thoughts, Vandalis takes a deep drink from the cup and hands it back to Boronwë. Boronwë recognizes the challenge in Vandalis' eyes and knows she cannot refuse. Besides, this is the Princess of Swords, and her request is the same as a demand. Boronwë drinks. The drink is vaguely similar to the ceremonial drink, but has a strong, flowery smell and a bitter taste that is not entirely disguised by the honey that has been added. Vandalis demands that Boronwë finish it and she does.

The Daughter of Death watches from the shadows.

Once I received the penciled pages, I worked out the final script on tracing paper laid over the art. Here is a photocopy of the pencils for page 13 with my lettering, balloons and captions added.

Figure 6.19

I then put the script into a more standard script form for the letterer. The underlined words in the dialogue indicate they should be lettered in **bold**. Here is the script for page 13.

PAGE 13

PANEL 1

BORONWE(THOTBAL): For the first time since Kelki ran away, I feel content to be alone.

DELANI: Boronwë, I'm glad I found you!

PANEL 2

DELANI: I want you to know . . . I'm sorry about the way I acted this afternoon. Now I see how childish it was . . .

BORONWE: We're sisters, Delani! That's all that matters.

PANEL 3

VANDALIS: You have not yet shared a cup with me!

PANEL 4

VANDALIS: Why do you look so wary, cadet? We have had harsh words in the course of duty, but this is the purpose of the Ritual, to tear down old barriers and find new resolutions!

VANDALIS: Do you refuse to drink with me, as one sister with another?

BORONWE: I can hardly refuse the Princess of Swords, though I'm sure I don't deserve this . . . honor!

BORONWE(THOTBAL): All my peace . . . shattered! What does she want with me? Could it be poison?

PANEL 5

VANDALIS: I'll drink first, to relieve the fears you conceal so poorly!

PANEL 6

VANDALIS: Well?

BORONWE(THOTCAP): She makes it a challenge . . .

PANEL 7

BORONWE(THOTBAL) . . . one that I <u>must</u> accept!

Finally, here is the finished page. You may notice that the letterer accidentally turned one of the speech balloons in panel 4 into a thought balloon instead.

Figure 6.20

Here is what those same pages would have looked like if the script had been written in DC script style. (For additional comic script samples, please visit http://www.christymarx.info)

PAGE 13

PANEL 1

Boronwe stands alone momentarily, but Delani comes over to speak to her.

BORONWE(THOTBAL): For the first time since Kelki ran away, I feel content to be alone.

DELANI: Boronwë, I'm glad I found you!

PANEL 2

Close on Boronwë and Delani sharing a moment of friendship.

DELANI: I want you to know . . . I'm sorry about the way I acted this afternoon. Now I see how childish it was . . .

BORONWE: We're sisters, Delani! That's all that matters.

PANEL 3

As Delani leaves, Boronwë reacts to a cup raised in her direction.

VANDALIS: You have not yet shared a cup with me!

PANEL 4

Boronwë turns and faces off with Vandalis, who is the one holding out the cup in an obvious challenge that leaves Boronwë wary and confused.

VANDALIS: Why do you look so wary, cadet? We have had harsh words in the course of duty, but this is the purpose of the Ritual, to tear down old barriers and find new resolutions!

VANDALIS: Do you refuse to drink with me, as one sister with another?

BORONWE: I can hardly refuse the Princess of Swords, though I'm sure I don't deserve this. . .honor!

BORONWE(THOTBAL): All my peace . . . shattered! What does she want with me? Could it be poison?

PANEL 5

Vandalis drinks first from the cup.

VANDALIS: I'll drink first, to relieve the fears you conceal so poorly!

PANEL 6

Again, she holds out the cup as a challenge, knowing full well that a mere Cadet cannot refuse to drink with her.

VANDALIS: Well?

BORONWE(THOTCAP): She makes it a challenge . . .

PANEL 7

Boronwë drinks from the cup.

BORONWE(THOTBAL) . . . one that I must accept!

PANEL 8

Nearby but unseen, a Daughter of Death lurks in the shadows and watches them.

NO DIALOGUE.

CHAPTER 7

Breaking and Entering

Breaking into comics solely as a writer is a challenge. It's easy for an editor or publisher to evaluate an artist's portfolio at a glance. Writers require more effort.

Obviously, if you're an established pro in another area — such as TV, film, or novels — it's easy to call a comics company, lay out your background, and make inquiries into writing for their books. Well-known TV and film writers are especially welcome.

If you're a new writer without credits in other areas of writing, you'll need to prove yourself by having a lot of creative story pitches, then do your best to get those pitches read by editors.

The worst way to do this is submitting by mail without a personal contact. Never, under any conditions, submit an unsolicited pitch or script, meaning a script that no one knows is coming. Most likely, an unsolicited script won't even be accepted for the slush pile, and will be returned unread at best, or will hit the circular file. In rare instances, a company throws open its doors and announces it's looking for material. They will provide rules for submission — rules that you should follow carefully. However, editors quickly become inundated with material when they have open calls for submission like this, and the odds of getting anywhere amid the mountains of material they get are a zillion to one.

Your best bet is to establish a connection with an editor to the point where you can pitch story ideas. This is also a delicate and tricky process, but it can be done. The first step is to *meet* an editor, preferably in person.

Here are some of the possible methods:

- Conventions
- Workshops, seminars
- Clubs or associations
- Mail or e-mail contact
- Personal appointment

Conventions

A primary meeting ground is a comic book convention, and the mother of all comic book conventions is Comic-Con International (http://www.comic-con.org) in San Diego. It's held sometime in late July or early August. When I first began attending Comic-Con in the late 1970s, it was a small, cozy gathering of comic book people and comics dealers. Now it is a massive, gigantic, sprawling convention that covers comics, animation, anime, TV shows, movies, and videogames—usually, but not always, with some connection to comics. All the major and independent publishers have booths with editors and creators there to meet the public. Plus, there is a section for the small independents to display their books, an artists' alley, and the gigantic dealers' room (now selling a lot more than just comics).

This is also a good place to look for an artist, if you're looking to team up with an artist and produce your own book.

The plus to Comic-Con is that nearly everybody in the business comes to it. The downside is that nearly everybody in the universe comes to it—which means the chance to have a quiet, intimate conversation with an editor is pretty much nonexistent. However, it's a place to start, and certainly an invaluable place to get a feel for what's happening in the business. And there's always the chance you can get invited to a party where you'll get that opportunity for a more personal conversation.

At the very least, strive to meet the editor and exchange a few memorable words, maybe hand her a business card and get an O.K. from her to submit some story pitches. If she says yes, *get her business card*. If she's out of cards (it happens), get the pertinent mailing info from her or from an associate.

Do not—repeat, ***do not***—try to pitch to her or hand her your pitches to read at a convention. The last thing an overburdened editor needs is someone's unknown work to haul around in luggage all the way back to New York or wherever. Nor do they want to be bombarded with story pitches when they're insanely busy and distracted. They have too much to deal with already, and this will not endear you to them.

If you get an O.K. to submit some pitches, do not delay. The minute you get home, send off your ideas, with a short, polite, simple cover letter indicating that you met at Comic-Con and that said editor asked to see your ideas, so here they are, with a brief indication of which books or characters you're pitching. Editors are busy people and need to have the info at a glance. They don't have time to read tomes.

A good cover letter should include three short paragraphs and run no more than one page long: one paragraph to remind her that you met, where and how, and that she gave you permission to submit; one paragraph with a brief listing of the pitches; and one closing paragraph in which you should say anything about yourself that might help sell you as a writer (such as having sold other pieces of writing, writing columns or articles for a fanzine or prozine, a self-published comic you've put out, that sort of thing).

If you want the pitches returned, be sure to enclose an S.A.S.E. (self-addressed, stamped envelope for mailing the material back to you). If you don't care about having it sent back, indicate in your cover letter that the material doesn't need to be returned, so the editor will know why you didn't include an S.A.S.E. In that case, you might at least enclose a regular letter-size S.A.S.E. to cover sending you a rejection or comment letter.

If you can't make it to Comic-Con, search out other comic book conventions that you can get to, and find out whether they will have editors there as guests.

Workshops, Seminars

Once in a rare while, a company or creator may hold introductory workshops or seminars. These will occur in large cities, so won't be easily accessible to everyone. You'll need to keep abreast of general comic book news to stumble across these. See the resources chapter for links to Web sites.

Clubs or Associations

Another route is to search out comic book clubs or associations that might have regular meetings and might sometimes have a comic book pro as a guest. That was how I met Roy Thomas, which led to my selling him my first story for *Savage Sword of Conan*. This is likely only if you're in or near a large city, though.

  If you have a comic book retailer in your area, check with them to see if they ever have comic pros make appearances at their stores. Again, this tends to happen mainly with stores in or near big cities, and depends on how savvy the owner is with setting up such appearances. Maybe you could offer to help with that, and thereby become personally involved in contacting pros to make visits to the store. If you can't go to the pros, be creative in finding ways to bring them to your area.

Mail or E-mail Contact

Neither of these next two methods is recommended, but if you're simply too far away to attend conventions and can't travel, you may have no choice. Most editors will probably ignore e-mail inquiries, unless they get to know you and welcome hearing from you.

  A cold inquiry letter should follow the basic guidelines laid out above in following up a contact at a convention. You should have several usable story ideas ready to send, so if by chance you get an O.K. to submit, you'll have them ready to go.

Personal Appointment

Back in the 1980s, I contacted the editors at DC and Marvel and made appointments to meet with them and pitch ideas to them in person. I had a few small writing credits behind me by that time, but I think the editors were also impressed that I was willing to travel from California to New York to have meetings.

  The catch here is to have strong ideas to pitch, with the hope that the editors might actually let you in the door. It's a tough form of cold-calling, but what have you got to lose? Other than the cost of travel?

  It would require a polite phone call to the editor's assistant, explaining that you want to travel from the Far Ends of the Earth to have a half hour of the editor's time to pitch your ideas. They will undoubtedly want to know more about you, which you should be ready to provide. Even if a personal meeting isn't on the agenda, try to leverage it into an invite to submit by mail. Most importantly, don't be obnoxious, overanxious, or a pest. Keep it light, friendly, and professional. If you don't make progress, don't call on a daily basis. Maintain a written record of when you call, whom you talk to, and what they said. If waiting for a response, allow several days between calls. Give it a try, but if you get the feeling they don't really want to see you and are trying to discourage you, you should quickly backpedal and ask if you can submit by mail instead. Most of all, remain polite at all times and be able to take no for an answer. Thank them for their time and move on to someone else.

What to Send

Here are a few methods for choosing what to send as a pitch:

METHOD NO. 1: If you're approaching an editor at one of the Big Two (DC or Marvel), pitch a stand-alone or fill-in idea. By stand-alone, I mean one that could easily fit into the series, stands on its own (not a continued story), matches the tone and feel of the book, and doesn't include any changes in the series' continuity. In fact, much of the pitch advice I give in the animation section applies here as well. For example, don't kill off, maim, resurrect, or give a sex change to any major character. You're not trying to revise their continuity; you want to show that you can come up with good, *usable* ideas.

METHOD NO. 2: If you're submitting to one of the Big Two, pick one of their characters or books that hasn't been active for a long time and isn't currently being utilized. Come up with your unique, updated approach to bringing back that character or set of characters. This is trickier because you'll have to be very, very good at it and come up with an approach that grabs the editor's interest. If you have the guts and a fantastic "hook" for revitalizing the character, go for it. Even if that particular approach doesn't work, you could get the editor interested enough in you to pursue other work.

Alternatively, you could pick some minor, secondary character that appeared in one of their books, then disappeared. If no one has done anything else with the character and you can see some potential there, you might come up with a spin-off idea utilizing the character in a new and interesting way.

METHOD NO. 3: Submit something that is your own, original idea. This is a tougher road to go down because few publishers are really looking for new books from unknowns.

Peter David (*X-Factor, Friendly Neighborhood Spider-Man, Fallen Angels*) has this advice: "I always recommend that [the prospective writer] should come up with story springboards (five, six lines) designed as "evergreen" (or as we used to call them, fill-in stories) that could be used for popular characters in multiple books, such as *Spider-Man, Superman,* or *Batman.* Then send them, not to the editors of the respective books, but the ASSISTANT editors. Why? Because no one ever writes to the assistant editors, so they'll actually open the envelopes and read the contents. That's the biggest problem right there: getting your material in front of people's eyes. Now I don't know for sure that that will actually work, but it seems a good theory."

Kurt Busiek (*Astro City, Superman*) has written an excellent essay called "Breaking In Without Rules" (*Write Now!* #13). He gives a cogent and vital piece of advice: there *are no rules for breaking in.* You must be clever, inventive, and creative in finding the method that will work for you. Each writer will have a different story for how he or she broke in. In most cases, the only thing the writers will have in common is dogged persistence and enough talent to pull it off.

Kurt says, "The trick to it, if there is one, is to remember that you're a craftsman with something to sell, and if you're trying to break into the business, you need to find someone

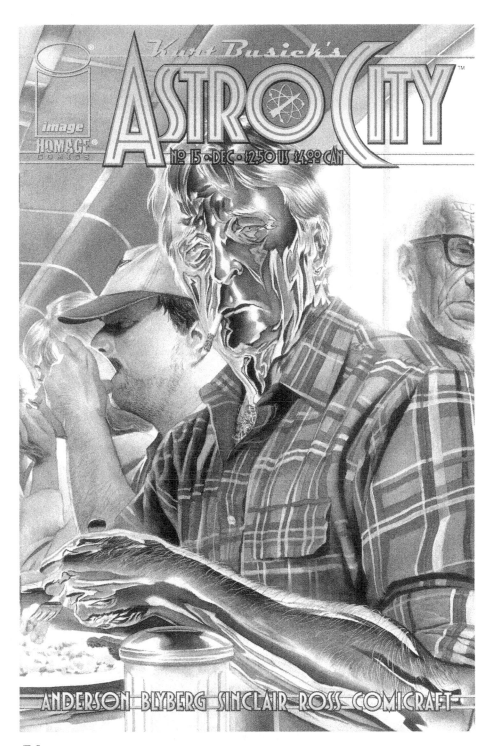

Figure 7.1
Astro City by Kurt Busiek. Cover art: Alex Ross.

willing to buy it. No one will hire you to write *X-Men* just because you really, really want to. They won't even hire you because you've got really good ideas for how to revolutionize the *Batman* books—they have experienced pros lined up for those assignments. What you have to do is find someone who needs what you have to sell."

He emphasizes the need to study the market. "That's half the job anyway, and you'll need to keep doing it even after you break in. Look for opportunities. Make the best of them. And then look for another."

"These days, there are far fewer openings at the bigger companies for new talent—but the good news is that there are a ton of smaller companies that didn't exist when I was looking for opportunities. They need books to publish, and they might need you. But it's up to you to do the research, to figure out who's out there, what they're publishing, where your particular skills might fit best—and where they're most likely to need you, which is even more important—and approach them."

For the independent and smaller companies, Method No. 3 is your best bet. With indies, Method No. 1 isn't quite as useful, because the books tend to be more-personal creations of a specific writer and/or artist, unlike the corporate fare of the Big Two. And Method No. 2 doesn't apply very well either, for the same reason.

Indies are usually interested in finding new creators, and are more willing to look at proposals for a new series. The drawback is that an indie is more likely to require that you have an artist attached. If submitting original material to an indie, that is probably the first question you need to ask—will they look at your series proposal on its own, or do they want to see a full-fledged book with an artist attached?

Create Your Own Comic

This provides more challenges to the writer than to the writer-artist because it means you have to find an artist who is willing to work with you, either for free or because you can pay him or her. But if you've exhausted other avenues and are hungry enough, this could be your best bet.

Your first effort doesn't have to be a full-size color book. If you can find a like-minded artist to take a risk along with you, you can start by creating a black-and-white ashcan of your idea. Then send that sample to editors and publishers. Sell it at conventions and hand it to any editors you meet there. An ashcan is small, light, and a quick read, so it makes a nice calling card—provided it's of professional quality. You must be a good judge of the quality of art, and recognize that vague but crucial borderline between amateur art and professional-quality art. Poor-quality art will do more damage than good, because the reader's lasting impression will be of the art first and the writing second.

Many independent creators have done well for themselves by creating their own black-and-white series, which they produce consistently year after year so they build a following. The main examples that come to mind are writer-artists: Wendy Pini's *Elfquest* (fig. 7.2), Terry Moore's *Strangers in Paradise*, the Hernandez brothers' *Love & Rockets*, Stan Sakai's *Usagi Yojimbo* (fig. 7.3), Colleen Doran's *A Distant Soil*, Donna Barr's *The Desert Peach*, and Dave Sim's *Cerebus*.

A special example that must be mentioned is *Teenage Mutant Ninja Turtles*. What became a multimillion-dollar powerhouse phenomenon spawning animation series, movies, toys, and tons of merchandising began life as a small indie black-and-white comic book parody. It's a

Figure 7.2
Wendy & Richard Pini's *Elfquest*.

Figure 7.3
Stan Sakai's *Usagi Yojimbo.*

bit of a fluke, but if the commercial potential is there and the right people discover it, this kind of success can happen. There are movie-production companies formed with the express purpose of finding comic book properties to turn into movies, so it never hurts to think of a self-published comic as a launching platform to other media.

    Your task as a writer is to find an artist who is willing to partner with you, who is not only a good artist, but is reliable and professional enough to keep working on a long-term basis.

One or both of you need to have the funds to get your book published, promoted, and distributed. You must, must (I can't emphasize this enough), *must* have a written agreement with your artist partner to lay out who owns what part of the art, the rights to the book, how the copyright will read, how you'll divide the money and responsibility, and so forth. You should have a lawyer well versed in copyright issues draw up an agreement for you. There should be no surprises that can destroy your working relationship later on. Both sides should know very clearly exactly what they're putting into, as well as what they're getting out of the partnership.

It would take an entire book to tell you how to self-publish a comic, and that's not the purpose of this one, though I will recommend some books in the Resources section following this chapter. You will need to research self-publishing and learn a great deal about printers. When getting quotes, it will immediately become clear why the indies go for black and white rather than color. You'll need to learn about promotion, as well as how and where to buy ads. You'll need to contact comics distributors and find out how they operate and what they'll demand of you. Mainly, they'll want to see the book, and they'll want to know whether you can continue to put the book out on a regular basis. Maintaining a regular, dependable output is one of the single most important elements of succeeding in self-publishing. Nothing is more ruinous to establishing a career than a book that doesn't come out on a dependable schedule. It doesn't have to be a monthly schedule, as long as it's a consistent one.

Places to look for an artist partner:

- Local or nearby art schools
- Specialized art schools that teach comic book illustration, such as the Joe Kubert School of Cartoon and Graphic Art (http://www.kubertsworld.com/kubertschool/KubertSchool.htm), the Center for Cartoon Studies (http://www.cartoonstudies.org/), or the Savannah College of Art and Design (http://www.scad.edu/academic/majors/seqa/index.cfm). Planet Cartoonist (http://www.planetcartoonist.com/services/schools) lists art schools (some of which have courses in comics art) by region.
- Comic book conventions
- Through your local comic book store, where aspiring artists often hang out
- Comics club (though they may be too fan oriented, thus making it hard to find professional-quality artists)
- Advertise by placing an "Artist Wanted" ad in a comics-oriented publication (either paper or online). However, be careful how you word the ad, and be prepared to sort through the flakes who may answer. I had extremely dubious results via this method early in my career, so I don't highly recommend it.

On the Internet

Creating your own comic and putting it up on the Net, instead of publishing on paper, is another alternative. As with any alternative, it has pros and cons.

On the pro side, it's cheap and easy. You need a Web site and some basic knowledge to get the digital version of your comic onto the Web site, and off you go. You can do color without the associated costs of printing in color. If you have a good comic that will attract readers, and you do a lot of promotion, you can build up a readership that might eventually enable you to sell paper versions of the book.

On the con side, you don't make money from it. Charging people to look at a Web comic is out of the question. You can add banner ads and hope for some income that way. You can have an online store to sell associated products, such as T-shirts or mugs. All of this depends on building up a sufficiently large and loyal following, which again requires good-quality work put out on a regular basis.

What you mainly hope for with an online comic is attracting the attention of people who can do something more with it, whether we're talking about a regular comics publisher or someone from the TV or film business. I can't think of an instance where this has happened, but at least your work is out there and available if you don't have the means to do it any other way.

I would take a good look at how Scott McCloud adapted one of his *Zot!* comics to the Web site. What he did is creative and brilliant, and takes full advantage of how Web pages work. Check this out at http://www.comicbookresources.com/columns/zot/heartsandminds.shtml.

One interesting new tool for possible self-publishing is a piece of software called Comic Book Creator. This program allows you to create comic book pages by using images you import from videos, digital cameras, videogame screen captures, or images you've scanned. It has templates for panels, various types of balloons, text, and other features. With enough creativity, it might be possible to produce commercially viable comics, or at least something you could use as a sample.

Copyright and Ownership

If you're new to writing, you need to understand the difference between owning your material and doing work for hire. Anytime you're hired to work on an existing property or a property in development that belongs to someone else, you'll be employed as work for hire. This means that you have no ownership or rights at all on the work that you do. If you're hired to write for *Spider-Man* or *Superman*, it is obviously going to be a work-for-hire situation because these are corporate-franchise characters.

Copyright is a complex issue, and I urge you to become as informed as you can about copyright and trademarks. Here is a brief primer.

INTELLECTUAL PROPERTY

Here is a definition taken from Cornell University's Web site (http://www.library.cornell.edu): "Intellectual property refers to creations of the mind: inventions, literary and artistic works, and symbols, names, images, and designs used in commerce. Intellectual property is divided into two categories: Industrial property, which includes inventions (patents), trademarks, industrial designs, and geographic indications of source; and Copyright, which includes literary and artistic works such as novels, poems and plays, films, musical works, drawings, paintings, photographs and sculptures, and architectural designs. More information is available from the World Intellectual Property Organization (http://www.wipo.int)."

If you create an ashcan, single graphic novel, comic book series, online comic, or a proposal for a comic book, that is an IP. It's a creation of your mind, a creation that has commercial value—or at least the potential for commercial value.

COPYRIGHT

The word conveys exactly what it means—the right to copy. Once you create an original and unique work (be it a book, drawing, painting, song, movie, game), you automatically own the copyright to that work. That means that you and you alone can determine who will make copies of that work, how they will make the copies, what they'll pay you for that privilege, and where or how they can distribute those copies. You own that right to control the copies of your work by any means in any media. You get to decide how you will share, sell, or license any part of your copyright to others.

Although copyright law automatically gives you that protection from the moment of creation, the trick is having absolute proof of your creative ownership. A court of law isn't going to take your word for it. That is why you need to register your copyright as soon as you can, and before you set out to sell your work to anyone else. If you self-publish your own comic, it's a standard part of your business procedure to register each issue with the U.S. Copyright Office. It would be wise to do the same for an online comic.

You register your copyright by going to http://www.copyright.gov. Print out the correct form for the type of media you're copyrighting (for a comic series, it would be "Serials/Periodicals"; for a script or proposal, including illustrations, it would be "Literary Works"), fill it out, include a copy of your book or script, and send it in along with the registration fee ($30 at the time I write this). The Copyright Office Web site has lots of useful information and instructions.

You cannot copyright an idea or a concept. For example, you can't copyright "A series of adventure tales about warrior-women set on an island." You can copyright only your specific, exact expression of that idea in a finalized form—whether that form is a prose novel, a script, a comic book, a proposal for a series, or whatever. That is why it's possible to have two such different approaches to the same idea as DC's *Wonder Woman* and my *The Sisterhood of Steel.* Your specific expression of an idea is the only thing you can protect.

A copyright does have to be protected. Allowing other people to create fan-based material based on your copyrighted work undermines your copyright. If you freely allow others to make new creations based on your IP without exercising your rights or control, it is viewed as giving up ownership in your copyright.

Creative Commons (http://creativecommons.org) is a movement to allow a more flexible form of copyright, designed to make it easier to share creative works on the Net. You may want to investigate this and see if it suits how you feel about copyright.

TRADEMARK

The United States Patent and Trademark Office (USPTO) defines it this way: "A trademark includes any word, name, symbol, or device, or any combination, used, or intended to be used, in commerce to identify and distinguish the goods of one manufacturer or seller from goods manufactured or sold by others, and to indicate the source of the goods. In short, a trademark is a brand name."

You have to file for a trademark for each category where you want that protection. A comic book trademark would fall under "Publications," which would also cover other types of publications, such as coloring books, activity books, storybooks (paperback and hardcover), tape sets, magazines, and so on. If you wanted to trademark your character for an action figure, you'd have to trademark it under another class that includes such things as toys, games, playthings, dolls, action figures, stuffed animals, and miniatures. Clothing is a separate class, and so on and so forth. It's extremely complicated.

To register a trademark, you are best advised to use a legal professional who knows how to do the necessary trademark searches and applications. Filing a trademark is considerably more expensive (we're talking hundreds of dollars for each class in which you register your trademark), and you have to make sure there isn't already in existence a similar trademark with which yours might conflict.

For more information, the USPTO Web site is http://www.uspto.gov. The site does allow you to do a basic search by yourself, but the USPTO will do its own search once you make an application, and they could still turn you down. They don't refund your application fee if they turn you down, which is why you're better off using a lawyer who can make sure it will be done right.

The Ownership vs. Making a Deal Trade-off

Some publishers out there are looking for new ideas from new creators and can provide another way to break in. One of these is Platinum Studios, established by comics pros who know the field. Platinum has an emphasis on publishing graphic novels that can be sold as movie properties. *Men in Black* was one of their early successes. They've done well at making deals in the film and television arenas, and have the contacts to give your book a push in that direction if they take you on.

The trade-off is that Platinum will own the copyright. The creators are offered monetary participation if the IP is sold into other media, but as far as I know, there are no guarantees that the writer would be able to work on the other project.

If you're only getting started and this is your first chance to be published, you have to weigh the pros and cons of giving up ownership. It depends on your temperament and how important it is to you to get those first credits.

If you happen to sell a proposal to a large comics publisher, they will likewise want ownership. The major publishers have had creator-owned lines of books from time to time. That's why I still own all rights to *The Sisterhood of Steel*. I sold it to Marvel's Epic line, which was publishing creator-owned books at the time. If you want to sell your proposal to a big publisher and still own the rights, you'll need to research whether or not they have a creator-owned line of books in existence. Then you'll need to research what type of books they buy, and see whether your idea falls within their guidelines.

A manga publisher called TokyoPop was involved in a flap over the rights issue. In addition to Japanese manga, they offered deals for what many people labeled EOL (English Original Language) manga, meaning manga by English-language creators rather than Japanese creators. The flap was about this same trade-off—new creators were getting a break and getting books published in exchange for giving up a significant chunk of their copyright. Established creators who already had credits in the field were able to negotiate contracts that didn't require giving up ownership.

Is this worth it to get published? That's very much a personal decision. You may not have a problem with making that trade-off, or you may feel strongly about owning your material. It's something you need to think about if you get serious about trying to sell your IP to a publisher rather than publishing it yourself.

Getting Paid

Large companies use a voucher or invoicing system. Some of them provide you with vouchers, which are a type of invoice that you submit when you turn in work. Other publishers might require you to invoice on your own letterhead, and at other companies the editors may take care of the invoicing for you. You'll have to find out what the procedure is for the company that hires you.

It will be up to you to track pending payments to make sure you get paid on time. When it's a work-for-hire situation, you'll receive a contract first. Your contract must specify how your payments are broken out, what you have to turn in for each payment, how long they can take to pay you, and whether they have to accept or approve your work before you'll be paid. Be sure your contract sets a specific time for approval or acceptance of work that's turned in. Otherwise your payment could sit in limbo while you wait for an editor to accept your work or ask for revisions.

The larger companies offer royalties or incentives that will be based on how well your book sells. You might have a royalty that kicks in only when your book sells a certain number of copies, so you should do some research and try to determine how well certain books sell (this is not easy info to come by, I should add). Sales of comics have fallen tremendously over the past couple of decades. Setting a royalty that doesn't kick in until a book sells five hundred thousand copies a month, for example, means it's highly unlikely you'll ever see a penny in royalties.

Your contract should specify what percentage the royalty or incentive will be, what sales figures it's based on, and when such royalties or incentives are paid (quarterly? twice a year? once a year?). Unless you're a big name and have tremendous clout, you won't see a royalty based on gross (total profit from sales, with no publisher expenses deducted). You will be offered royalties based on net. What you want to watch for is exactly what are those expenses that will be deducted, because that will eat away what you receive. Again, unless you have some kind of clout, you won't have much chance of changing what they offer you.

If a company doesn't offer a royalty, they should instead offer a greatly increased amount of money up front to make up for this.

Going rates? It's tough to give a going rate in a changing business, but a rough guideline would be anywhere from $50 to $200 per page and up (possibly higher than that for writers who are under contract on a continuing basis). However, smaller companies or independents may ask you to accept a deal with no money up front and only royalties on the back end. They're asking you to share with them the risk of publishing. If they're a reputable, established company that doesn't seem like it might fold at any minute, and you can afford to do that in order to break in, then you should consider it.

"Per page" means the number of pages in the printed book. So if you get $100 per page for a twenty-two-page book, you make $2,200 for that script (plus royalties later, if any).

Location, Location, Location

At one time, where you lived was more of an issue than it is now. Marvel and DC are in New York City, and at one time that meant that you needed to live in New York to work for them. If you aren't an established or big-name writer, it still is helpful to live there if you want to work specifically for one of those Big Two companies. Living there gives you more opportunity to make personal contact and become known to the people who can hire you. That means meeting and getting to know someone on staff—an editor, another writer, artist, or anyone who can get you in the door. You might also try getting hired on as some type of assistant and work your way up from there.

But comic book companies sprout up everywhere, from Oregon to Florida, and most of them aren't going to decide whether or not to hire you based on where you live, as long as you have good Internet access for sending and receiving material.

If you're going to go the self-publishing route, what is probably more important is to live in a major city, or at least close to one, so that you have access to a larger pool of artists, letterers, colorists, printers, binders, retailers, and other people or services you might need. You don't have to live in the same place as your artist, but it usually works a whole lot better if you do.

Agents

There are no agents for writers in the comic book field. I had an agent for a while. He'd worked in the comics business for decades, had published the first-ever line of alternative comics that weren't undergrounds, had helped establish the direct market (selling to retail comic book stores rather than relying on newsstand sales), and really knew his way around. He set up an agency to represent writers, artists, colorists, letterers, and others in the field. Yet after putting a lot of years into it, he finally closed it down.

The resistance to agents is partly history. It's a business in which the creators never had any significant say and never had anyone to represent their interests, so there's no precedent for representation. It's in the interest of the big companies to avoid that. And because the majority of comic book deals aren't for big money, there's not a lot of payoff in it for the agents who have to battle this resistance.

It's possible that big-name writers from film or TV have their Hollywood agents negotiate comic book deals for them. The big names already have those agents, and by virtue of being a big name, they may be able to command enough money to make it worth the agent's while. I don't know of any agent, however, who actively tries to represent comic book writers. Plus, you run into the problem that a Hollywood agent won't know much about the comic book business. If they don't know any more than you do about the business, they're not of much help to you.

If you're breaking in and being offered a standard work-for-hire contract, there's not much you can realistically do except take what's offered. If you're selling an original IP where a contract needs to be negotiated, you should immediately hire a good entertainment or copyright lawyer. This will cost you, but it will be worth it to let the lawyer handle the negotiations and legal end of the deal. It's the only way to truly protect yourself.

Unions and Organizations

There is no union or organization that represents people in the comic book field. Artists and writers are notoriously difficult people to organize under any conditions, and as stated earlier in this chapter, there was never any precedent set for that type of representation.

Los Angeles does have some local groups, such as the Comic Art Professional Society (CAPS). This organization requires that you have professional credits to join. Joining is a nice way to socialize and network. There are other, less formal groups that I've heard of that meet for dinner once a month or get together for a "writers' lunch." If you get into the business, keep your ears open for groups like that and join in. Social networking is a great way to pick up work.

One group that everyone in the business should join is the Comic Book Legal Defense Fund (CBLDF), which fights to defend comic book creators and store owners who have been arrested, censored, or otherwise prohibited from exercising their First Amendment rights in comic books. The CBLDF uses donations to cover legal fees in fighting the good fight. Please give them your support.

Videogames

CHAPTER 8

History/Evolution
of Videogames

Many forms of entertainment have been created by and for computers. There are arcade games for a large machine that sits in a corner of your local pizza parlor and takes your quarters. There is entertainment created specifically for your personal computer (PC)—games that can be enjoyed individually, in a pair, in small groups, or with thousands of other people on the Internet. And there is entertainment designed for a special console box attached to your TV. The kinds of computer entertainment vary greatly, but they all have two things in common. First, they all came to exist thanks to the development of the modern computer and its components: the computer hardware, the software, the graphics display, and the interface for the player to control it all.

Second, and more importantly, they all are a form of *interactive* entertainment—computerized entertainment that allows the user to make choices that can affect the direction in which the entertainment will play out. It is input-active entertainment—in contrast to the receptive-only entertainment of books, TV, and films. For general purposes, I'm going to lump most of what I'm talking about under a general word to encompass all types of games played in this manner—*videogame*.

The Boundaries of Interactive Entertainment

I've read a lot of discussions about how to define a "game." Here, I'm going to keep it simple. I see a game as an activity one engages in, either alone or with others, that has a set of rules and has one or more goals. Thus, a game can be as simple as playing solitaire with a deck of cards, or a round of poker with tough-as-nails pros for big stakes. It can be a friendly game of touch football in the backyard, or it can be the NFL. It could be a complex board game that challenges the intellect, or a game of hopscotch on the front sidewalk.

Videogames can be straightforward "shoot your enemies" roller-coaster rides, or a sprawling, complex online game populated by thousands of people from around the world, where the player's options are fluid and vast. And of course, a videogame can also be a game of virtual solitaire or playing as a virtual member of the NFL. The possibilities are limited only by imagination.

A videogame is only one form of interactive entertainment. In print form, there are "Choose Your Own Adventure" books, which rely on extremely simple branching options to allow for multiple paths through a story. Attempts have been made to make "interactive movies," some using live actors, but they're cost intensive and didn't make it in the marketplace. There are *Dungeons & Dragons*–style role-playing games (RPGs), in which people gather to play their imaginary character. There are live-action role-playing (LARP) games, in which, for example, people get together in a real location to unravel a make-believe murder mystery as though they were the actors in a play. A rich variety of interactive entertainment exists, but the videogame is the one that's achieved the greatest market success.

Some experiments in digital, interactive drama fall outside the realm of games, such as *Facade*. This Internet-based program deals with interpersonal relationships where there's no "win" or "lose," and no specific goals other than exploring how the characters will react to what you do. I look forward to the day when the medium can get beyond the narrow definitions of "game," and accomplish daring new forms of drama, entertainment, and storytelling.

The Evolution of the Videogame

In the meantime, and for the purposes of this book, the subject will be the multimillion-dollar industry known as videogames, and how you can fit into that industry as a writer.

The following *brief* history is from my perspective as a writer, rather than detailing the march of technological development. It's an obvious given that videogames advanced as the technology advanced, and will continue to do so. Games in 2 colors gave way to 4 colors, then 12 colors, then 256 colors, and onward to the beautifully rendered, full-color masterpieces we see today. Ditto with sound and music. A similar technical progression is taking place in mobile games, made for cell phones or handheld units. Although the technology is a significant driving force, it can take a game only so far. Without a well-realized world, a coherent story, and some catchy characters, the best technology in the world can fall flat.

That is, unless you're playing *Tetris*, where all you have to worry about is sorting the colored blocks. I freely admit that there are certain types of games that provide entertainment on a simpler level. Let's rule those out, and agree that we're talking about the more complex form of videogame, where the participation of a writer makes sense.

Early computer games that wanted to tell a story were text based, relying on the imagination of the player to fill in the "world" in which he played. The only "video" involved was seeing the words on the screen. A small chunk of narrative was given, then the player was given two or more choices to determine what would happen next. After making the choice, the result of that choice was given in the next chunk of narrative, and a new set of choices were presented based on that result. The player could type in a response or chose a response from a numbered list by typing in the number. The earliest parsers (software that analyzes and processes the text input) could handle only extremely simple sentences, basically a verb-and-noun combination ("go west"), or a single descriptive word (such as "west"). The software had to parse the input and provide an appropriate response. Later parsers became more complex, such as the one created for *Zork*. *Zork* was a benchmark game of interactive fiction that let the player adventure through a huge underground labyrinth in search of treasure. It went beyond the simple verb-noun parser and used one that could understand full sentences.

Text-based games relied on the cleverness of the writer to set up the story and situations, to anticipate how players might respond, and to decide what to give them in return for those various responses. That, in turn, increased the sheer volume of writing that was required. The more options you give the player, the more variables you have to take into account and the more replies you have to write.

The next major evolutionary step in story-based games was to introduce graphics, the first one being *Mystery House*, a simple murder mystery with rudimentary animation. Rather than the player creating the environment in her mind based on text alone, she was given the environment in which to interact.

The early animated adventure games were also parser based. The player could move his character around on the screen using cursor keys, but had to type in commands in order to talk, look, take things, and make his character perform other actions. As with purely text-based games, the designer/writer had to anticipate whatever the player might want to do, then create a response for it. Design choices often included responses for the crazy things people may do while playing a computer game just to see what will happen—for example, cursing or typing nonsense, or purposely jumping their character off a cliff. As games became more complex, with more and more choices for the player, the scripts for these games became massive. My script for my first adventure game was a stack about a foot high. It was the equivalent of writing dozens of screenplays.

Along came the mouse. This called for an evolution in the interface of games. Game designers adjusted by switching from text input to screen icons that represented possible actions. Instead of typing in "take gold," the player used the mouse to click on a screen icon that represented "take" and used that mouse icon to click on the gold. An eye icon could be used to "look at" items represented within the screen environment, a talk icon could bring up a set of dialogue options, a map icon could bring up an interactive map, and so forth. The designer/writer had to shift away from thinking about every possible thing a player could type in, and instead focus on how to tell a story using a limited set of interface icons. The new interface eliminated puzzles or story choices that required typing in text that had to be parsed.

Though the interface became easier for the player, this form of interactivity could seem more limited than earlier parsed games that allowed more input from the player. To compensate for this, many early computer games insisted that the player get a response no matter where she clicked on the screen. This, once again, made for a massive amount of writing, nearly as much writing as a parser-based game demanded. If the writer wanted to have dialogue between the player's on-screen persona (avatar) and a nonplayer character (NPC, a character controlled by the computer rather than by the player), he had to provide both sides of the dialogue and allow the player to select from prewritten dialogue options. Each option demanded more writing. Because early computer memory was limited, the early computer games used a fairly simple branching-path dialogue tree. These memory restrictions meant that writers had to figure out how to hold the player's interest with the fewest amount of words possible.

The next step in the evolution of videogames was to minimize the interface to almost nothing. The two breakout examples in 1993 were *Myst* and *The 7th Guest*. Both of these games were minimal on story, and there was no NPC dialogue interaction—they were purely puzzle games. They provided visual puzzles to solve. Like previous games, *Myst* and *The 7th Guest* were 2-D—meaning their graphics were two-dimensional, and the ability of the player to move around inside the environment was restricted by that. However, both of these games provided stunning and detailed visuals (including video sequences with live actors), along with an interface so simple that anyone could easily master it. When the cursor passed over an interactive element (a "hot spot") on the screen, the cursor would visually change, and the player knew she could click on that hot spot—which would cause some piece of animation to happen or some object to move. Finding the solution to a puzzle involved figuring out how to move an object, or trying to decide in what sequence objects should be configured, or the frustrating "pixel hunt" (searching for the one spot on the screen that was a hot spot)—and that was the totality of the interface. The writing for such a game would have been limited to the designer's document detailing what the puzzles were, and scripts for the few minimal pieces of video to cover the thin story. Yet these games were wildly successful. *Myst* in particular became such a financial powerhouse that other game companies scrambled to produce look-alikes based on the same minimal style of interface. Nearly all of these imitators failed because the mere novelty of the minimal interface wasn't enough to support an entire genre. The lack of story and low level of interactivity didn't prove satisfying enough to players in the long run.

By contrast, *Gabriel Knight II: The Beast Within* was a game that heavily utilized live actors and a simple point-and-click interface like other games of its time period, but in addition it had a complex, character-driven story that set it apart from the competition. It was both a financial and critical success, one that should have proved the value of strong writing.

SimCity (1989) was responsible for another evolution, and created an entire segment of the videogame market unto itself. It was one of the first and most successful of the simulation-based "games." Though usually referred to and sold as a game, *SimCity* had no story and no preordained goals. It provided a giant playground in which the player was able to build a city any way he wanted to, managing resources and determining the zoning, taxes, and so on. The player had the freedom to build up, tear down, design, and rebuild any way he wanted. The game then simulated the results of those machinations and how the virtual denizens of the city reacted to them. These sims are also called "god games" because the player essentially plays god to his virtual subjects.

Other sims followed, leading to *The Sims*, in which the player gets to play god with a cast of NPCs whose lives she completely controls. She can determine how and where they'll live, when they eat, how they interact with other NPCs, and so on. Then the sim characters react to these decisions in a continuously evolving process based on their inherent drives, goals, and desires. The outcome of those godlike manipulations depends upon the game design, programming, and artificial intelligence of the NPCs, rather than on any kind of written story. Sims are a fascinating form of interactive entertainment, which may or may not use any form of story writing.

Doom (1993) established the popular form of play known as a first-person shooter (FPS), in which the action is seen as though the player were inside the game environment and looking through his own eyes. In this early type of FPS game, story was virtually nonexistent, and the goals were basic—shoot things, survive, shoot more things. *Doom* also took advantage of yet another significant graphic development, the 3-D game engine, which created a three-dimensional virtual world through which the player's character could move. Now the player could feel more immersed in the virtual world by being able to move around freely. The heightened sense of reality, combined with great sound and music, had a major impact on players. From a writing perspective, early FPS games had little to offer, because there was only the barest excuse for story, and none of the other elements that call for good writing, such as character development. However, these games set the stage on a technical level for immersive games *with* story—games that could push the boundaries of digital storytelling. Plus, the FPS itself has evolved so that the genre is now an important source of work for game writers.

The boom in console games has altered the videogame landscape because they eat up an enormous chunk of the money spent on videogames. This results in more development money being spent on console games than on PC games, which in turn affects which writing jobs might be available. However, it's worth noting a new trend of dual-platform launching in which a game is released in both PC and console versions.

For the writer and designer, what is significant about console games is their interface between the player and the game. Because a console controller consists of a limited set of buttons, the designer of the game is restricted to those limited interactive options with which to tell an interactive story. To convey story, console games make use of "cinematics"—noninteractive real-time animated scenes between NPCs. These are similar to "cutscenes" developed for PC adventure games, which are noninteractive, prerendered animated sequences or video of live-action scenes. One of the consequences of relying on scenes of this type is a trend toward giving console games more-linear storylines.

Finally, I want to touch on the development of the MMOGs (massively multiplayer online games). These games are a unique blend of adventure game, role-playing game, and social club. They have also opened new doors for content writers because the amount of writing that goes into them is especially massive and ongoing. An MMOG requires an enormous amount of writing to create the vast worlds and races it has to provide; the backstories for all those races and locations; an overarching quest of some kind; and endless numbers of smaller, individual quests, missions, and tasks. All of which to keep the legion of online players occupied for weeks, months, and years.

In the past few decades, videogames have grown from a small business run out of someone's garage into a gigantic industry whose products spawn movies, comics, animation, and toys—or whose products are based on one of those media. Sometimes they happen simultaneously, with a movie, game, and other merchandising being created at the same time.

One thing hasn't changed—within the videogame business, there is still a lack of recognition of the need for professional writers. This has improved slightly since I began designing games in 1988, but only slightly. A few enlightened producers or executives understand how much a writer can add to the quality of the game. More often, writers are brought in as an afterthought when a game is already partly or mostly completed, and someone suddenly realizes they don't have a coherent story—or because the dialogue needs to be done, and nobody else around the company has time to do it.

Mainly this comes from the reality that videogames first emerged through the creativity of programmers. You can have a game without visuals or music or professional writing, but you can't have a game without code. Consequently, programmers-as-writers were the norm in the beginning. Back when I began designing, I had an e-mail argument with a longtime designer-programmer who told me that I couldn't design games unless I knew how to write algorithms. I countered that you didn't have to know how to build an engine from scratch in order to drive a car.

As games have grown up, so have the budgets and amount of people required to produce them. This isn't necessarily a good thing, because game budgets have become enormous (if not outright astronomical), and the consequence of enormous budgets is that (a) it's harder to get a game made, and (b) companies are a lot more nervous about the whole process. They're less willing to take risks, and thus they become more dependent on existing licensed properties. The bottom line and marketing have largely come to dictate what the creative process will be.

The tiny good point in this evolution is that large companies, especially those that are part of or tied to major entertainment studios, are more likely to want a professional writer to be involved in the development process.

Nowadays, a typical game design team might consist of a producer or product manager, lead designer, lead programmer, lead artist/art director, composer, sound engineer/designer, and the teams of programmers and artists.

You'll notice I didn't include writer. They're rarely included in the initial design team. My own personal opinion is that from the earliest stages, the ideal design team should include a writer with some design experience. The trick is to get a company to budget for one. Instead, what you find is that companies expect to hire a lead designer with superhuman qualities who knows code, can use art programs, *and* can write on a professional level.

Beneath the surface, it gets back to the mistaken notion that anybody can write. Although a company wouldn't hire a programmer to create beautiful art, or an artist to write elegant code, they somehow think that any spare person can match the quality of an experienced professional writer. It's a hurdle that still needs to be overcome for anyone who wants to write for games.

Videogame Categories

Videogames can be broken down into the same genres as animation and comics—such as science fiction, fantasy, action-adventure, military, historical, and so on. But more commonly, games are defined first by their hardware-platform category, then by categories that describe their type of gameplay. The platform dictates how extensive or complex the gameplay can be. A desktop PC has vastly more computing power than a Game Boy (at the moment), and provides better screen resolution, so that is going to determine what sort of game can be played on it. The nature of the hardware interface will further dictate how complex the gameplay can be.

Following are the major platform categories:

- Console: A game-playing box that connects to a television set or monitor, with a hand-held controller for gameplay—such as the Wii, Xbox, or PlayStation (each platform having its own proprietary systems that aren't compatible with other platforms)

- Handhelds: Such as the Game Boy, PlayStation Portable (PSP), or any game-playing device that is its own independent system that can be held in the hands while played

- Mobile, wireless, Wi-Fi (wireless fidelity): Cell phones, PDAs (personal digital assistants), and other mobile/wireless devices

- PC: A desktop computer or laptop (further divided into computers using Windows, Apple, and Linux operating systems)

- Web-based games: Use the Internet and/or World Wide Web (and are therefore widely accessible to any computer)

Following are the major videogame categories:

- Adventure, action-adventure: Adventure games provide the avatar that the player will play throughout the game, along with a story and an overall large quest, subquests, NPCs, puzzles, combat, and whatever else makes for an interesting virtual adventure toward achieving a final goal. Examples include *Prince of Persia, Splinter Cell*, and *The Legend of Zelda: Twilight Princess*.

- Arcade games: Games made specifically for large, stand-alone game-playing machines with a screen and a panel of buttons or other game-playing controls. They provide a set amount of game time for coins or tokens. So named because they are usually found in arcades. They are only a tiny slice of the market at this point.

- Casual: A large, loose market that includes such subcategories as puzzle (for example, *Tetris* and *Bejeweled*), word and trivia, card and board, action and arcade, poker and casino, and pop culture. Not a writer-driven category, but one that must be mentioned.

- Educational: Games primarily for children, to teach through entertainment. Examples include *Clifford The Big Red Dog Reading, Zoo Tycoon,* and *I Spy Fantasy.*

- FPS (first-person shooters): As described earlier, these games are played through the first-person perspective of the player, showing whatever weapon he's holding. They usually involve a lot of running around and shooting things. Examples are *Doom, Quake*, and *Halo*.

- MMOG (massively multiplayer online games), also sometimes called MMORPG (massively multiplayer online role-playing games): This type of game combines elements of other games listed above, but adds a community of people from around the world, with hundreds or even thousands playing at the same time. These games involve large amounts of typical RPG play, but can be played from either first-person perspective, with no avatar on the screen, or third-person (looking over the shoulder of the character) perspective, where the player sees the avatar on the screen. They evolve in real time (an ongoing, persistent game world). They have some background story and plot, but differ in that they are more open-ended (new material is constantly generated). Players interact with one another in real time, sharing quests or missions, crafting, selling their crafts, chatting, socializing, or engaging in combat with one another. Examples include *World of Warcraft, EverQuest, City of Heroes*, and *Dark Age of Camelot*.

- RPG (role-playing games): A game in which the player plays the role of a particular character from a third-person perspective. These are usually more story based, involving long stories and a quest or mission to be achieved. The character is usually from a certain class type, such as "warrior," "ranger," "priest," "rogue," and so on. The player builds up the experience, abilities, appearance, and other characteristics of her character as the game progresses. Examples include *Final Fantasy* and *Dungeons & Dragons*.

- RTS (real-time strategy): A game that progresses in "real time" as the player plays, so that the action is continuous. RTS games usually have a combination of combat, strategic planning, building bases, directing individuals or units, and managing resources (such as gathering, manufacturing, production, and so forth). Examples are *Dune II, Starcraft, Command & Conquer*, and *Rome: Total War*.

- Sandbox: This is a recent and controversial category and I may get in trouble for even mentioning it, but it encompasses an important concept, so here goes with a very simplified definition. A sandbox game provides the player with a virtual space or environment, provides a lot of "toys" (objects, items that can be used), possibly some story, and then gives the player total freedom (as much as is possible) to do anything at any time to anyone or anything within that virtual environment. Some people quote *Grand Theft Auto* as the quintessential sandbox game. Other people argue that nearly any MMOG can be called a sandbox game. The main thing about the concept of a sandbox game is the amount of freedom given to the player to use or abuse the interactive environment in any way he wants without necessarily having to accomplish a goal unless he chooses to do so. Other examples are *Mercenaries* and *Destroy All Humans!*

- Sims (simulators): The idea of a sim game is to create a virtual reality in which the player has various levels of control over how that virtual reality evolves. A dating sim game lets the player explore various options and their consequences in virtual dating. A flight sim lets the player experience what it would be like to fly a plane. *The Sims* game lets the player explore what will happen to NPCs in a range of virtual-life situations as the player manipulation aspects of the virtual world. Other examples include *SimLife, Railroad Tycoon*, and *Project Gotham Racing*.

- Sports: Any sport you can imagine, from skateboarding to volleyball to football. A huge section of the market with huge sales—which is why it's listed here as a category rather than as a genre. Examples include *Madden NFL, Tiger Woods PGA Tour*, and Tony Hawk's skateboard games.

This doesn't cover every type of game out there, plus there will be games that combine elements of two or more types, but these are the significant categories.

Alternative Markets

In addition to the major categories listed above, there are some interesting alternative markets that deserve a mention.

ARGs (Alternate-Reality Games)

These games are often used for promotional and marketing purposes, such as creating buzz for a major movie or console game release. They represent a tiny market for now, but have potential for enterprising writers. An ARG uses real-world assets to "push" various pieces of a storyline to the participants—such assets being Web sites, e-mail, text messages, faxes, phone messages, diary entries or photographs on a blog or Web site, and so on.

To give a sense of what it's like to write for this niche market, I consulted with novelist Maureen McHugh, who has worked on ARGs. She said that getting work in this small field mainly involves being in the right place at the right time. "I got work in the ARG field because I'm a science-fiction writer and the head writer knew me. I had been following his work in one of the very first ARGs ever. I was enthusiastic about his work and the field because I loved what he was doing."

She points out that it's actually quite possible to set up a Web site and create your own ARG—if you can convince a couple of other people to spend eighty hours a week in this labor of love. However, McHugh also points out that she knows of at least one person who now does game design who started by running one of these games.

Most ARGs are seen as marketing and advertising, and many of them are designed and written by advertising firms. They are "pitched" by teams to potential clients. It's all very much a business.

McHugh describes this type of writing as highly collaborative, similar to the TV-writing process that is often done by a team of scriptwriters who rewrite each other's work and plot stories as a group process. "The writing on them ranges. The first big ARG, for the Steven Spielberg film *A.I.*, was very story driven. That rather set a kind of expectation that they would be stories told in interactive, innovative ways. Many of them are still very writing intensive, built around a design lead and writing lead working in partnership. Because they are often advertising for a movie or a console game, they are always done in a huge hurry. A nine-month development cycle is long. The pace is blistering for people used to the traditional game industry. When they are story heavy, the story can make or break the experience. An ARG has to have a sharp and innovative design, including an element of novelty (pay phones, T-shirts, phone calls, and live events) and a story so that once the innovation becomes familiar, the story pulls the players back again and again. On the games I've worked on, the traditional aspects of storytelling—interesting situations and compelling characters—have been essential. At the same time, each game must establish the conventions of that game. For example, that the game will be told entirely through diary entries, answering machines, stolen e-mails, photographs, and Web sites."

Serious Games

Sectors that wouldn't normally be involved in game design are learning to make use of the expertise of the game business to create "games" that are not simply for entertainment, but serve a more serious purpose. The United States Army created a game, *America's Army*, that was designed to teach people what it's like to be in the army. *America's Army* was intended mainly as recruiting tool. Other serious games have been developed to teach people how to respond to emergencies or how to perform medical procedures. Another example, *World Hunger— Food Force*, is about a United Nations food program, and is designed to educate players about world hunger and how the UN deals with it. There are now conferences that deal entirely with the category of serious games.

Virtual-Reality Worlds

A fascinating development is the success of online "games" that don't involve combat and are designed more for purely social interaction. What is unique about them is that everything in these virtual worlds is created by the players themselves. That includes architecture, landscaping, vehicles, clothing, accessories, and scripted actions such as dancing or gesturing. What these worlds don't have is writing or story content, because everything is user created, but those users can establish entire virtual-life subcultures and social groups. These virtual worlds operate on a different economic model that involves both subscription fees and real-world economics, such as buying and selling virtual assets for real-world money. Examples include *Second Life (secondlife.com)* and *There (there.com)*.

Figure 8.1
The *Second Life* virtual-world software provides extensive tools to create a player character. Every physical characteristic down to the smallest detail can be altered and manipulated so that each character is highly personalized and unique.

CHAPTER 9

Writing vs. Design

I am frequently asked how one goes about becoming a game designer, because people still tend to think that designer = writer of the game. To add to the confusion, the two are often combined. However, as game production becomes more and more specialized, so do these two roles. Given the scope and complexity of writing for videogames, it's important to understand the difference between design and writing. If you want to work as a writer, you need to understand how they differ and what a designer does, so that you'll know when you're being asked to be a writer or to go an extra step toward being a designer. To get some of the confusion out of the way, let's deal first with the issue of being a game designer.

The Game Designer

The role of game designer has evolved considerably since I began work as a designer. As explained earlier, the first designers were programmers for the simple reason that they were the only ones who knew how. As the games business grew and games became more complex, the role of designer became more of an entity unto itself. Back then (at least at Sierra On-Line), it seemed as though anyone who could come up with good ideas for a game and put them down in a reasonably coherent manner could be hired to design. It was more about having the creative vision and enough technical skill to know what could or could not be done within the existing programming and animation capabilities.

Today, the position of designer has become a more technical job. The designer must have the overall vision of the game, must understand the mechanics and fundamentals of game design, must have a very good grasp of what makes a game fun, is expected to know programming and art tools, *and* (in most cases) is expected to be a writer. Boiling it all down, it is the job of the designer to ensure that the game is entertaining, interactive, and functional. Bad design will kill a game faster than you can blink.

As game development teams grew larger, other designer roles were born. There is no standardization, so the job titles will vary from company to company, adding to the muddle. The designer at the top of the totem pole with the highest level of responsibility may be called the Lead Designer, Senior Designer, Head Designer, or just the Designer. You can have a Lead Designer assisted by a Senior Designer who is assisted by a Junior Designer, and the Lead Level Designer and his team of Level Designers. Or any combination of the above.

In MMOGs, there can be Content Designers (creating quests/missions, dialogue, and so on) and World Building Designers (creating the virtual terrain and everything in it) answering to a Creative Director or Producer or some other title. They can be senior positions or junior positions. Content design is closer to being a writing job, and world building is primarily an art job, but it's not entirely as clear-cut as that either. However, a Level Designer is a combination of design, art, architectural, and programming skills. An Art Designer is another term for an Art Director, someone in charge of the art and animation asset creation.

Still with me? The best way to understand what companies think any kind of game designer is, is to look at the skill requirements in job listings for designers. Many Web sites list designer jobs. The best place to go is Gamasutra (http://www.gamasutra.com), a site that is intensely useful for all things related to game development, and features plenty of job listings. High-tech headhunters have Web sites looking to fill the positions for the companies. The game companies often have job listings on their own Web sites.

For those who are interested specifically in being a game designer, looking at these lists of requirements will tell you exactly where you stand and what you need to acquire (experience, skills, education, and so forth) in order to qualify. Today, some colleges teach courses in game design, so there is at least a starting point now that didn't exist years ago.

You'll notice that 99 percent of these job listings will include "a passion for games" as one of their requirements. If you get interviewed, you can be sure they'll test you for your knowledge of and experience with playing games. If you go after a job with Company A, make sure you play as many games as you can that are made by Company A. Feel free to rave about the games to the person interviewing you. If you think the games suck, you'd better find something else to be positive and enthusiastic about (though one wonders why you'd want to work there anyway if you don't like their games).

No one will hire you right out of the gate to be a lead or senior designer. The most likely path to become the top person designing a game is to find an entry-level job and work your way up. Some people recommend finding any kind of entry-level job—for example, as a game tester (QA, for "quality assurance"). Other people contest this. The advice is all over the place. From what I've been able to distill, it depends on three big factors: the internal attitude of the company (will they promote from within, or do they look down upon lowly game testers?), how good you are at proving you can do design work, and luck.

Designer or Writer

The rest of these chapters will deal with being a writer for games, rather than a game designer. There will be additional info about game design in this chapter, because it can be intertwined with the writing. It's so intertwined that it can be hard at times to sort out where writing ends and design begins, but you need to be able to sort that out because you should be paid differently if you are doing design work in addition to writing, and you should receive a proper credit for it in the game credits.

Possible credits for your work could be Writer, Story Writer, Scenario Writer, Scriptwriter, Dialogue Writer, Content Designer, Story Designer, Narrative Designer, Writer/Designer, or something else invented on the spot.

This is extremely simplified, but my take is that the line between the two rests on whether or not you are asked to create the *interactive* elements. For example, on one game I was hired to write a story and character bible; however, it was a martial-arts fighting game, so none of the backstory or biographies affected the actual game design or the gameplay. This material added background and flavor, but created nothing interactive.

In contrast, on another game I was hired not only to create the world bible and biographies, but I also had to come up with the backstory, game story, overall quest, the story-related subquests, how the story would be expressed from the beginning of the game through all the quests to the end, plus write cutscenes and dialogue. I didn't design the combat system or the magic-using system or the interface, but the game story and quests are at the heart of the interactivity of the game, so that is design work all the same.

If you're hired as a writer and are asked to create new elements that are definitely generating interactivity in the game, you should discuss with the client whether or not this should be considered as some form of design work.

This doesn't extend to writing dialogue. It's true that dialogue is interactive, but if you didn't create the interactive elements that generated the dialogue, it isn't design work.

Videogames and Hollywood

There's much traffic between Hollywood and the games business. Movies, TV series, and animation are turned into games, whereas games are turned mostly into movies, but could easily become TV series and animation as well. One announced project was an MMOG and reality TV series created in tandem.

Words that mean one thing in Hollywood can mean something extremely different in games. The most important of these is **development.**

In Hollywood, development is mainly a writing process. It's about acquiring a concept (script, book, newspaper article, or whatever), hiring or acquiring a scriptwriter, getting it written and rewritten, while possibly attaching creative elements such as a director or star actor to help ensure it will get made. Once development—meaning the script—is finished, the project is either killed or is greenlit. If it gets a green light, the movie or show can go into pre-production, and finally, with luck, into actual production. A studio or an executive or whoever has the power can take credit for "developing" the project.

In games, development is the process of *making the game.* The development team (the developers, or devs for short) consists of the people creating every aspect of the game design and game assets. That includes the producers, designers, programmers, artists, animators, composer, sound editor, QA, and so on. Game development begins with the initial concept for the game and continues until the game is done and shipped.

Another term that can cause confusion is **scripting.** In Hollywood, everyone knows what a scriptwriter is—the person who writes the TV or movie script. In games, however, a "scripter" or a "scripting" job refers to writing code using software such as Python or Lua, programming languages commonly used in game development. If you're a writer looking for writing jobs in the games business, be careful not to get snagged by jobs looking for scripters or people able to do scripting. It's a programming job, not a writing job.

Another term to avoid is **world building** or **world builder.** It's a term that sounds useful for a writer, but in games it's a technical term for the work of a level designer who creates the geography/architecture for a level or region in the game.

Using a hyphenated term to describe oneself is another area where games depart from standard Hollywood terminology. I have done both game design and game writing, so for years I referred to myself as a writer-designer (or designer-writer). I was so accustomed to the use of hyphenates in Hollywood, it never occurred to me that people in games would have a negative reaction to the usage. In film or TV, if someone is a writer-director, writer-actor, or writer-producer, it's well understood that this person can do either or both of these jobs, not necessarily at the same time. Oddly enough, though, there seems to be more acceptance in the games business of the term designer/writer or writer/designer when a slash is used instead of a hyphen.

In general, the belief is that the combined terms confuse the issue and leave game people unsure whether you want to write or you want to design; or worse, they'll worry about hiring you as a writer, and you'll end up trying to meddle with design when they don't want you to. Most games people think it's essential to have two separate résumés: one purely for the game writing work, and one purely for game design work (if you do both).

Terminology

The terms below are a tiny fraction of the huge vocabulary that surrounds the process of making games. I've subjectively grabbed a batch of the terms that I think are useful for a writer to know, especially if you're not already familiar with games.

The first few definitions pertain more specifically to terms that a writer absolutely needs to know. The rest of the definitions relate more to playing games in general.

Writer-Specific Terms

ASSETS

Any digital file that makes up part of the game—such as art, animation, code, sound, music, voice recording, text dialogue, or whatever. If you write dialogue for a game, each piece of dialogue is an asset.

CINEMATIC

A noninteractive scene that is part of the game story and is rendered in real time by the game engine. It's a scene that the player can only watch, but cannot affect (other than to skip over it). A cinematic can be used to convey a key story point, give the player an extra "pat on the back" for completing some important section of the game, create atmosphere, provide clues to the player about what to do next, and so on. See also *Cutscene*. The two terms, cinematic and cutscene, are used interchangeably, however, and most people no longer make a distinction between them.

COMMENTING OUT (USING ; OR //)

Putting a semicolon (;) or double backslashes (//) in front of a line indicates you are "commenting" or "commenting out" that specific line as a piece of information, rather than writing a line of script or a line of code. When a line is commented out, it tells a programmer (and the program itself) that this is information only, and not something to be acted upon. It's used to make a note of explanation or other information about the piece of code or script that immediately follows it.

CUTSCENE

A noninteractive, prerendered scene written for the game, the same as a cinematic in purpose. A cutscene, however, might use art assets beyond what the game itself can provide. For example, a cutscene could be shot with live actors, or it might use a higher resolution of animation. The two terms, cinematic and cutscene, are used interchangeably, however, and most people no longer make a distinction between them.

DELIVERABLES

A term commonly used to refer to game assets that have to be delivered to meet a milestone (a game development deadline). In the case of a game writer, deliverables would be such things as a story treatment, a quest, dialogue for a particular character, or some other specific chunk of writing.

DESIGN DOCUMENT

This can vary from company to company, but ideally a design document contains the design specifics for every aspect of a game, from the game bible, explanation of the interface, world-building description, character biographies, lists of NPCs, and indications of all the interactive elements and what they are and how they work. In short, it is the complete blueprint for the game.

FMV (FULL-MOTION VIDEO)

Prerendered video (animation or live action) done in broadcast-quality resolution (thirty frames per second) and played like a minimovie. Note that as game platforms continue to advance in their ability to render high-quality animation, there may no longer be a need for FMVs. They have been used primarily as opening trailers for the beginning of the game to set up the story, situation, or environment, or for cutscenes.

MILESTONES

Game schedules work to milestones rather than deadlines. A milestone is a date by which a certain chunk of the game design must be done, or the assets created, or code implemented, and so on. For a writer, chunks of game writing will be assigned as milestones.

WALKTHROUGH

A written description of how to follow one or more paths through a game. A walkthrough generally tells the player how to get to locations, how to find the necessary NPCs, what to do there, and other details that help the player find his way through the game.

Game-Development and Game-Playing Terms

AGGRO, AGGRO RADIUS (AGGRO = AGGRESSION)

Aggro refers to how likely it is that a mob (see definition below) or object in the game will attack your avatar (see definition below). If the mob has high aggro, it's more likely to attack you. Your own level as a player can also affect this—for example, a higher-level mob will tend to have more aggro toward you if you're a lower level, while a very-low-level mob may completely ignore you if you're a much higher level than it. Aggro radius is the size of the area around the mob that your avatar must enter in order to trigger the aggressive action. You might be able to run right into or through some mobs without triggering an aggro response, but other mobs might attack you when you're yards away.

AI (ARTIFICIAL INTELLIGENCE)

In computer science, AI is a computer system that is programmed to "think" like a human, to reason, to learn, and to perform cognitive functions that mimic human intelligence. In games, AI is more loosely used to refer to the level of intelligence programmed into the computer-controlled NPCs and other objects to determine how they'll respond to the player or to other objects in the game. The AI given to the human characters in *The Sims*, for example, is much higher than a role-playing game's AI for a minor NPC who needs to have only a specific and limited set of things to say or do.

ATTRIBUTES

Used mostly in role-playing games to refer to the vital statistics that a player can control and improve for their avatar, such as strength, agility, speed, stealth, spirit, and so on.

AVATAR

The avatar is the player's character in the game and is always controlled by the player. There are games in which a player can control more than one character, but the player has only one avatar. The secondary characters are NPCs, even though the player controls them. The avatar may be a specific character that is created for the player (such as Lara Croft in *Tomb Raider*), or a character the player builds from scratch and assigns a unique name, as in RPGs and MMOGs. Note that although the term "avatar" has been around for a long time, some companies may use other terminology, such as "player character" or "hero character." (See also *Toon*.)

BETA TESTING

A stage of game testing in which people outside the company (meaning potential customers) are invited to test the game shortly before it is officially released. The idea is to find as many bugs (see below) as possible and fix them before the game is released. It can also build a loyal customer base and give the game good word of mouth (you hope).

BOSS

A boss is a mob that is a higher level than the others around it (the "boss" of the lower level mobs), thus posing a greater challenge to the player. A boss is usually the last one the player fights, as the payoff for getting past all the lower mobs. (See also *Elite*.)

BUFF

A spell or other effect cast in the game that benefits the player's avatar, usually for some limited period of time. For example, an avatar might get a boost in strength or an increase in agility or stamina, or might gain an ability, such as turning invisible, and so on.

BUG

An error in the programming code that causes a game to work incorrectly. The bane of a developer's existence.

DEATHMATCH

A player-vs.-player mode of combat that occurs in the multiuser versions of a first-person shooter. In deathmatch mode, a player can respawn (reappear) in the game either immediately after dying or after a very short delay.

DPS (DAMAGE PER SECOND)

A common stat that indicates how much damage your avatar or avatar's weapon/spell can do to NPCs or other players, and vice versa.

DUNGEONS

In game usage, this refers to special spaces set aside for dangerous exploration and combat—usually, but not always, underground. It typically indicates a large and complex space with lots of room for the player to get into trouble, rather than a single room or simple cave. "Dungeon crawlers" are games built entirely around large, multilevel dungeons where all the action takes place.

ELEGANT

If you hear a programmer refer to something as elegant, he means that it's a beautifully written piece of code that is clear, clean, easy to understand, well commented, and works with minimal problems.

ELITE

A boss mob or NPC that is high level, extra-powerful, and difficult to battle. It can also refer to a dungeon or quest in which such bosses or NPCs are found.

EMOTES

Typed commands that cause the avatar to perform some emoting action, such as waving, dancing, cheering, flirting, bowing, blowing a kiss, slapping, and so on.

EXPLOIT

A bug in the game or a loophole in the game design that allows a player to exploit the flaw in some way that wasn't anticipated, isn't necessarily desirable, and is advantageous to the player, giving him an unfair advantage over other players. For example, a player might discover a bug that allows him to get unlimited numbers of some item and sell them, thus becoming very rich very quickly in a way that wasn't intended and unbalances the game's economy.

FEATURE

To put it simply, the features are the actions you're able to do in a game via the interface. Being able to save a game at any point is a feature. Being able to craft or manufacture something in a game is a feature. Being able to customize the appearance of your avatar is a feature. There's an old joke among programmers: "It's not a bug—it's a feature!" This is another way of saying: "It's not really broken—we meant it to work badly like that." The joke is sometimes applied to bad design decisions. Another aspect of feature is "feature creep," which refers to new features being added to a game after the initial game design is done because they seem like a cool idea, but which can seriously mess up the budget and schedule. Adding a feature means adding code, art, and possibly other assets, so a good producer or game designer needs to keep feature creep under control.

FRAG

Killing another player, most commonly used in the deathmatch mode of FPS games.

GRIEFERS

People who play multiuser games for the purpose of interfering with or taking unfair advantage of other players. They cause grief, hence "griefers."

GUI (GRAPHICAL USER INTERFACE)

The Mac operating system was the first to use GUI (pronounced "gooey") when it created graphic elements on the screen (symbols, icons, drop-down dialogue boxes, and so on) that could be clicked on in order to perform a program action, rather than having to type in text instructions to tell the program what you wanted to do. This was a revolution in interface design because it made interacting with programs friendlier and easier (or that's the theory). Now GUI (such as Windows) is the standard.

HIT POINTS (HP)

A mathematical value that represents how much damage the player's character can take before dying.

INSTANCE, INSTANCING

This applies to MMOGs in which there can be hundreds to thousands of players sharing the same game locations or zones, so special zones will be set aside to be instances. This means that many copies of the zone can exist on the same server, so that one particular group of players can enter that version of the zone and carry out a quest or mission without the intrusion of any other players. Basically, an instance is your own private universe for your group of players. Simultaneously, any number of groups can be playing the same quest or mission within their own versions of that zone. For example, a particular dungeon can be set aside to be an instance. As soon as the player or party of players enters the dungeon, they are in a unique version of it that is accessible only to them and not to any other players. Instancing is often used to avoid overcrowding in significant quest areas so that players get a quality experience for that quest. There is much debate among designers over the use of instancing, and what constitutes too much or too little.

INTERFACE

The software and hardware controls used by the player to interact with the game. The hardware part of the interface can be a keyboard, mouse, console controller, joystick, and so forth. The software part of the interface can be icons, symbols, or other input areas on the screen that are used to play the game.

INTUITIVE

Game designers use this word a lot when discussing the design of the game interface. Every designer strives to make the game interface and design as intuitive as possible—meaning extremely easy and natural for the player to understand and use. The idea is that the player intuitively understands what something does or how it works, rather than having to be trained in how to use it or having to read a complex manual.

LEVELS, LEVELING UP

A dual-purpose term that can refer to a zone (region or location) of the game (for example, a desert, a range of mountains, a swamp, a dungeon, a city, an entire country, a neighborhood, or even the single floor of a huge building structure). It can also refer to the levels achieved by the player when she has racked up a certain number of experience points (or similar stat). The player then "levels up" (usually a numeric level, such as going from level 40 to level 41) and gains enhancements, such as increased strength, spirit, stamina, or other abilities.

LEVEL DESIGNER

Again, there can be variance in this job description, but basically a level designer is responsible for using art and programming tools to create a geographic region or zone for the game, including the design, placement, and functions of flora, fauna, terrain, architecture, NPCs, and mobs.

MOB (MOBILE OR MOBILE OBJECT)

A mob is any NPC or other humanoid, creature, monster, or object that is mobile within the game and is controlled by the computer. More commonly, it refers to mobile objects that can move around and attack or chase the player, rather than an NPC who simply stands around and gives out information, such as a quest giver.

NPC (NONPLAYER CHARACTER)

An NPC is any other game character that is not an avatar. NPCs are usually controlled by the computer, but there can be NPCs, such as a squad of soldiers or a set of quest companions, that are controlled by the player.

NERF

Means to weaken the abilities of a character class or other game object that is considered too powerful. For example, *World of Warcraft* players who feel that the Paladin class is too powerful will ask the devs to "nerf the Pallies." In order to have a weakening or negative affect on them, this would mean having to change the underlying rules that govern what that character class can do.

PATCH

In general computer terms, a patch is a software update that is meant to fix bugs or other problems with an earlier version of the software. In games, the patch would not only fix bugs, but might include changes to the gameplay (nerfs, buffs, new features, and so on) and new graphics, new sound, or new music to go along with new features. One example of a patch to improve gameplay would be adding the ability to have changing weather, such as a rainstorm, in a game region.

POLYGONS

What cells are to the human body, polygons are to 3-D digital art. A single 3-D character or building can be made up of thousands of polygons, which are tiny individual shapes that fit together to create the whole object. The more polygons, the more detailed and the better the resolution of the art, but also the greater the demands on the processing power of the hardware and software.

POWER-UP

A game item or commodity that can be acquired that gives the player's character an advantage over other players or against mobs. These items often have a limited usage or limited time.

PvE (PLAYER VS. ENVIRONMENT)

An MMOG option where the player is primarily playing against the game environment and the NPCs and mobs in it, rather than against other players (unless the player specifically chooses to do so). It's considered a safer form of gameplay because the player can enjoy the game without constantly having to worry about being jumped by some other player.

PvP (PLAYER VS. PLAYER)

An MMOG option where the player is always playing against other live players in the game environment, as well as with the NPCs and mobs in it.

QA (QUALITY ASSURANCE)

The process of testing a game (by playing and playing and playing it) to find bugs so they can be fixed before the game ships. Most companies have a lead QA person who runs a team of QA testers.

REPLAYABILITY

A game that contains enough entertainment value and variability that the player will play it two or more times to see what the alternative game experience is. *The Sims* has infinite replayability. A strongly linear game with little difference in how it plays out from one time to the next has low replayability quality.

SPAWNING

When a mob or monster or NPC suddenly appears in the game world, it has "spawned"—that is, the game engine has caused the entity to appear in a designated spot to carry out its function.

SIDE-SCROLLERS

Games that use 2-D graphics so that the background scenery has to scroll from side to side (or top to bottom) as the player moves his avatar.

SPAWN CAMPING

The practice some players use in order to keep killing over and over again (for loot or experience) by first killing the mob then sitting and waiting at that spot for the mob to respawn, then doing it all over again.

STATS (STATISTICS)

Stats are vital to every sort of game, whether they're an obvious part of the interface (such as RPG character and weapon stats) or a hidden part of the game (underlying code). In RPGs in particular, the player is constantly trying to improve the stats of her characters—stats governing characteristics such as strength, speed, agility, stamina, spirit, and so forth. Stats also apply to what damage or effect an attack, weapon, spell, or other effect will have on the player, other players, NPCs, and mobs.

STRAFE

In combat, moving the avatar from side to side (often while using a weapon) rather than moving forward and then turning. It's a technique for dodging attacks.

TOON

Slang word for an avatar, used mainly by people playing MMOGs.

TRIGGER, FLAG, HOOK

These are all programming terms that indicate a piece of code that checks for specific conditions and activates the correct response depending on those conditions. The response can be an action (fight, run away, give something to the player, and so on) and/or it might be a piece of dialogue. For example, if the player clicks on an NPC that's a dwarf, the NPC code might check to see what character class the avatar is, what level the avatar has achieved, whether or not the avatar is shown as friendly or hostile to the NPCs character class, what the avatar is carrying in inventory, or any other number of variables. Thus, the NPC might respond one way if the avatar is a hostile, low-level warrior ("Get lost, bud"), and a very different way if the avatar is a friendly, high-level dwarf ("Hail, friend—here's some gold to help you out").

Mobs and some NPCs may have a trigger radius around them, meaning a set distance around them which the avatar must enter before an action or response is set into motion.

TWINKING

Done when a higher-level player helps a lower-level player rise more quickly in levels and experience than would be possible in normal play, usually by providing the lower-level player with money or useful game objects (such as money, weapons, gear, or armor).

WAYPOINTS

In the virtual terrain, these are specific points that are used to determine the movements of NPCs or other moving objects (which are coded to move from one waypoint to another, or within a set of waypoints). Another example might be satellites positioned in space in order to serve as waypoints (spatial and navigational guidance) for the player in a spaceship so she can figure out how to get from one star system to another.

XP (EXPERIENCE POINTS)

The points an avatar gains by accomplishing missions/quests, killing, exploring new locations, and so on. These points are used to determine when the avatar will level up.

Fundamentals of Game Design

Before getting into writing specifics, such as script formats (see Chapter 10), let's take a look at the larger issues that affect writing for games. These issues have to do with the nature of interactivity and the peculiar demands of videogames. Although many of these issues are the responsibility of the designer, a game company will want to have a writer who understands how this type of writing differs from the linear modes of writing. In order to understand that, we'll need to address some fundamental issues of game design.

Linear vs. Nonlinear

The biggest learning curve for someone entering games with a background in writing for linear media (books, movies, TV) is how to think of story and dialogue in a nonlinear way. That is, how do you convey story or allow a character to grow and change, or allow a story to unfold, when you can't entirely control the sequence in which the player will experience the story elements? As a writer, I'm all about putting as much storytelling into a game as I can. As a designer, my mantra is *empower the player*. The trick is to find a way to both empower the player and infuse the game with story and character development.

There's a constant tension between storytelling and interactivity. Storytelling, in the traditional linear sense, depends upon a specific sequence of events. This sequence includes a beginning, a middle, and an end. The writer controls how the reader/viewer will experience this sequence, and the sequence leads to only one conclusion. Thus, the writer determines the structure of the story.

Note that linear storytelling can be nonlinear in the chronological sense, such as using flashbacks, flash-forwards, telling the story backward (from end to beginning), or showing events out of chronological sequence (*Pulp Fiction* being an excellent example).

However, in games, what we mean by nonlinear is that it is the player—not the writer—who has significant control over when and how and in what order she experiences those events. Furthermore, the input of the player can potentially be significant in the direction or resolution of the story.

For example, in both of my adventure games, I offered the player options that were moral choices. In *Conquests of Camelot*, the player's avatar was King Arthur. Along the way, Arthur was put into situations where he could either rescue or decide not to rescue three of his knights, including Lancelot. If the player let his knights die, he could still complete the game, but when he placed his hands on the Holy Grail (the object of his quest), he was found not worthy and was burned to dust, rather than taking the Grail home in triumph.

In *Conquests of the Longbow*, the player's avatar was Robin Hood. On numerous occasions throughout the game, Robin Hood had various options for dealing with NPCs—which could include killing, helping, bribing, convincing by talking, and so forth. The options chosen by the player, along with various other actions during the game story, determined which of four endings the player would get—ranging from the best result (a full pardon from King Richard plus the restoration of his title as earl and the hand of Maid Marian) to the worst result (being hanged as a good-for-nothing robber).

The essence of games is interactivity, which means putting the player in control as much as possible. There is still structure and there are still rules, but they are designed to give the player as much freedom as the structure can allow. Videogames can be nonlinear and interactive and still have a basic three-act structure. More about this later under Game Structure.

It's easy to see how a linear story (fig. 9.1) can progress from one story node to another, with later story nodes able to build on or make reference to earlier story nodes.

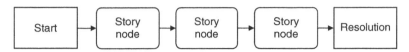

Figure 9.1
A simple linear story line.

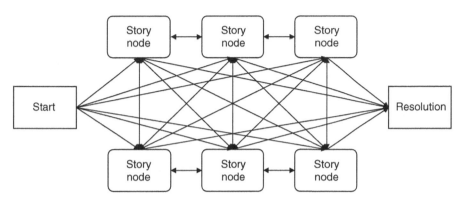

Figure 9.2
A nonlinear story line.

In a completely nonlinear story (fig. 9.2), each story node has to stand alone and be self-sufficient without depending on the other story nodes or making reference to them in a specific sequence.

Most games will fall somewhere between these two extremes, as other examples will show.

Basically, what it gets down to is this: the more interactivity (player freedom) the game allows, the less linear story the writer can tell. You can visualize it as a seesaw, with story at one end and interactivity at the other. A game that is weighted heavily with story is light in interactivity. If heavy in interactivity, the game will be light in story. Trying to balance the two issues so the seesaw is horizontal isn't necessarily the right answer. The type of game will determine where on this seesaw scale the game will fall.

Many console games have quite linear stories threading through them, and the interactivity is mainly about the combat system and what/whom the player gets to fight along the way. PC games demand a higher level of true interactivity, with the player able to command a wider range of choices. MMOGs demand a high level of choice. Because they are ongoing, these games provide an additional design challenge in how to keep thousands of players hooked on the game world, the story, and the quests for months and years on end. MMOGs in particular are more about creating a compelling environment—the game world—and the activities in which the player can take part within that environment.

Some games are designed specifically for the hard-core gamers, in which case the design emphasis is definitely on gameplay at the expense of story. Hard-core gamers aren't known for caring about story. Other games look to attract a wider market of players who like a more rewarding story experience or want something more out of a game than twitching their thumbs on a controller.

When writing for games, you'll encounter many variations of this design mind-set, and you'll often feel that story must take a backseat to gameplay. How much story or character development is woven into a game will be up to the attitudes and preferences of the designer or producer—which leaves you, the writer, with the task of balancing your writing input with the requirements of the game design.

Game Structure

Game structure is a huge subject. To fully understand it would require reading a book entirely about game design, but if you're hired to write a game story or text for missions/quests or dialogue for the NPCs, you'll need to understand the structure of the game in order to do a good job of it.

Understand that "game structure" is my own wording, and other game designers may have any number of words or terms to cover this. To me, the structure of the game is its underlying architecture, which determines how linear or nonlinear it is, and what parameters are used to create or control the nonlinearity. I would further divide this term into two major components: gameplay structure and story structure.

Story Structure

Although all games have at least a beginning, a middle, and an end, a game that contains story structure should fall under the basic three-act structure of drama—Act 1: *setup (exposition),* Act 2: *conflict (complications),* and Act 3: *resolution.* The three-act structure is about the development of emotional response in a story, the building of dramatic tension, and the final release of that tension in the resolution. Games that contain these elements have story structure. Games that lack any of these elements consist entirely of gameplay structure.

An example of a game consisting only of gameplay structure is a casual game such as *Tetris,* which is about manipulating colored blocks as they fall from the top to the bottom of the screen. It has a beginning with the starting positions of the colored blocks, a middle as the player must deal with the new blocks descending, and the end when the player either wins or loses the game. What it doesn't have is story.

Myst was about 95 percent gameplay (the puzzles) and 5 percent story. I'd put most MMOGs at about 90 percent gameplay, 10 percent story (though not story that the player can truly affect). The story-driven action game *Max Payne* is about 50–50. My adventure games probably fall somewhere around 60 percent story to 40 percent gameplay structure (in other words, in these games, the story dictated the gameplay slightly more than the gameplay dictated the story).

Setting aside games that don't depend on story (such as puzzles, cards, chess, sports, sims), every game requires some kind of Act 1 story setup. There must be at least minimal backstory about how the current situation, world, or conflict came to be; information about the avatar or character that the player will be playing (if applicable), or about the general race or class to which the avatar belongs; and what the current situation is that faces the player at the start of the game, which includes some sense of what the player is meant to achieve.

Along the way, there need to be the Act 2 complications that affect either the gameplay or the story, or ideally a combination of both. A more-story-driven game might even have an *inciting incident.* In drama, an *inciting incident* (or catalyst) is usually the turning point between Act 1 and Act 2, and is the event that starts the forces of conflict in motion.

Max Payne had a good example of that. The setup of the first game is that Payne's family has been killed by crazed drug users. At the beginning of the game, Payne is an undercover cop who is out to find and stop those killers, as well as to find the source of the drug. Very quickly, however, he finds himself framed for the murder of his partner, and is on the run from the law while on the hunt for the criminals. This is a classic inciting incident. It ups the ante and reshapes his goals. Now Payne must not only find the killers and stop the drug trade, he must clear his name while on the run. The game storyline throws various other turning points and conflicts in his way as Payne's search leads him from location to location (each location being a "level"), and from NPC to NPC.

Conflict doesn't just mean physical conflict. Top-notch TV writer Stephen J. Cannell has an online advice column (http://www.writerswrite.com/screenwriting) in which he also mentions "social conflict, emotional conflict, spiritual conflict, cultural conflict, internal conflict, relationship conflict, psychological conflict."

Finally, games with story require an Act 3 resolution. The hero wins or fails, achieves the quest or not, finds the killers or dies. Those resolutions may vary (more than one or two endings for a game), but there has to be a resolution. If the player wins, that resolution needs to be a satisfying payoff for the effort she has put into the game. The satisfaction level will depend on how thoroughly the player has gotten involved in the story and the characters, and how the player is rewarded for that involvement.

To be most effective, the three-act structure should be applied to individual scenes or sequences, to entire levels, to entire missions, and finally to the overall game story. In other words, the game should have a large three-act structure, but should also have numerous mini-three-act structures within it.

Resolution is a sticky problem for MMOGs. An MMOG can have the usual amount of setup, but is more about presenting the player with an ongoing world and leveling up within that world than it is with creating a through-line of story complications. There can be references to the background story, but it's extremely difficult for an MMOG player to impact an MMOG world in a significant way along with many thousands of other players doing the same things. All the same, the levels need to add up to something once the player reaches the top level. In *World of Warcraft*, for example, there is a climactic scene for the level 60 players and a big quest to pay off reaching that high level. It's a resolution of sorts, but not a true resolution because the game doesn't end there. There must be new material, new quests, and higher levels to achieve, or it will feel as though the game has reached a dead end.

Game Parameters

So we begin with the assumption that a game with story will have something akin to a three-act structure. The next big question in how to implement that story structure will be to work out the parameters of the gameplay structure.

"Parameters" is my own terminology. It's not an official game design word, and there can be any number of ways of expressing this part of game structure. The important thing is to understand the underlying concept of game parameters. Those parameters have a major impact on how, when, and where story can be injected into gameplay, or how the story elements will be carried out.

If game structure is the architecture, then parameters are the walls, floors, ceiling, doors, windows, and pertinent fittings. For example, if the room is a bathroom, it may or may not have a window, but it will have enclosing walls, floor, ceiling, and a door as the basic structure parameters. It will also have a sink, toilet, tub, and fixtures for running water as the basic interactivity parameters.

Parameters for a game structure control where a player can go, when she can go there, and what she can do there. A sandbox game has fairly wide-open parameters, allowing the player to go nearly anywhere at any time. A more linear console FPS game might have more-restrictive parameters that determine where the player can go and when and what she can do there. Sometimes two or more parameters work together to control or guide the player. Some parameters will apply mostly to gameplay, some will apply more to story, and many will apply to both.

Here are some examples of typical parameters:

- Zone (location, region, terrain)
- Time or phase
- Player level
- Acquisition of game objects
- Acquisition of a quest
- Predetermined events

Zone

Note that "zone" is only one word that might be used for the concept of a restrained area, and each game company could use a word of its own, such as region or level. The concept is the same. A zone could potentially be a single room, an instanced dungeon, or an entire geographic region. Using a zone to strictly control a player's movements means that the player is restricted to that zone until the right conditions are met to move on to the next zone. In *Conquests of Camelot,* Arthur's castle was one zone. It consisted of various rooms, corridors, garden, and the main gate with portcullis. Arthur had several tasks (subquests) to complete before he could safely leave through the main gate. Once outside Camelot, there were other geographic zones available that could be visited in any order and that required various local subquests to be completed (fig. 9.3).

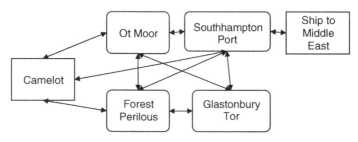

Figure 9.3
The various zones for the England portion of *Conquests of Camelot.*

Once the subquests for all the zones in England were completed, it opened up the ability for Arthur to get on a ship and travel to the Middle East, where the next zone was the town of Gaza, then a desert to be crossed, and finally the zone of Jerusalem. Because we didn't have the ability to make the game terrain endless, we had to build in restricting parameters. There was a safe path through the desert, but players who wandered off in other directions died of thirst.

If a zone is inside a building, the parameters will consist of doors that are either locked or can be opened only under the right circumstances, or other ways to get in and out. If the exterior geography or terrain is wide open, the player must eventually be blocked by something—whether it's an ocean, a sheer cliff, impassable mountains, a locked tunnel, monsters that can't be defeated, or severe conditions that block the player from going in that direction.

Zones don't have to be entirely restrictive. Certainly in MMOGs, the player has the freedom to travel extensively through various zones, but those zones will have mobs and other conditions of varying difficulty. In beginner zones, the mobs are low level and easy to defeat by any player, so those zones are fairly safe to wander around in. Other zones increase in difficulty. If a beginning player wanders into a zone populated with higher-level mobs, the player tends to get killed in short order. Players are quick to figure this out, and the zone boundaries become as effective as impassable mountain ranges. This is where two parameters (zone, player's level) work together to guide where the player should go or not go.

Zones are defined by appearance, theme, surface textures, color palettes, sounds, music, and other elements that help set the visual and audio boundaries for that locale. Those elements can potentially relate to story parameters—for example, a dark, forbidding atmosphere, unsettling sounds, and creepy music set the stage for certain types of quests or story elements. A haunted, misty forest will create a different mood for a quest than would a bright, sun-filled valley of flowers. As a writer, you want to mesh what you're writing with the look and feel of the zone in which it will take place, as well as understanding the parameters of the zone.

Time or Phase

In some games, the parameter might be time based or defined as a "phase" or similar term. In *Conquests of the Longbow*, I divided the gameplay and story elements into "days." The player was free to wander around Sherwood Forest and various other locations, so the zones were only a partial restriction. A set number of quests and events were programmed to occur each day in varying zones. They could be done in any order, but the day didn't end until they had been done (fig. 9.4). Then there was a nighttime cutscene that wrapped up the events of the day, depending on how they had gone. The game progressed this way through day after day, night after night, until reaching the resolution.

For another game, we divided a large, sweeping overall story into five phases, which were defined by evolving story elements, plus the player's level in which he advanced from the pilot of a single fighter spacecraft to squadron leader and up the ranks to Admiral of the Fleet. As the player advanced in rank, the story elements for each phase increased in scope and complexity to keep pace with his greater ability to have an effect on the gameplay. This meant that missions written for phase 1 had to work for someone who could operate only a single fighter as part of the space battles, but missions written for phase 4 had to work for someone who had advanced to commander of a group of battleships. However, missions also had to be written for every rank below commander, because there was always the chance that the player had failed or had chosen not to advance in rank.

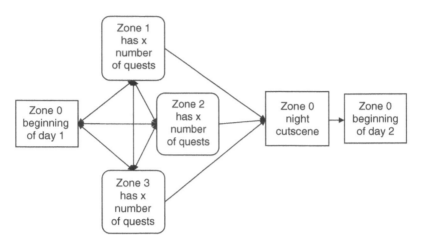

Figure 9.4
Story structure divided into day and night components.

Some games also introduce a timer that requires the player to complete a quest, task, or set of actions within a specific amount of time, such as having to kill some number of mobs within fifteen minutes. Usually such timers will be limited in use, applied to a single quest or small section of the game. Some players like the extra pressure of having the clock ticking down as they try to do something; other players prefer to do things at their own pace. And of course, some sports games use timers to mimic the playing times of the real games, as in football and basketball.

Player Level

As touched upon above, games such as RPGs and MMOGs advance the player by levels that govern his stats and abilities, what sort of weapons he can use, what sort of armor he can wear, and so forth. Some aspects of story and gameplay might be unavailable to a player depending upon his level. That level might be numerical, or it might be expressed in some games as a rank (squad leader, captain, admiral). The player-level parameter often works in conjunction with a zone parameter, as already mentioned.

Player Race, Faction, or Class

There can be any number of terms for this, and it applies to RPGs in which the player selects a particular race, faction, class, or type of avatar—such as Elf, Orc, Human, Dwarf, Gnome, Terran, Martian, or whatever. Within that larger race or class, there are usually subcategories for what type of that race or faction the avatar will be—for example, Warrior, Priest, Merchant, Rogue, Thief, Paladin, Explorer, Trader, and so on. The game engine can track the faction or race to which the avatar belongs.

Both parameters could be used to determine who gets to do a certain quest. There might be quests written that are offered to a Human or Elf, but not offered to an Orc or Troll, and vice versa; or quests that are offered to a Warrior but not a Rogue. If not every player gets to do every quest, it can obviously affect whether the player sees any story elements tied to those quests.

Zones can also be restricted to certain class or faction types. In the *Earth & Beyond* MMOG, there were three factions, and each faction had certain planets that only their members could visit in order to access special trainers for that faction. The effect this had on writing dialogue is that for those faction-only sites, dialogue had to cover only the one faction. In other sites in the game, dialogue had to take into account which of the three factions the player belonged to, and alternate dialogues had to be provided.

Acquisition of Game Objects

A smaller parameter that could affect story or gameplay structure would be requiring the player to acquire or win certain game objects before the next step of the game can unfold. An example would be requiring the player to acquire a cloak of invisibility before being able to sneak into a prison and free a prisoner. Freeing the prisoner could both set up the next stage of gameplay and reveal key story elements.

Acquisition of a Quest

A type of parameter is to require the player to be on a specific quest before other game elements become available. For example, a player takes a quest to enter a fortified area. Taking the quest triggers the appearance of an NPC who provides the means for the player to get in.

An example of a combination of the two types of acquisition parameters working together would be a key that the player can find and acquire only after she has taken a mission to get through a certain door. Once she has that key, she can unlock the door to access a new level of the game.

Predetermined Events

A game could be structured around predetermined events that will always happen as the player progresses through the game. These are usually going to be cinematics or cutscenes that drive the story forward, rather than being gameplay elements. *Max Payne* has a cutscene in which Max is knocked out, has a nightmare about his slain family, and wakes up in a new situation that he has to deal with. The scene provides a transition from one gameplay and story level to another, as well as adding to the emotional story content of the game.

In *Conquests of the Longbow,* I had key scenes or moments that happened on various days in which Robin would have to encounter Maid Marian. The first one was a rescue to bring the two together, whereas other scenes included both story and gameplay elements with the purpose of making the player feel connected to Marian so that in one of the major predetermined events—Marian is sentenced to burn as a witch—the player would feel compelled to save her, which in turn had additional major story and gameplay effects. It was a secondary thread running in parallel to the primary body of the gameplay and game story (which was to raise enough ransom to free King Richard from captivity). A writer would think of it as a subplot, but those predetermined events shaped both story and game elements.

A predetermined-event parameter indicates a more linear or story-driven game structure (fig. 9.5), and can be combined with other parameters.

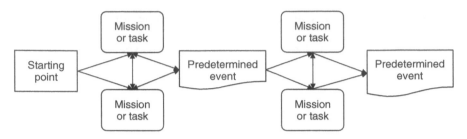

Figure 9.5
Example of a structure organized by predetermined events.

More Things You Need to Know

Next up are some additional topics that deal with other key aspects of being a game writer. The following topics are covered:

- What if . . .
- Variables and flexibility
- Gradients
- Choice
- The interface
- Immersion
- The player's mind-set

What If . . .

When a writer sits down to create a linear work, there is a constant process of asking "What if . . ." Creating our characters involves asking endless questions. We ask what if we use this or that type of character, what if this character were female instead of male, what if they have this trait or that trait, is old or young, have this set of beliefs, live here or live there, and on and on. What if my character leaves her cell phone uncharged when she's about to get into danger? What if my character says no instead of yes to a proposition? What if I give the character a child to protect? What if there is an ex-wife or ex-husband in the mix?

There are the countless what-ifs as we create the plot and the locations, determine the sequence of events, decide how those events will play out, and pick the one ending that feels right out of all the possible endings.

The nonlinear writer goes through the same process of asking the what-if questions—with the key difference that she doesn't necessarily have to pick only one answer. Instead of, "What if Robin Hood has to get inside Nottingham?" having only one answer, the game writer may have to cover several what-if answers: what if he tries to enter as himself? (he dies); what if he tries to enter disguised as a foolish merchant? (he gets to trick the Sheriff out of money); what if he enters disguised as a beggar? (he can enter safely and explore the town); what if he enters disguised as a monk? (he gets the corrupt Abbot drunk and steals a precious ring from him); what if he enters as a one-eyed yeoman? (he enters the archery contest and wins the golden arrow); what if he never enters at all? (Maid Marian dies for lack of a rescue).

Now, all of those things could happen in a linear story, but in order to empower the player, a game needs to make them all available as options that the player has to (*a*) discover, (*b*) choose to act upon (or not), (*c*) choose *how* to act upon them (Robin wants Merchant's clothes—does he kill, threaten, or bribe the Merchant to get the clothes), and (*d*) carry out the action (which could succeed or fail).

This is also expressed as "*if this, then this* . . ." because each of the what-if decisions requires a subsequent game response. For example, *If* Robin decides to bribe the Merchant, *then* we have dialogue between the two, money leaves Robin's purse, there's an animation of the Merchant removing his clothes, animation of the Merchant leaving, and the Merchant's clothes appear in Robin's inventory as a usable item. *If* Robin decides to threaten the Merchant, *then* we have animation of Robin aiming an arrow at the Merchant, a different set of dialogue between them, animation of the Merchant disrobing and leaving in anger, and the Merchant's clothes appear in Robin's inventory as a usable item. And so forth.

Other what-ifs can deal with story consequences. What if Robin simply kills the Merchant for his clothes? *If* he kills the Merchant, *then* the Merchant doesn't appear during the trial at the end of the game to testify in Robin's behalf, with his absence thus reducing Robin's chances of winning a pardon. What if Robin threatens the Merchant? *If* the Merchant appears at the trial, but has only bad things to say, *then* he has a negative effect on the ending. What if Robin bribes the Merchant instead? Then the Merchant will appear at the trial with good things to say, which will benefit Robin.

Granted, most of these are design decisions you might not be called upon to make as a writer, but being able to think in terms of *what-if* variables and the *"if this, then this"* connections are key components to nonlinear thinking.

Besides which, you *will* be called upon to base what you write upon such what-ifs, which brings us to the subject of variables and flexibility.

Variables and Flexibility

Every one of the options (the various disguises) for getting into Nottingham is a variable. Each method for dealing with the NPCs is a variable. Additional variables might include where they occur in the game sequence (for example, before or after Marian is sentenced to be burned as a witch), or other events that affect using the disguise (for example, whether or not the Sheriff has seen Robin in that disguise before). For example, if Robin uses the merchant disguise to trick the Sheriff out of money, what if Robin tries to enter Nottingham a second time using the same disguise? What if Robin uses the merchant disguise once, but doesn't interact with the Sheriff? Does he get a second chance to enter in that disguise and trick the Sheriff?

You can expect to be asked to write story components or dialogue that takes into account the numerous variables in the game. To be a game writer, you need the mental skills to keep masses of interrelated details in your head. You need to be well organized and detail oriented.

Another important quality for a game writer to have is flexibility. A game writer must also be ready, able, and willing to make sudden, sweeping changes to the story and writing if technical requirements or last-minute changes in game design take place. A change in one part of a game might affect variables in other parts of the game. The game writer must be able to follow the cascade of potential effects, catch any problems, and compensate for them. This requires having the overall structure of the game in your mind, from a large overview down to the small details. You might be the main person who can know whether pulling out a particular thread will unravel a large part of the game tapestry. This is a critical ability for a game writer to have.

Most often when significant changes are made to a game story, it's due to time or budget considerations. On one console RPG, I wrote a large, complex story full of secondary quests in several different geographic areas, with allowance for the player to return to those areas more than once with some variability in the story. For reasons of both time and budget (because in games, *time = money,* the same as in TV and film), we had to cut one large chunk out of the story to eliminate returning to one region. Although returning to that region didn't require new art assets, it did require significant programming work, which in turn affected how long it would take the programmers to complete the game. Fortunately, the story was modular enough that it was possible to remove that chunk and still make the overall story work, but I had to run through the entire range of variables that would be affected by the deletion and make sure they were accounted for during the rest of the game. Regarding the change, a number of questions needed to be asked: how did it affect the overall story quest; how did it affect other secondary quests; where there significant objects the player needed to get there; how did it affect the behaviors or use of NPCs; and how did it affect NPC dialogue, which might refer to it or be dependent on it?

Gradients

Good game design incorporates the use of gradients, in which the player is presented with easy tasks in the beginning, then tasks that become increasingly more difficult and complex as the game progresses. The idea is to give the player a lot of wins at the beginning in order to encourage her and keep her playing. This allows the player to become adept at the interface on a gradual basis, rather than trying to master too much all at once. A player who is given a batch of fairly quick and easy tasks at the start will feel empowered and more motivated to master the next level.

If you're writing quests or dialogue for them, you'll want to have an understanding of where they fall in the design gradient, so that you can have that in the back of your mind as you write. This may not have a significant impact on what you write, but it deepens your knowledge, which is always beneficial. It's not that you want to talk down to a player who is at the start of a game, but you do want to make sure the information you need to get across is clearly explained or stated for someone who isn't familiar yet with how the game works.

Choice

Boiling interactivity down to its essentials, it's about *choice.* In linear writing, the writer is making all the choices. In games, the player makes the choices from whatever options the designer and writer make available. The options made available to the player may be restricted by how much of the game budget and schedule can be spent on creating the extra assets to go along with those options. If every choice offered to the player requires a significant amount of new animation and programming, that will affect how many choices can be offered. This is where game design and story choices have to strike a balance between what you'd like to offer and what you can realistically afford to offer.

Choice empowers the player. And the choice must be a real choice, or else the player will feel cheated. As Spock said in the James Blish *Star Trek* novel, "A difference that makes no difference is no difference."

Getting back to Robin Hood's disguises, there is a different consequence for each choice in how to get the Merchant's clothes (killing, threatening, bribing). If there were no difference in the consequences, it would make no real difference which option the player chose. If killing the Merchant yields the same result as bribing him, there's no reason for the player to care about the choices.

Looking at a simplified example, let's set up a situation in which a player has to choose between taking one of two corridors. In this example, we see that whether the player chooses to go left or go right makes no difference, so having two corridors to choose from is a fake choice (fig. 9.6).

However, if there is something significant to be experienced or found in one corridor that affects the rest of the gameplay, those choices become real choices. Ideally, the player will be "pushed" (given some hint or guidance earlier) as to which corridor to take. For example, the player may have been told ahead of time to watch out for the corridor to his left because it's dangerous, they're guarding something there, whereas the corridor to his right is safe. But the player is looking for something that is being guarded, so this is a hint that what he's looking for could be in that corridor. The player has been presented with genuine choices (fig. 9.7)— take the safe path and risk passing up something useful, or take the dangerous path and get a valuable object that leads to the next step of gameplay. Notice also that although the player

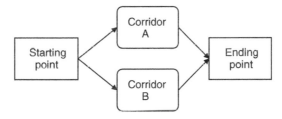

Figure 9.6
Example of a fake choice.

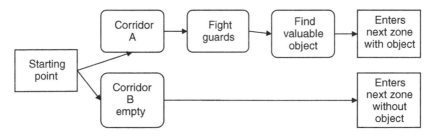

Figure 9.7
In this example, the choices are meaningful because they affect gameplay.

arrives at the same end location either way, you effectively have two different paths of action to track: one with the object and one without the object.

As game producer Ellen Guon Beeman sagely puts it, "Players want to win." Writers should think about that before they create a lot of alternative content that is seen only if the player continues down a losing branch.

Choice has a profound effect on linearity and storytelling. The greater the player's freedom of choice, the more the writer has to account for the variables created by allowing those choices. In the most linear storytelling form of games, such as many console games, the "choices" are nonchoices from a storytelling point of view, and are mainly gameplaying choices, such as battle strategy, type of weapon or spell to use, how to fight types of mobs, and so on. In an adventure- or action-oriented game with a distinct storyline, the choices should affect how the story plays out as well as what the gameplay elements will be. In a sandbox or MMO game, the player has enormous choice in a range of activities and gameplay, but there may be little to no storytelling impacted by those choices.

The Interface

Although a writer will have no control over the design of the game's interface, I consider it vital to understand how important the interface is, for two reasons: *(a)* a bad interface is almost guaranteed to doom a game, and *(b)* the interface dictates precisely how story and dialogue are implemented in the game.

Much of what I wrote about the evolution of games dealt with the changes in game interfaces. There's a significant difference in writing for a game that has a minimal interface *(Myst);* compared to writing for a console game with an interface that can contain many on-screen elements, but are all controlled by a limited set of buttons; compared to writing for a PC-game interface, which can allow a wide range of actions using keyboard and mouse or other devices.

Interface is where the rubber meets the road. Think about the interface for driving a car. What are the essential parts of that interface? You must have a wheel to steer, a pedal to make it move, a pedal to make it stop, something that controls the gears, and a set of tires. That's about it. The essence of controlling that car—speed, direction, avoiding obstacles, and reaching the goal—is dependent on those five basic interface elements. Everything else— such as speedometer, oil gauge, heater, air conditioner, windshield, radio, rearview mirror, side mirrors, adjustable seat, seat belts, and so on—provide nice extra features that make the experience more enjoyable or safe while not being essential to the fundamental interface.

So it is when designing a game. There are interface components that are absolute necessities, and there are the extra features that further enhance the gameplay. One of the designer's main responsibilities is designing a good, clean, intuitive interface and balancing the essential gameplay needs with the additional features (fig 9.8). The needs of the game and the requirements of the gameplay will dictate the interface, and the interface will be the only means you as a writer have of providing story or character interactions to the player.

In *Conquests of Camelot,* the player had word riddles to solve, and I could do that because my interface included the player's being able to type in words that the game engine could parse. In *Conquests of the Longbow,* I had a specific set of mouse-click icons I had to use, and no text-typing input, which eliminated doing a puzzle such as a riddle. Then we look at the MMOG, which has keyboard input only for chatting with other players or for using emotes, but nothing that affects the gameplay. For most PC and online games, the mouse click

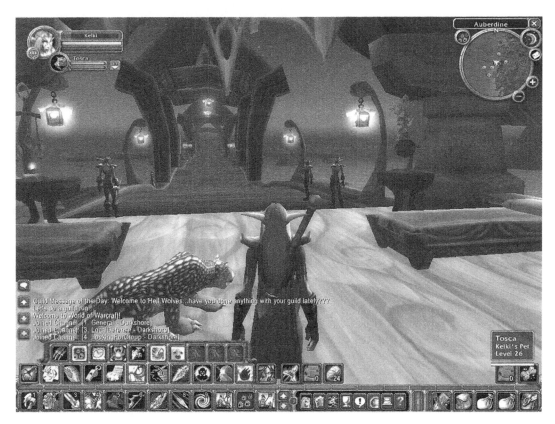

Figure 9.8
This screenshot from *World of Warcraft* shows an interface that conveys a vast amount of game-play information at a glance, yet is intuitive and easy to use.

is the vital hardware interface—whereas, in console games, it is mashing the buttons on the controller that is the vital hardware interface. Yet both methods can have a wide range of effects depending on how they interact with the game interface on the screen.

The interface elements on the screen fall into two categories:

- Those that are under the control of the player—such as deciding the direction in which to go, moving the camera around, selecting a battle mode, picking a weapon or spell to use, putting on or taking off armor, getting and buying and selling objects, and so on.

- Those that are controlled by the game—such as which NPCs or objects will be click-able, and what that clickable action will be. Examples include a "talk," "buy/sell/trade," or "quest giver" icon for an NPC; a "fight" icon for a mob that can be targeted; an "open" icon for a treasure chest; a "magnifying glass" icon for an object that can be looked at in more detail; and so forth.

Study the many types of interfaces that exist in a variety of games. Study the use of icons and symbols in conjunction with mouse clicks or button mashing. Study how, when, and where the interface allows the player to make a story choice or interact with an NPC in action or in dialogue. Imagine how you would try to convey story elements using the interfaces you encounter.

Immersion

Good designers and writers strive to create a game world, story, and gameplay that are so well meshed that the player can easily feel immersed in that virtual reality. Achieving immersion for the player means finding a way to disguise the obvious game mechanics and make them organic parts of the game world. This can be tricky when the player needs to learn to "Hold down button 1" to achieve a particular move. Anything that reminds a player that he is only playing a game is something that destroys the player's immersion in that game-world reality. Some players dislike traditional cutscenes because during a cutscene, control of the game is taken away from the player, an obvious reminder that this is a game rather than an alternate reality.

Most of the issues of creating immersion are the designer's responsibility, but as a writer, you should always look for the ways you can contribute to creating immersion. Is there some way to convey a particular piece of training to make it sound more "real" and less gamelike? Can training be seamlessly integrated into a series of easy initial quests rather than being a stark tutorial? Is there a way to convey a particular piece of story element without putting it into a cutscene? Can the cutscene be interactive instead of noninteractive?

Immersion is also about word choices, tone of language, avoiding anachronisms, and setting a consistent story mood or theme that meshes with the overall game world.

The Player's Mind-set

To write well for games, it's helpful to play enough games to have a sense of what the mind-set is of a person who plays the type of game you want to work on. If you want to write console games, you need to understand what a console player expects. If you want to write MMOGs, you need to play one or more MMOGs to understand that mind-set. This isn't an absolute necessity for someone who wants to be hired purely as a writer, but it improves your ability to deliver something that fits the gamer mind-set.

For those who have played a lot of games already, this may be a no-brainer, but when I began, I knew nothing about games at all. The first thing I did upon being hired by Sierra On-Line (today known as Sierra Entertainment) was to sit down and play all of the games that Sierra had produced. I wanted to become familiar with how their games worked, but also to tap into the mind-set of a typical Sierra player. I needed to meet—and hopefully exceed—that typical player's expectations. Playing a lot of games also helped me decide which design flaws I wanted to avoid. If something annoyed me as a player, I assumed it would annoy other players.

Being a person of logical mind, I tended to write dialogue and text responses in the order I figured a player would try. My mentors quickly pointed out that I was being too linear. I thought I understood their guidance, and I reworked my scripts trying to take that into account.

But I didn't have the One True Revelation until we had *Conquests of Camelot* about halfway done (the entire England chunk of the game) and took it to a convention to let random people bang away at it. I spent the afternoon watching how players interacted with the game, how they tackled the puzzles, how they approached dealing with the NPCs. By the end of the day, I had the One True Revelation. I finally *got* it.

The One True Revelation is this: players are the Forces of Chaos. They will do *anything* in *any* order, whether it makes sense or not. They use trial and error rather than figure out your clever clues. They throw logic out the window.

Therefore, I share this with you, the potential game writer: expect anything and write accordingly, and always remember—players are the Forces of Chaos.

CHAPTER 10

The Script Format

The first thing to know about writing for games is that there are absolutely no standardized formats for game scripts. There is no such thing as "a game script." None, nada, zip. This is especially true when dealing with dialogue writing, where every company may have its own unique method or some proprietary software that is used to create and incorporate dialogue. If you're an in-house writer (full-time employee), there will nearly always be specialized game-engine tools you'll use to create your material.

For the contract writer, there are a few rough guidelines I can give, but don't consider them to be hard-and-fast rules. The producer or whoever hires you may have a clear idea of what she wants you to do. If not, it may be up to you to decide what format to use.

First, you need to know what you might be expected to do. There are certain types of jobs you can typically be hired to do as a game writer. They are:

- FMV or game intro
- Design document
- Game bible
  - Game-world creation
  - Character biographies
  - Game backstory
  - Game story
- Quests or missions
- Cutscenes/cinematics
- Dialogue
- In-game text

- Naming NPCs and game objects
- Technical material or game manual
- Web site and promotional materials

FMV/Game Intro

As defined in Chapter 9, full-motion video is of broadcast quality and is usually of higher quality than the animation that can be generated by the game engine. With technology constantly advancing, FMV may become obsolete, but what won't change is the desire for a really hot, enticing game intro, something that gets the players' juices flowing and gives a taste of the game world. Essentially, it's the trailer for the game, and runs maybe one to two minutes. It's like writing a trailer for a movie or TV show, except that you'll have to distill the intro from whatever game materials the company provides.

You may be called upon to write an actual introductory scene of some kind—or more likely, it will be a montage of images to capture the mood and feel of the game, as well as to show off the significant game elements (race types, locations, special effects, enemies/monsters, and so on). If it's scenes, you'll be writing dialogue for live actors to record. If it's a montage, there may be some narration to be recorded, or it might have no voice and be done with music only.

This will be noninteractive and will be storyboarded, then created by animators; consequently, you can feel safe using a standard scriptwriting format. My recommendation would be to use an animation-script format, because you will almost always be dealing with animation rather than live action.

If you aren't familiar with the animation-script format, go to the first section of this book to read up on animation writing. All the basic rules of animation writing apply here, including the need to keep recorded dialogue (if any) minimal, strong, and pithy.

Design Document

It is highly unlikely that you, as a writer, would be asked to write a design document, because this is a designer-level piece of work. However, you need to be aware of what this is in case it comes up in conversation. As defined in Chapter 9, a design document is the complete blueprint of the game. It should be written by the lead or senior designer(s), though many people may contribute to portions of it. The design document needs to contain basically everything that everybody working on the game needs to know about the game—ranging from story elements (descriptions of world, characters, mobs, and so on) to gameplay and technical specs (such as interface, combat systems, lists of items and mobs, stats for items, mobs, and NPCs). Each type of game will naturally require its own sort of design document.

What you would most likely contribute to a design document as a writer are the portions dealing with the game bible, as discussed below.

Game Bible

There isn't a standard format for game bibles either. What you'll be hired to write can vary according to the type and nature of the game, and whatever it is the company wants.

Generally speaking, the format of an animation bible works every bit as well for games, so I recommend going to the Animation section of this book and reading up on animation bibles.

How much you do on the bible may depend on what stage the game is in when you're hired. You could be hired at the very beginning of the game development to create the game bible from scratch (with input from the producer and designer). You might be hired when the game is already well into development and they want you only to polish up a bible that is in rough form, or perhaps to flesh out only certain portions of it, such as expanding the character bios or adding more depth to the history of the locations.

You could also be asked to describe weapons, vehicles, or other related elements, to come up with a chronology of quests, or any number of other tasks. Consequently, you want to be sure that the company is very specific about what elements you'd be covering if hired to write a game bible. You will want to know how much material already exists and how much you will be expected to create on your own.

A game bible will be whatever the person who hires you wants it to be, but these are what I consider to be the main ingredients of a good game bible:

- Game-world creation

- Game backstory

- Game story

- Character biographies (both avatar and NPCs)

- Mobs/monsters/bosses

Game-World Creation

Game-world creation is writing the description and explanation of the entire setting of the game, which covers descriptions of geography/terrain, key locations, history of regions or places, descriptions of the various races or NPC types, histories of races, and other related information to create a coherent whole for the world of the game.

To be a good game-world creator, you should have at least some knowledge of a wide range of subjects—such as geography, sociology, politics, economic structures, mythology, personal combat, weaponry, war, military strategy and tactics, religions, foreign cultures, linguistics, physics, art, architecture, technology, weather, biology, plants and animals, trade systems, various professions and skills from primitive to technological, the development of civilization, government power structures, and all forms of human interaction. There's your reading assignment for the afternoon.

Depending on when you're brought into the project, you may be asked to create a world from scratch, or you may be given existing assets that have to be stitched together, or you may be working from a preexisting property (such as a comic book or movie) that will dictate what you can do.

A good example was the work I did on a PS2 RPG called *The Legend of Alon D'ar*. I was brought in to create the game bible, including the game story. What existed were the art designs for the world and its zones, for the main characters and races, and some mobs. The world was a chunk of land torn from a planet and floating in space, which presented an interesting challenge right there, because by the usual law of physics, nothing could live there. Because it was a fantasy-themed game, there had to be a mystical or magic-based explanation for how this world could exist. It was great fun to work out a history to explain its existence, histories and descriptions for the zones and characters and races, and come up with names for everything and everyone, inspired by the wonderful artwork alone. Plus, it all had to work together and, most importantly, have an inner consistency that allowed it to make sense within the rules I established.

Imagine how the cataclysmic event that created this Floating World must have affected each of the races, the impact it would have not only on their histories and mythologies, but on their native psyches. Imagine the unique pattern of "day" and "night" such a world would have. What about weather patterns? Imagine how the people inhabiting this terrain deal with having a clearly defined edge to their world beyond which there is only an infinite Void. Why are some of the races human, whereas others are reptilian or amphibious? How does that affect their natures, how they live, what social structures they have, what they believe in, what goals or desires they have? World creation begins with such questions and expands from there.

The same cataclysmic event that created the Floating World provided the hook for the deep backstory of the world, which in turn provided the jumping-off point for the game story and overall big quest that drove the player through the game.

You'll find the game bible and story for *The Legend of Alon D'ar* at www.christymarx.info.

The largest amount of game-world creation is done for fantasy and science-fiction games, understandably. In the game bible I wrote for *Tao Feng*, I gave the game an alternate-history twist, so that rather than building an entirely new world, it was a matter of detailing how a turning point in real-life history had created a recognizable, but altered, version of the real world in which the Chinese immigrants to what would have been California in the 1840s established the independent nation of New China, spanning most of the western states.

Game Backstory

The backstory is often woven into the game-world creation. The backstory is everything that is pertinent to the game story up to the point the game begins. With *The Matrix Online*, the first three movies, comics, and animated stories made up the full backstory leading up to the point where the MMOG began. Some characters—such as Neo, Superman, Spider-Man, James Bond, King Arthur, or Robin Hood—are well enough known that there wouldn't be much need for a detailed backstory. The backstory can be full and deep, or short and concise, depending upon the need of the game. *Shadow of the Colossus*, an award-winning game, had only the sketchiest, most minimal kind of backstory that set up the goal of the game, without feeling the need to explain how or why the hero's situation or the monstrous colossi he must fight came to exist.

How much of the backstory is conveyed in the game is another issue. It may be relegated to the game manual, it may be given in the trailer to the game, or it may be woven into the game itself (for example: the player goes into a library, and there is a book containing details of the backstory that can be read if the player so chooses).

Game Story

This would be the story that drives the game by providing the overall quest/mission/goal that resolves the game, plus subquests and secondary tasks that provide the twists and turns. It should cover the locations and the NPCs that are critical to the story. It should specify and describe significant puzzles, obstacles, and other vital gameplay elements, along with what, when, and where quest objects are required, obtained, and used. It may need to specify what, when, and where cutscenes or cinematics will occur to convey pieces of the story.

The game story is intertwined with the interactive elements of the game because the story is not simply about what the goal is or achieving the goal, but *how* the player can achieve the goal. Some of these stories can be quite linear (often the case with console games), or may need to be highly nonlinear, allowing the player a multitude of possible paths for completing the game, with story components that can be accessed in a nonsequential order. The more linear the story, the more likely the company would be to use an outside writer. The more nonlinear, the more likely that the story will be written by a designer.

It's not unusual to be hired when a game is quite far along and the company has suddenly realized it needs a story or other background material. My friend Katherine Lawrence used to call this "reverse engineering," because the writer has to come into an existing game world and work backward to come up with a story that fits into it.

Character Biographies

The two categories of character biographies are the player's main character (the avatar) and the NPCs. An avatar can be a specific character or can be left deliberately vague. How much detail is needed for the avatar's biography will depend on a couple of factors: *(a)* how much detail the company wants, and *(b)* whether the avatar has dialogue in the game. An avatar who will have meaningful (not generic) dialogue in the game needs to be fleshed out well enough to establish that avatar's "voice," meaning how the personality and character traits will come out in dialogue. Will the avatar speak in a formal or casual manner (contemporary approach or based on some historical time period)? Will he use slang? If so, what kind of slang? Is he sly, droll, sarcastic, ribald, poetic, philosophical, timid, loving, hard edged? Young or old? Shaped by what sort of life experiences?

An example of avatars with bios attached would be Lara Croft *(Tomb Raider)*, Max Payne, or hard-edged spy Sam Fisher *(Splinter Cell)*. In *Shadow of the Colossus*, the player's avatar wasn't even given a specific name (he is referred to only as "Wander"), and all the details surrounding the avatar's background and relationship with other characters are left undefined and open to the player's interpretation. For most RPGs and MMOGs, it's up to the player to create the avatar from a set of character options, so the player is creating her own avatar's biography, if any.

Consequently, the bulk of the work lies in creating bios for NPCs. These might be nothing more than a few lines of description, depending on how significant the NPC is. For example, a minor NPC might have a bio that is nothing more than "Mortar Pestwhistle is a Leprechaun engineer with a sly sense of humor and an overbearing pride in his creations." In *The Legend of Alon D'Ar*, the player had three NPC companions that he could control as a group along with his own avatar, so I gave those three characters detailed bios—including their own subquests, needs, and goals—which were featured in cutscenes along with the avatar.

In the game bible I did for *Tao Feng*, besides writing the character bios, I included a paragraph on how each character would interact with or behave toward each of the other major characters. Because there were twelve major characters, that meant an additional eleven paragraphs for each character to cover these relationships. This is typical for an animation bible, but somewhat unusual for games.

Mobs/Monsters/Bosses

Most mobs or monsters are usually described by their general race characteristics in the game bible, but if a mob is important enough (a boss or a major villain), it might rate its own special description and possibly a biography.

Quests or Missions

This is another area that dovetails with design, because a quest or mission is a primary interactive element. If a game is big enough, especially something such as an MMOG, there can be a lot of work involved in coming up with and writing quests/missions. A quest needs to have an appropriate reward or payoff—such as XP, money, a quest item, vital information, or unlocking the next piece of gameplay.

Here's a list of common types of quests:

- Collecting/gathering: Asks the player to bring back an object or x number of objects—such as "Bring me a bottle of cologne" or "Bring me 5 enemy satellites" or "Bring me 15 black tulips." This could be a quest that simply involves finding and getting the object, or it might involve having to kill mobs or NPCs in order to get the object(s) as drops—such as "Bring me 10 pirate eye patches" or "Bring me 5 chimera snouts."

- Courier: Asks the player to deliver an object or message to an NPC (sometimes referred to as "FedEx quests")—such as "Take this letter to X" or "Deliver this crate of weapons to Z."

- Talk to: Asks the player to find a certain NPC and talk to him/her/it. Usually that NPC will have a quest for the player. It can also be used to "push" the player to discover a new location or zone.

- Escort/protect: Asks the player to escort an NPC from point A to point B. This will usually involve being ambushed or encountering danger of some kind while protecting the NPC.

- Fighting mobs: In most cases, tells the player to kill x number of a mob—such as "Kill 10 raging chimeras" or "Kill 20 Putrid Bandits." It can be combined with a collecting quest—such as "Kill 20 Putrid Pirates and bring me their eye patches as proof."

- Fighting elite mob: Asks the player to kill a specific boss mob or NPC, which is more powerful and dangerous than the usual kind—such as "Slay Big Badd, the pack leader of the raging chimeras" or "Destroy the planet-eating Doomship."

- Scouting: Asks the player to scout a dangerous location—as in "Scout the inside of this mine and report what sort of monsters inhabit it" or "Travel to the Sagittarius Sector and determine whether there are enemy ships in the sector."

- Rescuing/setting free: Asks the player to rescue an NPC from a dire situation. This can be similar to an escort quest if it involves helping the NPC get out of the location. Or it might involve bringing something to the NPC instead (such as a potion to cure a mortal wound). A variation on this is completing a task or bringing a quest object that will free an NPC from some form of imprisonment.

- Finding person or object: Asks the player to locate an NPC or game item, which may or may not involve doing anything with them or bringing them back—such as "My husband left for Nasty Valley days ago and hasn't returned. Please find out what happened to him." The player could end up talking to the husband to resolve the quest, or might find the husband's bones and have to return with this info (or a token found on the body) to the original quest giver.

- Capture person or object: Asks the player to capture an NPC, mob, or object, rather than kill or destroy it—as in "Take this rune and use it to enchant a raging chimera, then lead it back here to me" or "Capture the supply depot."

- Unraveling clues: Gives the player clues to unravel some sort of mystery. This is often used with a linked quest (see below).

- Chained, linked: Many quests are chained together so that the first quest leads to a second related quest, which leads to a third related quest, and so on. Any of the above quest types (or others not listed here) can be combined in a chain of quests. Usually the tasks become more difficult as the chain progresses.

Cutscenes and Cinematics

These are more commonly used in the linear types of games and can serve more than one purpose. Most cutscenes/cinematics are used to reveal key pieces of the story and to advance the story for the player. They can have an emotional payoff, or they can be bald chunks of data. They can also be used to validate the player for accomplishing something special (a pat-on-the-back "way to go!" moment).

You will want to have a discussion up front with the producer or designer about what the game engine can or can't do in creating the cutscenes/cinematics. A lot of times, there will be "easy" and "hard" ways to do the scene in the engine. For example, changing the camera angle in the middle of the scene could be either easy or incredibly hard, depending on the engine design. Another example: on one PS2 game, I was initially told that the characters wouldn't be able to move their lips, let along do lip-synching. With that in mind, I carefully wrote the scenes using animation-writing techniques to minimize the amount of time the camera lingered on a character's face, such as using over-the-shoulder shots for the speaking character rather than looking at the speaking character from the front.

Most frequently, cutscenes/cinematics are noninteractive. Control of the game is taken away from the player, who is then expected to stand and watch the scene unfold. A wise designer will allow the player to click past the cutscene/cinematic if he doesn't feel like following the story thread.

In *Half-Life 2*, a clever approach was taken in which the cutscenes/cinematics would play out inside an enclosed environment so that the player couldn't conveniently leave right away, but the player was allowed to continue interacting with the environment. This gave the player the option to do something else in the location, and either ignore the scene or pay attention to it if she wished. There are occasionally minicinematics in *World of Warcraft* where a short scene plays out between a couple of NPCs, with the player free to watch or move on to another part of the game (in this case, however, the cinematics don't affect an overall game story).

The important thing to remember about cutscenes/cinematics is that they should be *short*—preferably one to three pages in a standard live-action-script format, slightly more if written in an animation-script format. Again, apply the general rules of animation writing. Keep the dialogue minimal, strong, and pithy.

If you're writing the story that includes indications for the cutscenes/cinematics, there are two things to bear in mind as you create the story:

- There is probably a budget and time limit to how many cutscenes the developers can put into the game, so determine ahead of time what the limit is. Craft the story so that you could lose two to three cutscenes should there be a cut in the schedule or budget.

- Be careful not to craft a story that requires big chunks of exposition or too much explanation of events in the cutscenes. Try to limit each cutscene to revealing *one* key piece of story, maybe two, but not three or four. Cutscenes need to be tiny nuggets of story, not big chunks of exposition.

You'll find a few examples of cinematics from *The Legend of Alon D'ar* at www. christymarx.info.

Dialogue

Setting aside cutscenes/cinematics, 99 percent of dialogue you might be hired to write will be for NPCs. Common types of dialogue include the following:

- Giving quests/missions.
- Giving information, training, directions (to a location).
- Giving hints: "Did you go to Sagittarius Sector yet?"
- Generic greetings: "Hi, how ya doing?"
- Generic threats: "Die, mangy cur!"
- Generic default replies: "I don't know what to do with that."
- Generic vendors (selling and buying game items): "Buy from me. I'll give you such a deal."
- Adding flavor: for example, a storyteller who relates tales that may not be significant to the story, but adds general flavor to the background material.

You'll want to know up front whether the dialogue will be done as text or as voice. Some games will combine the two and play audio while also showing the dialogue as text. Both ways present you with limitations in terms of length, so once again apply the rules of animation writing—keep it short and pithy. If it's text, you could potentially have a more specific limitation, such as a certain number of characters (letters) and spaces per speech so that it doesn't occupy too large a balloon or dialogue box when on the screen.

Because voice is expensive, time-consuming, and creates large sound files, it tends to be used sparingly. You should read audio dialogue out loud to yourself to make sure it's easy to say and sounds right when spoken. Better yet, record yourself speaking the lines and play them back to yourself. A line that looks fine in text can sometimes be a clunker when spoken out loud. Saying the lines out loud will call your attention to speeches or sentences that are too long.

If the developer has devised specific methods of integrating dialogue into the game, you may be required to learn a special piece of software. This method can be different for each company, so you need to be good at adapting to new software. And because of this, there is nothing like a standard format. However, it is a common practice to put game dialogue into a TV/film-script format when it's being given to actors for recording.

Writing game dialogue can involve two of the game-design elements described in Chapter 9: variables and choice.

Variables

The variables that affect dialogue depend upon the programming "flags" that need to be checked before the correct piece of dialogue is fed to the player. These flags are conditions the game code looks for. This gets back to the "*If this, then this* . . ." formula. "*If* this condition exists, *then* this dialogue is given." There can be an infinite number of such conditions, but here are some of the most common ones:

- What level is the player?
- Is the player on a certain quest?
- Is the player incomplete on the quest?
- Has the player completed the quest?
- Does the player have a certain game item or quest object?
- If buying something, does the player have enough money?
- Has the player spoken to the NPC before?
- Has the player spoken to some other NPC yet?
- Does the player belong to a certain race or class?
- Does the player have a race or class bias in relation to the NPC (for example, friendly, neutral, hostile)?
- Has the player been to a certain location yet?
- Has the player done a specific action yet?

There might be only one variable/condition tied to a piece of dialogue, or there could be two or several in combination—or there could be none, of course. Some games don't have these complexities of dialogue. But for those that do, it will be vital to you as the writer to have a full and detailed understanding of what variables/conditions will affect the dialogue, so that you can tailor the dialogue accordingly.

You'll need to be good at juggling these variables in your head and making sure one piece of dialogue doesn't contradict another, especially if they can be accessed in a nonsequential manner.

For example, an NPC could have dialogue that pertains to a particular quest that can be given only once the player is level 10, and only if the player is of the warrior class, but any player is free to talk to the NPC at any time. The variables and attendant dialogue might look something like this:

;This NPC is just there to give the player hints about the Sagittarius quest if the player is a warrior, or to push the player to another zone if not a warrior.

//if player is a NOT a WARRIOR:

> NPC
> I hear there's a guy in the Betelgeuse sector that's
> looking for somebody like you.

//if player is a WARRIOR and is LESSER THAN level 10, and has NOT spoken to the NPC before:

> NPC
> You've got the look of someone who's hunting for
> trouble. Get some more experience under your belt,
> and I might help you with that.

//if player is a WARRIOR and is LESSER THAN level 10 and has spoken to the NPC once or more before:

> NPC
> You're too green to bother with. Get yourself more
> experience before you bother me again.

//if player is a WARRIOR and IS level 10 or more and does NOT have the Sagittarius quest:

> NPC
> You look like someone in need of a job. Talk to
> Larry the Leech over there, if you're up to risking
> your neck.

//if player is a WARRIOR and IS level 10 or more and does NOT have the Sagittarius quest and has spoken to the NPC once or more before:

> NPC
> Do I look like I have nothing better to do than give
> advice?

//if player has the Sagittarius quest and has NOT spoken to the NPC before:

> NPC
> So you're the Leech's new sucker . . . ah, I mean
> recruit. Good luck to ya.

//if player has the Sagittarius quest and has spoken to the NPC once before:

> NPC
> Why are you hanging around here? Aren't you
> supposed to be in the Sagittarius sector?

//if player has the Sagittarius quest and has spoken to the NPC twice or more before:

> NPC
> What do you want, a medal? Get a move on.

//if player has COMPLETED the Sagittarius quest and spoke to the NPC BEFORE taking the quest:

> NPC
> So you worked for the Leech and got out in one
> piece. I'm impressed. I'll spread the word that you
> can be trusted.

//if player has COMPLETED the Sagittarius quest and has NOT spoken to the NPC before, use any one of the following dialogues chosen at random:

> NPC
> Nice day, if we don't get sucked into a black hole.

> NPC
> Something you want?

> NPC
> What do you want, an autograph? Move along.

Hopefully, what you have noticed about that example is that the more variables the game design allows in the NPC dialogue, the more specific the dialogue can become (making the game feel "smarter"), but it also increases the amount of both coding and dialogue writing that has to be done. In that short example, there are a dozen or more conditions that a programmer has to code (including flags that must be *created* by talking to that NPC), which is one reason for a push to keep game dialogue limited. In game design, there is a constant tension between wanting to make a game feel smart and more aware of exactly what the player is doing vs. the need to keep the writing and programming from getting out of control.

One more thing about the example above—it's one-sided and nonbranching. Only the NPC has lines, assumedly initiated by the player clicking on the NPC, and there is no input of player dialogue. It's minimally interactive because the player can't affect it and can't do anything other than read or hear it. Once you go the extra step of adding player dialogue, you move into the area of player choice and branching dialogue.

Choice

The biggest mistake a non–game writer tends to make is assuming that game dialogue always consists of simple branching-dialogue trees. Many games avoid using branching dialogue,

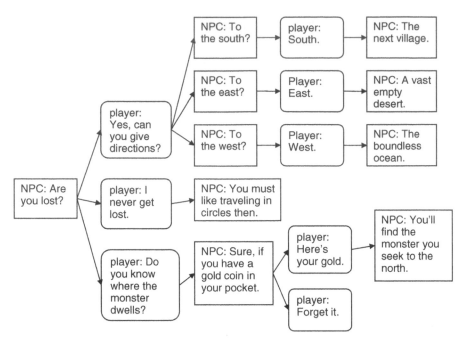

Figure 10.1
Example of branching dialogue.

or have adapted it to be more variable. However, because you could encounter some form of it, it's a good idea to understand the basics as well as the pitfalls. The trick with branching forms of dialogue (fig. 10.1) is to keep the dialogue from branching out of control. At some point, each branch has to come to an end or become a dead end, or the branches could become infinite. Notice from this simple example how quickly branches can proliferate.

In the above example, one branch dead-ends pretty quickly. One branch will lead to useful data about a particular direction, but only if the player pays for it. But the remaining branches allow the player to deduce the right direction without paying (assuming the player has the same dialogue options to choose from each time he talks to the NPC).

The other pitfall to avoid is creating branches that don't serve a real purpose and create only an illusion of choice. You would never, for example, want to do this (fig. 10.2).

That's a waste of the player's time—and frustrating to boot. Every branch and each dialogue option should have a purpose, or it shouldn't be there. At the same time, each branch has to end somewhere, with the player feeling that taking the branch was worth it—either in getting useful info, receiving something (reward), opening up an option to do something (such as buy, sell, or trade), getting backstory flavor, or, at the very least, being given something amusing (a joke or insult).

Bear in mind that branching dialogue will be further complicated by the same types of variables and conditions as nonbranching dialogue. On one MMOG, we wrote branching dialogues for numerous variables (checking for player level, phase of the game, what step in a quest the player had reached, whether a reward was due, and so forth), with some of the branches linking to other files of branching dialogue with more variables and conditions. In more-complex cases, we had up to six interconnected files of complex dialogue trees that linked via special branches from a main file.

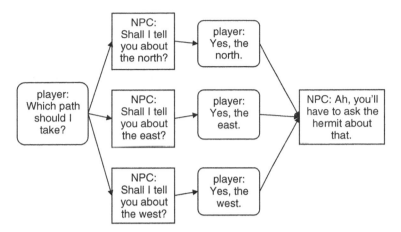

Figure 10.2
Example of branching dialogue with false branches.

Another variable that could come up in some games is the race or class bias that could be attached to both the NPC and the player. Being friendly, neutral, or hostile toward a particular race or class could require different dialogues to account for the bias.

In summary, writing dialogue can range from fairly simple to intensely complex, but one thing remains the same—you must be able to write clever, compelling, useful, and entertaining dialogue limited to a few sentences at a time.

Slang and Fantasy Language

You will find this section in the Animation chapters, but it bears repeating here.

Using contemporary slang will make you sound hip, but will also quickly date the game. Many clever writers get around this by inventing slang that doesn't really exist, but sounds appropriate for the genre. This is even more useful when dealing with a futuristic or science-fiction game where you don't want modern slang to sound out of place or archaic . . . unless that's by deliberate intent.

If you're going to use foreign slang, *do your homework!* It's embarrassing to hear or read slang—say, for a contemporary Australian—that hasn't been used for twenty years except as a joke.

Then there's fantasy. When writing a pure fantasy game, it's easy to forget how modern some of our phrases are. "Fast as lightning" is fine, but "faster than a bullet" is a problem if your characters use only swords. Unless you're writing a total parody, you don't want to hear a medieval knight say, "Wow, cool." Be careful to avoid anachronistic slang.

I came up with the Marx Fantasy Dialogue Scale to differentiate the various ways in which fantasy dialogue could be spoken, ranging from colloquial/modern (No. 1) to High Epic/Poetic (No. 5). Here's an example:

1. He doesn't know what he's doing.

2. He does not know what he is doing.

3. He does not know what he does.

4. He knows not what he does.

5. He knows not what his purpose is, for confusion lies heavy upon him.

You would rarely want to use No. 5, because it's wordy and sounds least natural to modern ears. Using purely colloquial language can sound jarring in some fantasy settings. Creating the right fantasy dialogue depends a great deal on how you use contractions, the word arrangement and sentence structure, and the vocabulary you employ.

In-Game Text

This is written material the player might come across in the game. One example mentioned previously is finding books that can be opened and read. Other examples would be letters, journals, dispatches, notes, briefings, decrypted code, and other such items that can be found or are given to the player as part of a quest. It might be text that appears on a monitor, PDA, or other communication device that the player uses in the game.

Technical Material or Game Manual

In addition to the game itself, there is writing that needs to be done to explain to the player how the game works and other technical-writing needs. When I was making adventure games for Sierra On-Line, I wrote the game book that came with the game. The book gave backstory and other general information about the game and interface. I also wrote the "hint book," a separate book that the players could consult for hints when they felt stuck or unable to progress.

You could be asked to write other game-related material that falls outside the game—such as compiling a list of quest objects and where they're found, a chronology of quests, a walkthrough, and so on.

Web Site and Promotional Materials

Most games have a Web site to help promote the game and create a sense of community for it. You could be hired to write material—of either a technical nature or purely promotional—for the Web site, or you could be hired to write marketing material for other media.

For example, for *The Matrix Online*, I was hired to take the brief descriptions of the many skills and abilities the player could learn in the game and "*Matrix*-ize" them, meaning rewrite them in a way that would fit with how data are downloaded into someone's brain in the *Matrix* movies. Those descriptions were intended as additional material for the game's Web site. On another game, I was asked to recraft the game bible into a shorter version that could be used by the marketing people in PR releases.

Beyond the Basics (Advice, Tips, and Tricks)

Some writers who have expressed an interest in writing for games have worried about what level of technical skill they need to have, in terms of knowing programming or special software.

Because each company can have its own approach, there isn't any particular software to learn ahead of time, but—and this is a big but—you should be technically inclined and able to quickly learn new pieces of software. Obviously, you'll need to know one of the major word-processing programs, such as Microsoft Word. Microsoft Excel is another program that is heavily used in the business, and though it doesn't relate directly to writing, it would be useful to have some familiarity with Excel.

You don't need to know programming or be able to write code. However, you could potentially be asked to incorporate bits of code, so it doesn't hurt to pick up whatever basics you can along the way. If you can write some basic HTML or use Flash, you have taken a good step toward proving that you can handle a basic scripting language. If a company wants you to incorporate bits of code, they'll provide you with the necessary training or instructions. They won't expect you to come in the door knowing it.

Version Control

You need to have good organizational skills and the means to track the many versions and variations of the work you do. It will be vital to have good communication with the producer, product manager, or senior/lead designer (whoever the point person is) on how to name your narrative or dialogue game files. If you're writing only a game bible, this may not be as crucial. But if you're writing numerous files, such as dialogue for lots of NPCs or a large batch of missions, it is absolutely crucial.

Either they or you need to establish precisely what identifiers will quickly and easily tell anyone working on the game what that file is about, what it attaches to, what NPC or zone it belongs to, and so forth. Additionally, there must be an identifier (such as a date) that will immediately indicate which is the most current, latest, and/or approved version of the file.

Without careful version control, you end up in the hell of version confusion, with no one quite sure which is the latest or approved version, or what goes where in the game. Some companies have "data wranglers," whose job it is to oversee such assets and make sure there's a workable system of asset identification and version control.

Once you plunge into a game-writing project, make sure to find out whom to deal with and what system they want to use for version control.

Recording Dialogue

If you write game dialogue that will be recorded by actors, the chance is slim, though not impossible, that you'll be asked to attend the recording sessions. If you do get the chance to attend, you should go for it. As the writer, your input to the voice director and actors could be invaluable, because you will know better than anyone else what the context is and what the emotional tone of the dialogue should be. Plus, it's a good way for you to learn what works or doesn't work in spoken dialogue.

Because that *is* rare, you should be aware that the overwhelming majority of the time, actors will record their lines alone, not in the presence of other actors. A game that has a superbig budget and uses big-name movie actors might go the extra step (and considerable expense) of getting their big names together at the same time in a recording studio so they deliver their lines to one another in a more natural way. That would be the exception.

Instead, what you have are actors with sheets of paper that usually show only their lines. If they're really lucky, the actors might be given a full script so they can see what other characters are saying, but you can't count on that. A voice director will feed other lines to the actors (if it's back-and-forth dialogue), so that the actors at least have something to respond to. And hopefully, above the line of dialogue, there will be a line or two of additional information that gives some idea of the situation or circumstance in which the line is delivered. Though if you look at the sample presented earlier in this chapter, the descriptions of the game variables may not provide the actors with much help. A good actor will draw the meaning out of the lines, but some lines may not by themselves clue the actor in to how the dialogue should be delivered.

For that reason, I recommend the free use of parentheticals when writing audio game dialogue. If you've read the Animation chapters or are familiar with scriptwriting, you know what this means. For those who don't, parentheticals are one or two words in parentheses beneath the character's name, indicating the emotional tone or attitude for the line.

Consider this line:

NPC
You don't want to go there.

Imagine how many different ways a line like that could be delivered, if the actor had no indication of what to do with it. If you include a parenthetical, you greatly increase the odds that the line will be recorded in the emotional tone you intended.

Here are some possibilities:

NPC
(friendly concern)
You don't want to go there.

NPC
(condescending)
You don't want to go there.

NPC
(afraid)
You don't want to go there.

NPC
(impatient)
You don't want to go there.

NPC
(angry, stern)
You don't want to go there.

NPC
(cool, indifferent)
You don't want to go there.

This is not to say that you should overdo the use of parentheticals. Limit them to the pieces of dialogue that could be interpreted in more than one way.

One more item that is tremendously useful for a recording session is to include along with the recording script a paragraph or two of background information about each character. That way, if the actors haven't been provided with other information beforehand, they will at least have something that fills them in on the nature of the characters they're portraying.

Game Bible, Game Story, and Cinematic Samples

You will find the game bible, game story, and examples of cinematics that I wrote for a PS2 action RPG titled *The Legend of Alon D'ar* available to read and study at www.christymarx.info. The developer was Stormfront Studios, and the publisher was Ubisoft.

CHAPTER 11

Breaking and Entering

This was the most challenging chapter of the book to write. Although it's difficult to break into any creative field, and difficult enough to break into animation or comics, it was far more challenging for me to come up with cogent, useful advice for breaking into game writing. The advice in this chapter is culled from a large pool of game producers, designers, developers, and writers to supplement my personal experience. Given the rapid pace at which videogames and the videogame market evolves, my advice is subject to change at any time.

There's one especially pesky question that is asked all the time, so let's get it out of the way and move on.

The $64,000 Question

The question usually comes framed something like this: "I have a great idea for a game! How do I sell it to a game company?"

The short answer is—you don't. Game companies do not buy game ideas from outside people. They don't need to. That's why they have designers working for them, or why designers establish their own companies (for example, Sid Meier, cofounder of Firaxis Games, creator of the *Civilization* game series; and Will Wright, cofounder of Maxis Software, creator of *SimCity* and *The Sims*).

This leaves you with three choices:

- Work your way up from within and try to get the company to do your idea, understanding that you will have to give the company ownership of the idea.

- Make it yourself. This would require creating a prototype or demo (demonstration) of your proposed game, which you could then show to game companies or venture capital investors in the hope that they'll fund you to a full game. You would need to have the necessary programmers and artists to carry this out, or be so incredibly talented that you can do it yourself. There is some do-it-yourself game-creation software out there, such as DarkBASIC, if you have the inclination to master it, but this software provides only the programming end of the equation. You would need additional art software to add to it. If you have the courage and energy to go this route, you'll need to find some books or courses on how to make games, which is way beyond the bounds of this book. One more alternative is software from online casual-games company PopCap. They offer free casual-game-creation software via their PopCap Developer Program (http://developer.popcap.com). If PopCap is impressed enough with the game you create, they may publish it.

- Develop an intellectual property in some other format (book, comic book, movie, brand name, and so on) that you own so that you can sell the rights to a game company. If you can be the creator and owner of an IP, you will be in a position of power far better than being a designer. A classic example is Marc Ecko, a young hip-hop artist who created a multimillion-dollar line of clothes, shoes, watches, and accessories, then turned his brand-name power into a videogame.

If you come from a teaching or educational background with a good educational résumé, you might have some luck breaking into educational children's games (sometimes referred to as edutainment) as a consultant. Such games are more linear and focused on the teaching elements. It's a rather specialized area of game development, and many of the educational-game companies have teaching experts on staff or as consultants. This is to ensure that the games follow the proper educational guidelines, especially if the company wants to sell them to schools. You should contact the game companies that make educational games, and put yourself forward as a consultant. From that position, you can learn more about creating a game and perhaps eventually move into designing them.

Publishers and Developers

When sorting out how to break in, it's important to have a grasp on the business structure of game development. Making a game is one thing; having the know-how or resources to handle production, sales, promotion, and distribution is another. In the 1980s, some game companies did everything: created the game; had an art department that created covers, game booklets, ads, posters, fan magazine, and so on; had a production line where the disks were copied, packed into boxes, and shipped; and had sales reps who sold the games to stores. Rarely would a game developer now do all these things, especially the production end. They simply can't afford to.

The business structure has sorted itself out in tiers of publishers and developers. Generally speaking, the development studios create the actual game, and the publisher handles everything else—production, marketing/promotion, sales, distribution, inventory. This may vary according to the type of deal that is worked out between publisher and developer, and it can apply to any kind of game—PC, console, or MMOG.

The tiers look like this:

- Publishers/Platform Owners: Sony, Microsoft, and Nintendo are in a class by themselves because they are not only enormous publishers, they are the companies that invent and sell the hardware platforms on which console games are played—that is, PlayStation, Xbox, and Wii. They license to developer studios the rights to develop games for their platforms. They can control development by funding games to be made solely for their respective platforms.

- Publishers: The big-name publishers are companies such as EA (Electronic Arts) and Ubisoft, plus the games-publishing arms of major entertainment studios such as Buena Vista Games (Disney), Vivendi Universal Games, Warner Bros., and LucasArts. Other substantial publishers include Take-Two Interactive, THQ, Midway Games, and Activision. Overseas publishers include Capcom (Japan), Namco (Japan), NCsoft (South Korea), Webzen (South Korea), Atari/Infogrames Entertainment (France), 1C Company (Russia), SCI Entertainment Group (United Kingdom), and CDV (Germany).

- Internal (in-house) developers: These are usually independent or external development studios that were acquired by a publisher and have become subsidiaries run by the publisher. It's easier to acquire an existing development studio than to build one from scratch. This allows a publisher more control over the development process than going to an external developer.

- External (third-party) developers: These studios either make their own games and make deals with publishers to distribute them, or they're hired to make a game based on some project or property controlled by the publisher.

This publisher/developer structure affects writers in three ways: (*a*) where and how you look for work, (*b*) how much you are paid, and (*c*) whether the project makes it to completion.

One of the unhappy realities of game development is that many games don't make it all the way through the development process to be released. Games can be canceled for any number of reasons, most commonly because the entity funding the game loses confidence in the project and decides not to keep throwing money at it.

Ellen Guon Beeman, a highly experienced game producer with more than a dozen produced games on her credits, summed up the status of game-project development as a food chain. At the bottom of the food chain are those mostly likely to lose out in the event of a budget reduction or game cancellation, moving up the food chain to those least likely to be cut.

The food chain is also cyclical. Historically, the game publishers have tended to shift every few years between funding in-house projects and using third-party (external) developers. In-house projects are generally more expensive, but the publisher can maintain more creative control. Third-party developers often (but not always) are less expensive, and the publisher can more easily cancel their projects in the event of a budget cutback.

At the moment, it looks like this in the game industry:

- The top of the food chain is made up of a publisher's internally developed projects. These are the least likely to be cut off if the publisher decides it's necessary to trim budgets—unless the publisher is a publicly traded company that wants to cut personnel to bump up their stock price. (It's always advisable to track your publisher's stock-price fluctuations.)

- Next down are internal producers who manage external projects, meaning a publisher's salaried producer who shepherds an external project to completion. If the publisher needs to cut budgets, guess who is usually going to get hit first?

- Next down are the external developers themselves. See the point above.

- At the bottom are the subcontractors (say, for example, contract writers) who work for the external developers.

Does this mean you should work only for publishers or internal studios rather than independents? Not at all. It does mean that when accepting work, you should be aware of how well established a studio is. Have they been around for a while? Have they produced a number of successful games? If not, do the people in charge have experience and good credentials in the business? Who is their publisher? For what platform(s) will the game be made? For console games in particular, putting out versions of the game for more than one platform is an indication that this game is a big deal, and therefore less likely to be canceled. If it's made for only one platform, is that because the studio has an exclusive deal with that platform publisher? Don't be afraid to research the studio or company before committing. If anything about the studio seems dubious, you will need to weigh how badly you want the work vs. how sure you are they will be able to pay you for it.

Looking for Work: Freelance or Employee

The first major decision you need to make is whether you want to have a career as a full-time employee at a game company, or as a contract writer (freelance) working for a variety of companies.

The Employee Track

As an employee, you will have a steady paycheck while you learn and hone your ability as a game writer, but it means dedicating yourself to that one type of writing full-time. Once you've built up a track record as a game writer, and have a network of contacts in the business, you'll be in a better position to try going freelance, if that appeals to you.

There aren't many companies that hire a full-time writer to be on staff. Publishers are less likely to make that kind of hire, because they primarily oversee the work done by developers. Consequently, your focus will be on developer studios, and even more precisely, on studios that create the types of games that might call for a full-time writer on staff.

MMOGs require the largest amount of ongoing content creation, so studios that create MMOGs are the best places to start the search. After that, you would need to research studios that create RPGs, FPSs, adventure, action, or other story-driven games.

Because the notion of hiring a full-time writer is fairly new, there are no established rules for the job. For an MMOG, they may post a job for a writer, content designer, or writer/designer because the writer will probably also be involved in creating quests or missions. Consequently, you should familiarize yourself with MMOGs and the other story-driven types of games, so that you have a sense of the design issues. At least one MMOG developer that frequently hires writers requires applicants to create a game-writing sample using their proprietary module-creation system. You must be technically prepared to learn, understand, and use their software—which is, of course, based on their game. Unfortunately, learning one piece of proprietary software doesn't mean you can use that precise knowledge anywhere else, because each company's software will be different, but it does show that you are capable of learning such software.

Today, there are more game design courses being offered in colleges, but still very few courses that deal specifically with game writing. A few schools touch upon game writing via game design courses or other media courses. You will find a sampling of schools in the Resources section.

However, good writing is good writing, so you should have education or training that shows you can write engaging stories with compelling characters. Game writers have debated whether a liberal-arts degree is sufficient, whether journalism is valid, and what other forms of writing best prepare a writer to get work in games. There is no consensus.

My recommendation is to study film and TV scriptwriting. These are the forms most closely associated with what you might do for a game company. Get any kind of writing you can under your belt. Write for paper-based RPGs. Write reviews and articles for game magazines or online game sites. Write a good script of any kind (screenplay, teleplay) that can serve as a sample of your work. It's hard to write a useful game-writing sample, because each game and each studio can have such different needs or expectations, but any potential employer will know how to read a teleplay or screenplay or short story. Any type of published/produced work — book, short story, script — will give you credibility.

With more and more games being based on existing properties — such as movies, TV series, and comics — you may also need to be familiar with those properties. One developer that was looking for writers asked the applicants to create a short sample to demonstrate that they could match the tone of the well-known TV property on which the game was based, as well as the manner in which the main characters spoke. The developer was appalled at how many applicants turned in utterly generic samples that completely lacked any flavor of the property, as though all game characters came from some bland cookie-cutter mold. Other applicants were openly scornful of the notion that games needed story or character development!

These are really great ways *not* to get hired as a game writer.

Your résumé should emphasize your education, training, and other writing experience, especially anything you've done that relates to games or multimedia work. Be sure to mention any awards or honors you've gotten for your work.

For the most part when applying for a full-time job, you'll be dealing with someone in the Human Resources (HR) Department. However, you should do the same kind of networking a freelancer would do. Making the right connection inside a company could be the break you need to get in the door. Read the following section to get more details on networking.

The Freelance Track

About the only way to establish yourself as a contract writer is to have experience and credits in another area of writing. In other words, you should already be a professional writer. Because contract game-writing work is scarce and hard to get, you are best advised to consider it as one of several arenas in which you can work rather than the only one. It is extremely difficult to work full-time or even most of the time solely as a contract game writer.

Developers that produce MMOGs, RPGs, FPSs, action, adventure, and other story-driven games are the most likely to want the services of a writer. Those that don't want to keep a full-time writer on staff will instead look for contract writers.

Looking for contract work requires having professional credits and solid writing samples. Set up your game-writing résumé to emphasize your writing strengths, especially anything that relates to games. If you have game-writing credits along with other types of writing, be sure to place the game-writing credits first on the résumé to call attention to them.

Note that if you are someone with both game-design and game-writing credits, you need to create two separate résumés — one strictly for finding design work, and one strictly for writing work. Once you're in with a company, you can demonstrate your various talents, but you really want them to be clear on who you are and what specific role they're hiring you for.

However, you will rarely get contract work on the basis of a résumé alone. Most producers don't know where to go to find the kind of writer they need—consequently, they'll go for a known name, whether it's known because of previous work the writer has done (on other games or in other media), known via a personal recommendation from a colleague (very important), or known because the producer is already acquainted with the writer in one way or another. Bob Bates, legendary game designer and writer, put it this way: "Producers are people with problems, and you want to be the solution to their problem." The hard part is making a producer aware that you are an existing solution.

Constant, consistent networking is vital to finding contract work. This requires a variety of approaches, including, but not limited to:

- Be involved in the IGDA (International Game Developers Association) community (consider serving on committees).

- Become a speaker for a lecture, workshop, or seminar for the GDC (Game Developers Conference).

- Take part in e-mail lists with other developers and writers (another benefit of belonging to the IGDA).

- Write articles about writing and game writing for whatever outlet you can (newspapers, magazines, Web sites, e-zines, blogs, and so on).

- Maintain a useful, informative personal Web site or blog that gives your credits, and have samples of your work available on the site. For the Internet search engines, include search tags such as game writer, narrative designer, content designer, and story designer.

- Attend every conference and trade show that you can, and schmooze like crazy (more info on conferences and trade shows later in this chapter).

- Speak at other conferences and trade shows (though GDC is always the best).

There are certain methods that are across-the-board *not* recommended, and it's good to know about those as well. At all costs, do not:

- Send out generic e-mail to any and all developers you can track down. They will treat you as spam, with everything that implies. Don't e-mail anyone at a developer studio or publisher unless you have already made contact with them so that they will know who you are and be receptive to your e-mail, or you're answering an on-line job posting in which you're directed to send email to their HR department.

- Call producers, designers, or other people at the studio or publisher. They are insanely busy most of the time, and the last thing they want is a phone call from an unknown (and therefore unwanted) person looking for work. Call only if you have previously made contact, and they have positively indicated that you can or should call.

- Send out flashy brochures that cost a lot to produce and mail, but can end up tossed into a forgotten file in some Human Resources office. I speak from personal experience here, having once tried this approach. I sent out hundreds of such brochures—which led to exactly no response, except for two postcards with a generic "Thank you for your interest in our company."

Sarah W. Stocker, producer extraordinaire, has worked as a game writer, game designer, and producer at a major independent developer for fourteen years; as an executive producer of mobile games; and most currently as a senior producer at Sony. She shares some exceptionally useful tips about searching for game writing.

Sarah points out that the need for writers, plus where and how writers are hired, also depends upon the budget and platform of the project. Here is a summary of her advice on that topic:

- Next-generation console games: At the time this book is being written, the industry is in what it calls a "transition year" because the major console makers are in the process of introducing their new, improved, and totally glitzy-awesome versions of their game consoles. The PS3 supersedes the PS2, the Xbox 360 supersedes the Xbox, and so forth. Games made for next-generation consoles are the equivalent of the blockbuster tent-pole summer movie, the one that got the megamillion budget and the big, big-name stars. The budgets for these games likewise reach into the tens of millions. Consequently, these are "star" games, and the company is going to be very selective about the writer to whom they entrust a megamillion-dollar project. The superior graphics and processing power of next-gen games raises the bar for quality storytelling to match. What producers on these games are looking for is credibility, and they will go for the writer who has the kind of credits that provides them with that credibility.

  The qualities these producers are looking for go beyond raw talent and creativity. They are looking for experience, professionalism, a proven ability to produce, and someone who knows how to work in a collaborative medium. This is where the writer with a name in movies or TV is most likely to be hired, especially if that writer happened to work on the original property on which such a game was based. These producers will be open to a writer with a track record of working on best-selling or critically acclaimed games. A name novelist with credits in the same genre as the game might also be hired to develop the story, though probably not for the more interactive elements of the writing.

- Last-generation console games: There are still plenty of games being made for the existing models of consoles (the ones being replaced by the next generation), but at lower budgets and with less stress on having to get a top name. Although producers of these games are equally concerned with having excellent content, the budget risk is lower, allowing them to take more risks with talent. These games provide a better chance for a writer to break in.

- MMOGs: As stated elsewhere, they have enormous writing demands, and some of them can have ten to fifteen writers working on them. Producers hiring for an MMOG would likely look for a writer with RPG or game-writing background, and would be thrilled if the writer had TV writing on top of it. They might also consider a novelist to do the story.

- PC: Huge numbers of PC games are still being made, so the opportunities for writing are out there. Given the many different genres and types of PC games, you should focus on the types that interest you the most.

- Casual games: This market is exploding. Many of these games are free downloads, and although there isn't a lot of writing in these games at the moment, there is at least some. This could be an easier way for someone without a lot of credits to break in, especially if you're willing to work for less money.

- Mobile games: This is another expanding market. Producers of mobile games use writers to create story and take the text that is written in-house by the company and rewrite it. This is short, limited writing (due to the limitations of mobile phones and handheld units), so it's not big money. Once again, though, this might be a way to break into the interactive field.

In contrast to my flashy brochures that didn't work, there is a type of mailed presentation that Sarah Stocker thinks is a good approach. She recommends an excellent, professional-looking presentation package that consists of the following:

- A short, well-written cover letter on a letterhead and personalized to the producer (*not* a generic letter)—meaning that you should mention or compliment the producer on his or her latest game, or at least on the company's games. The letter should emphasize your strengths and what type of writing you could best contribute.

- Your résumé

- *Short* samples of your writing. Note the emphasis on *short* samples. Although producers will appreciate the credibility of a published novel, they won't necessarily have time to read it. That's why sending a script is a better choice. The script could be a spec rather than something that has been produced, but if you have a produced script, so much the better. The producer will be looking for storytelling that shows the writer has a sense of visual direction, character development, and good dialogue. Although animation scripts don't have the same level of credibility as live action, one thing that an animation script shows is the writer's ability to storyboard a script. It's acceptable to include samples of game-writing work if they're in an easy-to-read format, but generally a producer will be more interested in a TV or movie script. A short story would also be acceptable, provided it demonstrates a cinematic sense of storytelling.

Where to Network

Various conferences and trade shows deal with games and electronic entertainment. For writers, it comes down to one that is absolutely vital, the Game Developers Conference (http://www.gdconf.com), which is held in March in San Jose, California. GDC describes itself as the official trade event "by game developers for developers" of computer, console, mobile, arcade, online games, and location-based entertainment.

GDC consists of an expo hall and job fair, plus workshops, lectures, and seminars covering all aspects of making games. It is the single most important event to attend in order to network and look for work. Unfortunately, doing the entire conference is highly expensive. As an alternative, go for an expo pass so that you can access the job fair and expo. Most companies have booths with HR people at the job fair. This is most useful if you're looking for an employee situation, not so useful for contract work.

For a contract writer, it's best to send in your résumé and samples ahead of time, then attempt to arrange follow-up meetings with someone at GDC. This gives the producer time to check out your credits and determine whether a meeting would be a good idea. Most people are solidly booked by the time they get to GDC, so spur-of-the-moment meetings just aren't going to happen.

Your strongest position for attending GDC is as a speaker. Each year, GDC invites people to submit proposals for workshops, lectures, and seminars. If your proposal is accepted, you will attend GDC free in exchange for being a speaker, with the extra benefit of a lot of free publicity. The conference lists its requirements for speaker submissions on the GDC Web site sometime in the summer for the conference the following March.

Another route for those on a tight budget to get in free is to volunteer as a conference associate (http://www.gdconf.com/register/caregistration.htm). As a CA, you get free entry in exchange for doing such work as guarding doors, monitoring conference sessions, checking badges at meals and special events, stuffing conference bags, and performing data entry.

In previous years, the monster trade show was E^3, which stands for Electronic Entertainment Expo. After the E^3 of 2006, the magnitude and expense of the show was no longer proving as effective as some of the major exhibitors desired, consequently at the time this book went to press, E^3 put out this announcement: "To better address the needs of today's global computer and videogame industry, the 2007 Electronic Entertainment Expo (E3Expo) is evolving into a more intimate event focused on targeted, personalized meetings and activities...."

What E^3 wasn't a great place to go job hunting, it had some usefulness as a place to network, set up meetings (in advance) and get a feel for what was happening in the business. How this "evolution" will affect the use of the show for writers, I can't say, but you'll want to keep an eye on it.

A more recent conference is the Game Writers Conference (http://www.gamewriters-conference.com). It's held in September in Austin, Texas, and focuses specifically on game writing.

For additional trade-show links and information, look at the GDC Web site and regularly visit gamasutra.com.

Timing

To understand *when* to send out your writing-sample package, you should be aware of another reality of game production—many companies aim to have a new game on the shelves no later than Thanksgiving in order to cash in on the all-important Christmas gift-buying season. A PC or console game can take anywhere from eighteen months and up to complete, meaning that it's common for new-game development to ramp up between January and March. This schedule doesn't apply to every game, of course—in fact, it has become more common for games to be released at other times of the year—so consider this only a rough guideline. In addition, companies often suddenly decide they need a writer when the project is halfway or more done, so they could suddenly be looking for a writer at any time of the year.

That said, it is often the case that in the months immediately leading up to Thanksgiving, projects are in crunch mode, with people working frantic overtime to finish a game and get it out the door no later than September in order to go through production and reach the shelves by November. Consequently, the least effective time to send out résumés and sample packages is probably between June and September.

Another time to avoid is immediately prior to and during GDC when producers are distracted by preparing for the conference.

MMOGs could need writers at any time. Development for something as large and complex as an MMOG could cover three to four years before it's ready to launch. And once it goes live (meaning in full operation online with paid subscribers), an MMOG continues to need writers.

How to Find the Right Person

Figuring out the right person to approach when you're looking for game work is one of the most difficult parts of this process. The employee track and the contract-writer track break out quite differently.

The Employee Track

You have two options—try to find a job on your own or go through a recruiter. Doing it on your own will take a lot of time and research, and writing jobs are rarely posted. Your search will have to be constant and thorough. This is a very tough way to go. You will need to do the following:

- Contact each company's HR Department to inquire about writing jobs, then send your résumé and samples (if requested).

- Check the company's job listings on their Web site, on the slim chance of a writing job's being posted.

- Follow up with HR every couple of months so they won't forget you exist.

- Network and make contacts that might alert you to writing jobs or help you get a foot in the door.

The other option is to go through a recruiter. The difficulty here is that because it's such a rare job, most recruiters don't place writers. Recruiters know exactly how to place a producer, designer, programmer, or artist. They don't usually know what to do with a person who is looking solely for writing work.

Also, be aware that recruiters *cannot* represent you to a company to which you have submitted your résumé in the past twelve months. If you decide to try using a recruiter, you need to take this route first before sending résumés to companies on your own.

Professional Electronic Entertainment Recruiters (PEER) is an organization of game recruiters. Their Web site (http://www.peer-org.com/members.htm) lists several reputable recruiters, along with links to the recruiters' Web sites. Be prepared to fill out the recruiters' online forms, and be sure to regularly check the job listings on their Web sites.

A lot of game jobs are listed on http://www.creativeheads.net, with a writing job occasionally among them. Once you sign up at their Web site, they will send you e-mails with job listings.

An important site for job listings is http://www.gamasutra.com, which is also a resource for learning about the art and business of making games.

Likewise, http://www.datascope.co.uk/jobs_by_email.html will send job listings after you fill out the form on their Web site. They cover both the United Kingdom and the United States.

Other sites to check include the following:

http://www.gamesjobnews.com

http://www.games-match.com

http://www.gignews.com/jobs/index.htm

http://jobs.awn.com (Note: this is the Animation World Network, but has been covering games as well as animation. Writing jobs occasionally show up here, but approach these jobs with caution. They often seem to be of dubious quality or are looking for people who will work for free.)

If you want to try getting in the door via technical writing, there are a few temp agencies that handle technical writers. Recommended ones include Sakson & Taylor (http://www.sakson.com), FILTER/TALENT (http://www.filtertalent.com), Excell Data (http://www.excell.com), and Volt Services Group (http://www.volt.com). However, doing technical writing may require you to live in a particular area to qualify for work, usually West Coast tech centers such as the Bay Area or Seattle.

The Freelance Track

There is no quick or easy way to get your résumé to the right person. This is why networking is so vital—much of the time, writing jobs are never posted, and someone is hired long before you might ever hear that a producer was even looking.

The next question is whether to go after producers at the publisher level or the developer level. A producer at a publisher can consider you for more games than can a developer who might work on only one game at a time, but more often it will be the developer that does the hiring. Publishers may be more involved in hiring a contract writer for a high-profile game based on a major entertainment property, but less involved with lower-profile games. The best bet is go after producers at either tier.

True, you could approach the lead or senior designers, because in most cases they are the ones who have the creative vision for the game, but designers report to producers. Producers make the decisions about hiring, firing, and budget—and that is why you will do better to focus on producers.

More specifically, first go after a senior producer on a project. If no one has the title of senior producer, go for producer. Avoid contacting executive producers. Executive producers are at such a high level that they tend to be more removed from the day-to-day running of a project, and may have multiple projects to handle at once making them far less likely to read your sample. A senior producer is more likely to be focused on a particular project, and consequently more aware of when a writer might be needed.

I wish I could tell you there was a simple, easy formula for finding producers, or a nice handy list somewhere. There isn't. This step takes time and research. You will have to look at the credits on games, search out credit listings on the Net, in magazines, and anywhere else you can think of to track down the names of producers. The Internet Movie Database (http://www.imdb.com) has some game-credit listings, as does the game-oriented MobyGames (http://www.mobygames.com).

Getting hired may involve a number of introductory steps. You might be asked to produce a sample of game work based on their specifications, which could be for free or could be paid work. You might be asked to come to the company and meet the development team, perhaps do some brainstorming, so they can get a feel for how well you work on a collaborative basis.

When you do finally get that meeting, producers will want to hear you talk about story and character. Producers in general have become more savvy about story arcs and character arcs. They'll want to hear what sort of writing or stories grab your enthusiasm. Feel free to gush about your favorite movie or TV series. What they don't want to hear a writer talk about is game design—unless, by some fluke, they are also hiring you to do design. In fact, talking about design could even lose you a job if they worry that you'll try to interfere with design issues rather than being focused on the writing. Understanding and being aware of design issues is a plus; trying to come across like a designer is a minus.

Getting Paid

The Employee Track

Game Developer magazine does an annual salary report on what people are making in the games business. Gamasutra posts the results on their site. Unfortunately, "writing" isn't treated as a category by itself, and instead is folded into "design." In the 2003 survey (the most recent one posted at this time), annual salaries in the design category ranged anywhere from $40,000 to $100,000, depending on level of job and level of experience. Because the data collected are provided on an entirely volunteer basis, this survey can be considered a rough guide at best, but it's pretty much all there is, other than what a recruiter might tell you. In 2006, I saw Senior Content Design positions at an MMOG offering around $70,000 (senior = experienced writers with design knowledge and impressive game or other writing credits). A purely writing position on an MMOG might offer less than that.

The Freelance Track

You should aim to be paid a flat fee for your work (one overall amount), which will be broken out into milestone payments. There are no established guidelines for what to charge for a game bible, cinematics, or other writing work. The best you can do is try to estimate how much time the project will take you to complete, and what you feel is adequate compensation for your time.

The amount also depends on various other factors: size of the company, status and budget of the project, type of writing that is needed, and your experience and credits. A big-name writer who is brought in on a high-profile (big-budget) game to create the entire story, lore, and game world from scratch is a higher level of work that might command around $60,000. The pay might be half that if a writer is brought in to polish an existing game bible, or simply to write a script based on existing gameplay. A small developer needing a simple bible might be able to pay only around $15,000 or less.

At the low end, for mobile games, they might pay around $300 to $1,000 to come up with a story for a very short game and a limited script of around thirty to sixty lines.

Some companies will want you to quote an hourly or weekly rate, especially for straightforward writing work such as dialogue, but there are no established rates and no easy sense of what to charge. Depending on the size of the company, the type of writing, and your level of experience, that rate can vary widely, anywhere from $35 an hour to $100 an hour. Rates between $1,400 and $2,000 a week are reasonable.

Note that game scheduling is built around *milestones* (as defined in Chapter 9). Consequently, you will be asked to turn in a certain amount of work (the deliverable) by a certain milestone (a date). As mentioned earlier, most games have a long development cycle—from one and a half years to many years. A contract writer is likely to be involved for only a number of weeks or a few months.

Whether talking about a flat fee or hourly/weekly rate, here are some additional factors to take into account when figuring out what to charge:

- Amount of work: If it's a game bible, get them to specify how many pages they are expecting, how detailed they want it to be, and precisely what it will cover. For cutscenes/cinematics, find out how many they plan to have in the game. Dialogue is much more difficult, but get them to be as specific as possible about how many characters or NPCs are involved, and how many lines for each (be sure to have them define what they mean by "lines," because game companies can view this differently than a TV or film company does). Then you have to do your best guesstimate on how much time you feel you need to create that work. Take into account the ramping-up time to absorb their game design, the time to get a handle on the interface and gameplay, and possibly time to play previous games (if this is a sequel).

- Scheduling: The company may be on a tight schedule with demanding milestones, though most of the time they will work out the milestones with you. You need to do a hard, honest assessment of whether you can meet their milestones, and whether there is any flexibility in the schedule.

- Approvals: Be sure to find out how many people can have notes, input, or right of approval on the work. Ideally, you will work with only one company representative who is the gatekeeper for all such input. Work out how many days the gatekeeper will require to evaluate your work and give you notes. If there are other entities (such as a movie studio) that require approval over scripts, be sure to add extra days in the schedule for that turnaround time. You don't want to have fixed milestones that suddenly become a scheduling nightmare because you had to wait a week to get notes from a third party.

- Rewrites: Specify how many rewrites you will do, and how those rewrites will be covered in payment and in the milestones. This is extremely important if you've worked out a flat fee—otherwise you could find yourself doing a lot of free rewrites.

- Additional work: Specify additional writing or work they may want you to do, such as promotional or Web-site material, or attending voice-recording sessions. You should be paid separate fees for that work, and the company should cover your expenses for attending voice-recording sessions.

- Travel expenses: It will be common for a game company to ask you to spend some time at their studio or office, particularly at the beginning of the project. They may have software to teach you, aspects of the game to share with you, and people you need to meet and work with over the course of the project. If the company is outside your immediate area, all travel expenses should be covered.

If you happen to be represented by an agent, the agent can handle most of the price negotiation and will handle invoicing and payments.

If no agent is involved, be sure to clarify who should receive the invoice, what the payment period will be (immediately upon receipt of invoice? in 14 days? 20 days? 30 days?), and keep careful track of your payment schedule. Make sure you specify precisely what deliverables are covered by each invoice.

Location, Location, Location

In the United States, there are some definite hot spots of videogame work. The main clusters are Seattle; the San Francisco Bay Area; Los Angeles; and Austin, Texas. Other major locations include Chicago, San Diego, and various cities on the East Coast. Game companies are popping up across the country, however.

In Canada, the main hot spot is Vancouver, with companies also in Montreal, Toronto, and elsewhere.

There are many companies in the United Kingdom. Scotland especially has been pushing the digital-media and creative industries established there. In 2006, Scotland boasted of an estimated annual sales of $6.1 billion, providing more than 100,000 jobs.

China, South Korea, and Japan are also strong international hot spots for game creation.

The Employee Track

Obviously, you must be ready to move to wherever the game company is located. If you have a definite preference for where you want to live, concentrate on companies in that area. But if you're willing to be flexible, you might find you have a better chance breaking into companies located outside the major game-production cities.

A major issue that has been a hot topic of discussion in the game business for the past few years is quality of life (QoL). Basically, it refers to what sort of working conditions a company provides for its employees.

The reason QoL has become such a significant issue has to do with the nature of the games business itself. Namely, it attracts a great many young and hungry workers who are so enthusiastic about working in games that they accept any kind of working conditions. Unfortunately, too many game companies have happily gone along with this, creating a workplace culture in which employees are expected to put in ten- to twelve-hour days, six to seven days a week. Theoretically, this should be restricted to extremely short time periods (meaning a few days to maybe a week) during crunch time. Crunch time is the all-out, last-minute push to get a game completed so it can ship by a certain date. However, some companies abuse this concept. They'll have extended crunch times, failing to understand that extended crunch times are the result of poor management, poor planning, and a poor grasp of what makes for effective productivity. Productivity actually declines after eight hours of intensive work.

A management that has disdain for QoL issues makes for a miserable place to work. It leads to exhaustion, burnout, and people who are unable to have any kind of life outside the workplace. You are strongly advised to ask questions about the company's attitude toward QoL issues, what sort of working hours are routinely expected, and how frequent or long are their crunch times. If you get the sense they expect endless hours of work just because working on their games is so very special, run away as fast as you can.

The Freelance Track

Although there is less emphasis on being in a specific location to do contract work, it certainly doesn't hurt to be in L.A., Austin, Seattle, or the Bay Area. You should be prepared to travel and spend some time on-site at the game company, especially at the beginning of the project—when you need to meet the team, become familiar with the design, and learn any software tools they may want you to use.

Agents

Having an agent to handle game-writing work is relevant only to the contract writer. You obviously won't be dealing with an agent if you're seeking full-time employment.

Until recently, there was no such thing as a game agent. For the most part, that remains true, though a couple of enterprising souls in L.A. have attempted to provide a talent pool of writers for whom they more or less work as an agent (though one such person rejected the term "agent," feeling that he was providing more of a production service). As far as I know, none of these people have made significant inroads in representing game writers. One producing entity that deals with game writers is Union Entertainment, a company that has set itself up to concurrently develop properties such as films, videogames, and comic books (and whatever else they can make happen).

The big Hollywood agencies have been adding to their rosters some agents who deal with game writing, but that is primarily as a service to their existing base of Hollywood scriptwriters. So far, there hasn't been enough demand to justify taking on clients who do nothing but write games. I suspect that mostly what that type of agent does is field inquiries that happen to come in from a game producer who is interested in a known Hollywood name.

Note also that it's important to understand that Hollywood agents are licensed and regulated. They can't take more than 10 percent of a writer's income. Other people or firms that set out to represent game writers may not be licensed, because this type of work is so new. If you should happen to find someone who claims to be a game-writing agent, check carefully into his background and experience, find out whether he's licensed in the same way as other talent agents, and determine what percentage of your money he wants, or how he intends to make money off you. Finally, have a serious discussion up front about how the agent can realistically find work for you or make contacts that you can't make yourself. Be extremely wary of anyone wanting more than 10 or 15 percent as a commission fee.

In the United Kingdom, there are script agencies or script consultancies, which are game writers who have pooled their resources to provide game scripts to companies as a group service. Joining a script agency isn't easy, but it's worth a try. This idea hasn't caught on in the States as yet, though one or two people are trying to make something work along these lines. The best you can do is keep your eyes and ears open for such agencies.

Is having an agent necessary? That depends. For the next-gen console producer who likes to find big-name writers, you might be considered an amateur if you don't have an agent. On the other hand, some producers and companies are resistant to dealing with agents. This is another one of those gray areas with no easy answer. If you're an established scriptwriter or novelist, you'll already have an agent. Then you can decide whether or not your agent or someone at their agency is qualified to handle repping you for game work.

Otherwise, worry first about getting in the door and getting game work before being concerned with the need for an agent. You may do fine without one.

Unions and Organizations

The WGA (Writers Guild of America) is working hard to represent the interests of game writers. I strongly recommend that you read the information in Chapter 4 about the protections and benefits the WGA can provide to you as a writer.

Within the WGA, the New Media Caucus (NMC) deals specifically with games, new and evolving media, and interactive entertainment in any form. Operating under the WGA's Organizing Department, the NMC has drafted two simple contract forms to use for interactive work—one for a single-game project, and one for online games. These contracts are for use as an addition to the basic deal you negotiate and their purpose is to guarantee that you also receive key WGA benefits.

One of the NMC's projects is an online database of game writers for members of the caucus. The NMC has also initiated a WGA writing award for game writing. For more information about the New Media Caucus, the qualifications for membership, how to join, or to download the contracts, visit their Web site (http://www.wganewmedia.org).

If you are a contract writer, you should seriously consider negotiating to have your work covered by the WGA. That way, you will gain pension and health benefits, as well as have a strong organization at your back in case of problems, such as ensuring that you receive a fair credit on the game. Realistically, many companies are uncomfortable negotiating with the WGA. Dealing with a union is unknown territory for them. Ask the company for WGA terms, but decide ahead of time how important that is to you. If a company balks at the notion of paying the additional pension and health benefits, you may be able to restructure the payment so that pension and health benefits come out of the overall fee. This means less in your hands up front, but the benefits can be worth it. That's a personal decision.

However, you will never *lose* a job by asking for WGA coverage. Furthermore, the WGA will bend over backward to help you achieve it in a way that works equally well for both the company and you. One more thing to consider—if a company doesn't think you should be entitled to have health insurance or a pension (via the WGA), then perhaps they don't value you much as a writer either.

The other equally important group to join is the IGDA (International Game Developers Association). According to their mission statement, "The IGDA is committed to advancing the careers and enhancing the lives of game developers by connecting members with their peers, promoting professional development, and advocating on issues that affect the developer community."

The IGDA has numerous SIGs (Special Interest Groups), but the one you want to become involved in is the Game Writers SIG, a great place to network and learn about the business. Go to http://www.igda.org/writing for more information.

The IGDA Web site also has white papers about writing for games, as well as a quarterly newsletter that is full of useful interviews and info.

Section III Resources

Books

HAMLET ON THE HOLODECK
by Janet Horowitz Murray

GAME WRITING: NARRATIVE SKILLS FOR VIDEOGAMES
edited by Chris Bateman

CHARACTER DEVELOPMENT AND STORYTELLING FOR GAMES
by Lee Sheldon

DIGITAL STORYTELLING: A CREATOR'S GUIDE TO INTERACTIVE ENTERTAINMENT
by Carolyn Handler Miller

BREAK INTO THE GAME INDUSTRY: HOW TO GET A JOB MAKING VIDEO GAMES
by Ernest Adams

CHRIS CRAWFORD ON INTERACTIVE STORYTELLING
by Chris Crawford

GAME DESIGN: THE ART & BUSINESS OF CREATING GAMES
by Bob Bates

THEORY OF FUN FOR GAME DESIGN
by Raph Koster

FIRST PERSON: NEW MEDIA AS STORY, PERFORMANCE, AND GAME
by Noah Wardrip-Fruin

SWORDS & CIRCUITRY: A DESIGNER'S GUIDE TO COMPUTER ROLE-PLAYING GAMES
by Neal Hallford and Jana Hallford

SERIOUS GAMES: GAMES THAT EDUCATE, TRAIN, AND INFORM
by David Michael and Sande Chen

Trade Shows and Conferences

GAME DEVELOPERS CONFERENCE
http://www.gdconf.com

GAME WRITERS CONFERENCE
http://www.gamewritersconference.com

E^3 (ELECTRONIC ENTERTAINMENT EXPO)
http://www.e3expo.com

HOLLYWOOD AND GAMES SUMMIT
http://www.hollywoodandgames.com/

MOBILE GAME CONFERENCE
http://www.MobileGameConference.com

SERIOUS GAMES SUMMIT
http://www.seriousgamessummit.com

Magazines

GAME DEVELOPER
http://www.gdmag.com

EDGE
http://www.edge-online.co.uk

COMPUTER GAMING WORLD
http://cgw.1up.com

Links

GAMASUTRA
http://www.gamasutra.com

INTERNET MOVIE DATABASE (IMDB)
http://www.imdb.com

MOBYGAMES
http://www.mobygames.com

PC VS. CONSOLE
http://www.pcvsconsole.com

ADRENALINE VAULT
http://www.adrenalinevault.com

GAMESPOT
http://www.gamespot.com

PC GAMER
http://www.pcgamer.com

GAMEPRO
http://www.gamepro.com

GAME INDUSTRY NEWS
http://www.gameindustry.com

GAMEDAILY
http://www.gamedaily.com

1UP
http://www.1up.com/

Unions and Organizations

WRITERS GUILD OF AMERICA (WGA)
http://www.wga.org

NEW MEDIA CAUCUS
http://www.wganewmedia.org

IGDA (INTERNATIONAL GAME DEVELOPERS ASSOCIATION)
http://www.igda.org/writing

Looking for Jobs

PEER (PROFESSIONAL ELECTRONIC ENTERTAINMENT RECRUITERS)
http://www.peer-org.com/members.htm

GAMASUTRA
http://www.gamasutra.com

CREATIVEHEADS
http://www.creativeheads.net

DATASCOPE RECRUITMENT
http://www.datascope.co.uk/jobs_by_email.html

GAMESJOBNEWS
http://www.gamesjobnews.com

GAMES-MATCH.COM
http://www.games-match.com

GIGNEWS
http://www.gignews.com/jobs/index.htm

EDGE ON-LINE
http://www.edge-online.co.uk

ANIMATION WORLD NETWORK (AWN)
http://jobs.awn.com

Schools: United States

ART INSTITUTE OF CALIFORNIA—ORANGE COUNTY
Santa Ana, CA
Conceptual Storytelling course.
http://www.education.org/artinstitutes/california_orange.php

AUSTIN COMMUNITY COLLEGE
Austin, TX
http://www.austincc.edu/techcert/Video_Games.html

BLOOMFIELD COLLEGE
Bloomfield, NJ
http://www.bloomfield.edu/academic/majorsandconc.asp

CARNEGIE MELLON UNIVERSITY
Pittsburgh, PA
http://www.cmu.edu

CHAMPLAIN COLLEGE
Burlington, VT
http://www.champlain.edu/majors/egame

FULL SAIL
Orlando, FL
http://www.fullsail.com

THE GUILDHALL AT SMU
Dallas, TX
http://guildhall.smu.edu

MIT (MASSACHUSETTS INSTITUTE OF TECHNOLOGY)
Cambridge, MA
http://www.comparativemediastudies.org

USC (UNIVERSITY OF SOUTHERN CALIFORNIA)
http://www.usc.edu

Schools: United Kingdom

SURREY INSTITUTE OF ART & DESIGN, UNIVERSITY COLLEGE
Farnham, Surrey
http://www.dgdu.org
http://www.ucreative.ac.uk/index.cfm?articleid=5638

Tech-oriented Temp Agencies

SAKSON & TAYLOR
http://www.sakson.com

FILTER/TALENT
http://www.filtertalent.com

EXCELL DATA
http://www.excell.com

VOLT SERVICES GROUP
http://www.volt.com

Section II Resources

Books

UNDERSTANDING COMICS
by Scott McCloud
As both an artist and writer, his book on visual storytelling is excellent. This is a must-read.

COMICS & SEQUENTIAL ART
by Will Eisner

ALAN MOORE'S WRITING FOR COMICS
by Alan Moore
Available from http://www.avatarpress.com.

WRITING FOR COMICS
by Peter David

WRITERS ON COMICS SCRIPTWRITING
by Mark Salisbury

PANEL ONE
edited by Nat Gertler
Contains comic book scripts by top writers.

THE DC COMICS GUIDE TO WRITING COMICS
by Dennis O'Neil
Focuses more on the art of writing and storytelling. By a highly respected comic book writer and editor with decades of experience in the business.

WRITERS GUIDE TO THE BUSINESS OF COMICS
by Lurene Haines
Focuses, as the title says, more on the business side—how to present oneself as professional, how to get organized. Contains interviews with thirty comic book writers on how they succeeded.

HOW TO SELF-PUBLISH YOUR OWN COMIC BOOK: THE COMPLETE RESOURCE GUIDE TO THE BUSINESS, PRODUCTION, DISTRIBUTION, MARKETING AND PROMOTION OF COMIC BOOKS
by Tony C. Caputo

REINVENTING COMICS: HOW IMAGINATION AND TECHNOLOGY ARE REVOLUTIONIZING AN ART FORM
by Scott McCloud

VISUAL STORYTELLING: THE ART AND TECHNIQUE
by Tony C. Caputo, with Jim Steranko

YOUR CAREER IN THE COMICS
by Lee Nordling

Trade Magazines

WRITE NOW!
The magazine about writing for comics, animation, and science-fiction, by Danny Fingeroth.
http://www.twomorrows.com

COMICS JOURNAL
http://tcj.com

COMICS BUYER'S GUIDE
http://www.cbgxtra.com

Links

ANIMATION WORLD NETWORK
This site will occasionally cover some comics news (such as announcing cons, workshops, and so forth), and has artists' résumés and job listings that overlap with comics on occasion. This might be another place to look for an artist partner.
http://www.awn.com

COMIC BOOK LEGAL DEFENSE FUND
http://cbldf.org

NEWSARAMA
Check out their forums for occasional workshop news as well.
http://newsarama.com

COMIC BOOK RESOURCES
http://www.comicbookresources.com

NATIONAL ASSOCIATION OF COMICS ART EDUCATORS
Promotes teaching comics in schools and has some script samples on their site.
http://www.teachingcomics.org

SCOTT MCCLOUD'S WEB SITE
http://www.scottmccloud.com

COMICS REPORTER
A blog.
http://www.comicsreporter.com

THE ENGINE
Forums run by comics writer Warren Ellis.
http://the-engine.net/forum

SILVER BULLET COMIC BOOKS
http://www.silverbulletcomicbooks.com

COMICS CONTINUUM
http://www.comicscontinuum.com

DIGITAL WEBBING
Has a talent-search section to help writers and artists connect for projects.
http://www.digitalwebbing.com/talent

COMIC BOOK CREATOR
http://www.mycomicbookcreator.com

Conventions

COMIC-CON INTERNATIONAL
http://www.comic-con.org

SUPER-CON
http://www.super-con.com

NEW YORK COMIC-CON
http://www.nycomiccon.com

Copyright and Trademark Information

U.S. COPYRIGHT OFFICE
Federal copyright and registration information.
http://www.copyright.gov

UNITED STATES PATENT AND TRADEMARK OFFICE
http://www.uspto.gov

Section I Resources

Books

HOW TO WRITE FOR ANIMATION
by Jeffrey Scott

ANIMATION WRITING AND DEVELOPMENT: FROM SCRIPT DEVELOPMENT TO PITCH
by Jean Ann Wright

THE COMPLETE BOOK OF SCRIPTWRITING
by J. Michael Straczynski

TELEVISION WRITING FROM THE INSIDE OUT
by Larry Brody

GARDNER'S GUIDE TO FEATURE ANIMATION WRITING: THE WRITER'S ROAD MAP
by Marilyn Webber

Trades and Magazines

VARIETY
http://www.variety.com

HOLLYWOOD REPORTER
http://www.hollywoodreporter.com/thr/index.jsp

ANIMATION MAGAZINE
http://www.animationmagazine.net

WRITTEN BY
WGA monthly magazine
7000 Third St.
Los Angeles, CA 90048
323-782-4522
http://www.wga.org

Organizations

WRITERS GUILD OF AMERICA
http://www.wga.org

ANIMATION WRITERS CAUCUS
http://www.wga.org/awc.aspx

LOCAL 839/THE ANIMATION GUILD
http://www.mpsc839.org

ASIFA (ASSOCIATION INTERNATIONALE DU FILM D'ANIMATION)
http://www.asifa-hollywood.org/

Education

WORDS INTO PICTURES
http://www.wordsintopictures.org

WRITERS BOOT CAMP
http://www.writersbootcamp.com/index.asp

ART INSTITUTE OF CALIFORNIA
Santa Ana, CA
Conceptual Storytelling course.
http://www.education.org/artinstitutes/california_orange.php

Informational Sites

ANIMATION WORLD NETWORK
Overflowing with general industry news. Also has a database of job offerings.
http://www.awn.com

TOON ZONE
http://www.toonzone.net/

HOLLYWOOD CREATIVE DIRECTORY
http://www.hcdonline.com/

THE WRITERS STORE
Articles and other useful info about scriptwriting in general.
http://www.writersstore.com/

U.S. COPYRIGHT OFFICE
Federal copyright and registration information.
http://www.copyright.gov/

FEDERAL COMMUNICATIONS COMMISSION (FCC)
Federal regulations on children's programming.
http://www.fcc.gov/cgb/consumerfacts/childtv.html

Writers on Writing

STEPHEN J. CANNELL
Top TV writer lectures on scriptwriting (full of excellent tips).
http://www.writerswrite.com/screenwriting/lecture.htm

WORDPLAY
Excellent Web site of Ted Elliott and Terry Rossio, writers of *Shrek, Pirates of the Caribbean*,
and other features.
http://www.wordplayer.com

JEFFREY SCOTT
Longtime animation writer.
http://users.adelphia.net/~getjeffrey/Home.htm

Obtaining Scripts

http://www.scriptcity.com
http://www.script-o-rama.com/table.shtml
http://www.movie-page.com/movie_scripts.htm
And of course, there are always writers' personal Web sites and eBay.

Creating Machinima

http://www.machinima.com

Index

407936

Lightning Source UK Ltd.
Milton Keynes UK
UKOW05f1411180616

276559UK00011B/207/P